Essay Ir

COLLECTED
ESSAYS

COLLECTED ESSAYS

W. H. HADOW

Essay Index Reprint Series

BOOKS FOR LIBRARIES PRESS
FREEPORT, NEW YORK

First Published 1928
Reprinted 1968

LIBRARY OF CONGRESS CATALOG CARD NUMBER:
68-20305

PRINTED IN THE UNITED STATES OF AMERICA

TO

GRAHAM BALFOUR

IN TOKEN OF FIFTY YEARS'

UNCLOUDED FRIENDSHIP

W. H. Hadow

CONTENTS

SOME TENDENCIES IN MODERN MUSIC[1]

1906

IF it be true, as Freeman said, that modern history begins at the call of Abraham, we can scarcely hope to find a more recent date for the beginning of modern music. As we trace back we find ourselves following the course of a continuous and unbroken record where every age takes its point of departure from something in preceding circumstances or conditions; where schools overlap, and methods interchange, and traditions alternate and weaken and revive; where even the most dynamic changes but liberate forces which were already operative. The *Neue Bahnen* of 1852 were trodden by a direct descendant of Beethoven and Bach, the Romantic movement began centuries before 1830, the *Nuove Musiche* of 1600 adapted the scheme of Greek tragedy to the Florentine stage, the counterpoint of the medieval Church grew out of the organum, and that in its turn grew from one of the most primitive employments of the human voice: there is no starting-point, there is no finality; and the only apparent gaps are due to our imperfect research. And all the while, to remind us of the continuity, comes criticism lagging contentedly in the rear, applying to each generation maxims derived from the practice of its predecessors, directing the advance by mapping out the ground already traversed, and issuing its marching orders at the moment when they are being superseded.

Yet, if the course has been continuous, it has also been rapid. As we lay down a score of Strauss or Elgar the old controversies seem curiously remote and alien: Mozart censured for a discord, and Beethoven for a modulation; Haydn accused of extravagance and Corelli of virtuosity. In 1835 Schumann was a dangerous revolutionary, in

[1] From *The Edinburgh Review*, October, 1906.

1855 he was upheld as the pattern of enlightened conservatism against the rebels of Zurich and Weimar. Gluck was assailed in terms almost exactly similar to those with which our elders attacked Wagner; the days are not far distant which will talk of Wagner as we talk of Gluck. Hence it is of some importance that we should now and again take stock of our present position, that we should endeavour to estimate contemporary methods and contemporary ideals, that we should look to the direction in which we are travelling and calculate our strength for the journey. The task is notoriously difficult; the road behind us is strewn with shattered prophecies and wrecked reputations: there are plenty of warnings against hasty judgements, against misapplied rules, against the tyranny of codes grown outworn and obsolete. Yet the same honesty of purpose which we claim from the composer he has an equal right to claim from us. The difference between truth and error is as valid to-day as it has ever been, and all who care for the welfare of music are responsible for its investigation.

One thing at any rate we have learned in course of experience: that music can no longer be appraised by the text-book and judged from the professor's chair. When Schumann bade his antagonists 'pick out the fifths', the voice of the grammarian was still heard in the land; it was still possible to say that an effect was wrong because it broke a canon of Marpurg or Kirnberger. When Brahms produced his first pianoforte concerto at Leipzig it was taken as a legitimate objection that he had not treated his solo instrument after the accepted form. From this kind of criticism we are at last emancipated. It is well to 'pick out the fifths' from a school exercise, for they are likely to be misused by inexperienced hands, but no reasonable man would any longer protest against their presence in a master's composition. It is well to bring up an artist on the study of past methods, since these will afford the securest basis for his own practice; but if he chooses to write a 'symphony with pianoforte obbligato', there is no longer any one to gainsay him. We have come to see, in short, that the true critic is simply the most enlightened listener; not standing aloof with a manual of arrogant imperatives, but taking his place among us to stimulate our attention where it falters, and to supplement our knowledge where it is deficient. His position is not to command, but to interpret, and we accept his judgement, as we would that of any other expert, as soon as we are convinced that it illuminates the point at issue.

This does not, of course, mean the abrogation of a critical standard. Such abrogation would reduce the republic of art to the level of Plato's democracy, where there is no government and no order, where Jack is as good as his master, and where the very beasts of burden contest your title to the roadway. But it means that the critical standard is determined by principles, not by rules; and that these principles are all ultimately derived from the sympathy which obtains between the artist and his public. Genius does not so transform a man as to put him out of all touch with ourselves: it is the acuter vision of that which we dimly see, the more eloquent utterance of that which we stammeringly confess, the revelation, by divine gift, of truths which we imperfectly recognize. Such sympathy no doubt implies that the artist on his side is unconscious of our presence. It is the charlatan who is constantly endeavouring to attract our attention by tricks and postures and laboured epigrams; the true genius has his whole mind centred on his ideal, and if he gives us a thought when the work is over it is only to feel, like Beethoven, that his new quartet 'will please some day'. He also is an interpreter, a prophet of the truth, and he has no right to soften or exaggerate a word of his message from any motive of catching our applause or conciliating our prejudices. But we on our side cannot be unconscious, for it is our function to hear and understand. There are many false shrines and false worships which, if we follow, we are traitors to the cause, and we cannot learn to discriminate by uncritical acceptance of authority. Even sincerity is not a sufficient touchstone; a man may be sincere and illiterate or unskilful, he may speak his own message through a temperament that is warped or embittered. There can be no great music without great ideas, no charming music without attractiveness of thought and ease of presentation: a cold art leaves us cold, a merely sensuous art crumbles at a touch into dust and ashes. But sincerity is of the very bed-rock of our foundation, and only when that is established is it time to look to the superstructure.

A single instance may serve to illustrate the type of principle which we have in view. When our symphonic form was young and unfamiliar, it naturally moved within the confines of a narrow structural limitation. Precisely the same reason which would have made a more adventurous scheme unintelligible to the hearer made it impossible to the composer himself. In course of time the artists of the eighteenth century so mastered these simpler forms that they could begin to experiment and develop; *pari passu* the auditors whom they had familiarized with the old scheme were ready to follow them into new directions; and so came the symphony of Beethoven, rendered possible, not only by his own genius, but by the place which both he and his public occupied in musical history. In this manner, through the succession of lesser and greater men, the bounds have been further widened, the range of invention has been further extended, until now we can comprehend a structural design which would have seemed chaos to a contemporary of Haydn or Mozart. But the principle has remained the same throughout. The need of some structural coherence and organization is fundamental; it is satisfied by different plans in different generations, but to each generation the requirement is equally imperative. A symphony of Brahms endeavours to meet it by a design drawn in terms of pure music: a symphonic poem of Strauss by the adventitious aid of a plot or story; each method has a right to be considered on its own merits, and in this matter the only relevant question is whether it fulfils its aim. *Zarathustra*, for example, ends on an implied discord. We may ask whether this is merely a piece of petulance and challenge, or whether it is the true outcome of the poetic scheme which Strauss is following; and our verdict will be blame or praise, according to the answer. But to say that an orchestral work ought to end on a tonic triad is like saying that a comedy ought to end with a marriage or a tragedy with a death. The sole principle is that the composer should present us with a coherent plan; the particular kind of coherence will depend partly on our receptivity and partly on his power of persuasion. And the case is the same with regard to his melodic and harmonic idioms, to his polyphony, to all the different varieties of phrase and sentence and paragraph through which he expresses himself. All rules in music are transitory, but the principles which underlie them are everlasting.

It is of interest to consider this point, for the last fifty years have seen some important changes in the musical perspective. These can be observed most easily by contrast with their background. Roughly speaking, the typical aim of the eighteenth century was proportion; the clear phrase, the symmetrical design, the style that is lucid, polished, and transparent. In the hands of genius this attained to the highest achievements of pure beauty; in the hands of mediocrity it degenerated into a formalism which mistook craftsmanship for inspiration. And because a certain degree of craftsmanship can be reached by any one who has skill and industry, the world soon became flooded with compositions which had all the qualities of academic art, and were accepted by an unthinking criticism which took no trouble to penetrate below the surface. In London the favourite composers, after Handel's death, were J. C. Bach and Sacchini; in Vienna, Mozart and Beethoven had to contend against Kotzeluch and Hummel and Adalbert Gyrowetz; and though, as we have seen, genius took the best intelligence with it, yet even the best intelligence was more inclined to accept than to discriminate. Any man could set up for an artist who had mastered the lessons of the drawing-school; any man was a composer who could write a fugue, or construct a sonata, or set smooth conventional melodies to a book of Metastasio. Then came a natural reaction. The so-called Romantic movement of Berlioz and Schumann was mainly animated by a protest against academic methods. Beethoven held expression and design in perfect balance: he was at once the greatest poet and the greatest craftsman of his age. Men like Hummel and Czerny copied the design, but left the poetry out: Berlioz—to take him as typical—followed the poetry without ever comprehending the musicianship. He honestly believed that the structure of the *Symphonie Fantastique* was formally perfect, and that the *Amen* fugue was written 'selon les règles les plus sévères du contrepoint'; he was so thoroughly preoccupied with his ideal of poetic expression that he had no time to repair, or even to recognize, the deficiencies of his artistic training. And here in one word is the strength and weakness of the school which he represented. It was full of ideas, it was vivid, picturesque, impressive; it had an extraordinary power of arousing emotion, of stimulating the senses, of suggesting action or scenery; but it never learned to make full use of its tools. Schumann, who was by far the best musician of the group, is always more interesting for what he says than for the manner in which he says it; we have but to place one of his quartets beside Beethoven, or one of his fugues beside Bach, and we see the inspired amateur in contrast with the unerring skill of the perfect master. Berlioz's magnificent orchestration does not conceal his poverty of style; the dexterity of Liszt is often set to embroider a thin or ill-woven texture: even Wagner's 'romantic' operas alternate their wonderful strokes of genius with passages of sheer clumsiness or vulgarity. And the reason is in all cases the same. Berlioz learned nothing at the Paris Conservatoire; Liszt began his public career at the age of eleven; Schumann's chief instructors in music were Thibault the lawyer and Jean Paul the novelist; Wagner graduated after six weeks of inefficient schooling. All these men, in short, had to make their own way by the force of almost unaided ability: they were saturated with the poetry of music, they were keenly susceptible to literary influence, they were full of fervour and passion, but they had not acquired the full artistry which cost Bach and Mozart so many years of patient endeavour.

Hence in the ultimate history of composition the music of 'the School of 1830' will be more valuable for what it suggested than for what it achieved. Already Berlioz and Liszt have almost gone; much of Schumann is trembling in the balance; and though Wagner's romantic operas will long hold the stage, yet every year is widening the distance between them and the true Wagner. But in two notable respects it has affected the methods and ideals of our own generation. In the first place it has killed academic art. The mere contrapuntist has no longer any patron or any audience, or, except as a teacher, any reason for existing; he takes his place in the training-ground and leaves the open field to a more adventurous talent. It is no more possible for a man to take rank as a composer because he knows the text-books than to take rank as a poet because he knows the classical dictionary; we have done for ever with the trim heroic couplets and the scholarly elegancies about Phoebus and Cynthia. No doubt we are forming our own conventions: every age does so; but at least we are not regarding them with complacency or taking them as evidences of merit. Indeed, it may be questioned whether we are not too wide in our toleration of revolt; whether we do not sometimes confuse extravagance with genius and bluster with conviction. In any case it is no small matter that we have learned to respect the artist who claims a free hand, and that we reserve the heaviest of our censure for a dull and timid docility. Again, the insistence on the poetic and picturesque aspects of music has enormously enriched the content of our own contemporary work. We have a different kind of poetry, but the line of derivation is plain enough. The direct appeal to our emotional nature, the desire to make music as far as possible descriptive, presentative, even articulate, the impatience of technical restraint, the prominence assigned to vitality of idea—all these form part of our present inheritance, and are counted in the wealth which it is ours to administer and bequeath. We can hardly estimate the debt which opera owes to *Lohengrin*, or song to the *Dichterliebe*: their monuments may be lasting or perishable; in either case they have been landmarks of the general advance.

Some metaphysicians tell us that a true cause works toward opposites, and assuredly no directions could be more widely divergent than those into which the School of 1830 ultimately issued. Half a century ago the two most important composers in Europe were Brahms and Wagner; each the complement and antithesis of the other. Wagner, already at the extreme left of the Romantic party, broke away still farther and occupied his ten years' retirement in developing a dramatic style which was almost as far removed from romantic methods as they were from classical. Music was no longer predominant, as with Mozart, nor admitted to equal partnership, as with Schumann; it was definitely subordinated to purposes other than its own. The *Ring* is to be judged not as music but as drama; the music is just as much an accessory as the costumes or the *mise en scène*. Its 'motives', often in themselves strangely vital and moving, are conceived, presented, and arranged solely for their bearing upon plot or character: outside the theatre the prelude to *Rheingold* is meaningless and the opening of *Götterdämmerung* barren. If we put a page of the score beside Beethoven, or a page of the book beside Goethe, we shall see, not that Wagner fails to achieve their respective aims, and still less that he succeeds in combining them, but that his art is projected from another standpoint and determined by relation to other laws.

Hence the roughness of style which would offend in a symphony may in the music-drama be a positive merit. The dramatist learns, not in the University, but in the school of life; he presents humanity to us, without intervention on his own part, and if he allows himself to be preoccupied by any other consideration—even that of artistic finish—he must needs give but a divided attention to the main issue. We all know the fate of 'literary' plays: *laudantur et algent*. The house rejects them, and if they are 'printed to shame the fools', they lead but a cloistered and secluded existence on the bookshelf. On the other hand, if a play is really human, its very vitality will enable it to set the canons of pure literature at defiance. Dumas, in an amusing passage, imagines Fénelon taking up a volume of Molière and, after twenty lines, closing it with the comment, 'Voilà un pauvre écrivain.' His moral is that from Fénelon's point of view the judgement is incontestable, and that from Molière's it is irrelevant. As a piece of French prose the passage is poor and ill-written; as a speech in a comedy it conveys its meaning in the manner that will most readily cross the footlights. And we may take, from the same preface, an even stronger example. In the famous and much-contested line:

> Je t'aimais inconstant, qu'aurais-je fait fidèle,

there is, as Dumas says, 'une abominable faute de grammaire'; but had it been pointed out a dozen times by candid friends, 'Racine, qui savait son métier, ne l'aurait pas écrit autrement'. The drama, in short, has its own laws, its own principles, its own perspective; and from these alone can it be properly judged.

It is for this reason that Wagner, supreme artist in his own craft, has been so dangerous a model in all forms other than dramatic. His musical speech is, in Mr. Dannreuther's phrase, 'a powerful rhetoric', wholly designed to interpret and heighten the spectacle on the stage; and of all devices those of rhetoric are most easily copied and degraded. The great man shows that certain conventions can be traversed; a host of little men believe that by traversing them they will share his secret. He follows at all hazards the higher issue; they take the hazard where there is no such issue to justify it. Again, the very imperfections of the *Ring*—its repetitions, its forced polyphony, its insistence on certain points of colour—while they pass almost unnoticed in the glow and splendour of its genius, have been doomed to reappear in a hundred tedious compositions which 'resemble Wagner' in their blaze of orchestration and their sedulous employment of the diminished seventh.

But within the walls of the theatre his influence, though not paramount, has been wide and salutary. It intimately affected the *Otello* and *Falstaff* of Verdi—two remarkable instances of discipleship on the part of a man already famous; it trained to good purpose many among the younger dramatists of France and Germany; it inaugurated a school which has been steadily growing in strength and reputation. The field is shared by two comrades: by lyric opera, with its twin forms of romance and comedy; by spectacular opera, which has taken the place of the old masque; but each occupies its station without rivalry or antagonism, and in future estimate Wagner's ideal will certainly be held of the most account. It is one of the ironies of musical history that a power so authoritative should be wielded by the man who was once a proscribed and persecuted outlaw.

Wagner, then, came to his full strength by throwing aside the traditional forms which he had never learned to master, which cramped and impeded his genius, and with which the particular character of his ideal enabled him to dispense. Brahms, on the contrary, found in the extension and development of these forms the fittest vehicle for the expression of romantic feeling. The descendant of Bach and Beethoven, he was no less the inheritor and disciple of Schumann, and it was his work to show how full a measure of the new poetry could be poured into the moulds of an exact and perfect musical design. The character of his music, grave, dignified, noble, made it specially amenable to intellectual control: at its most impassioned moment it never loses grasp, at the flood-tide of eloquence it never forgets restraint; it is wholly incapable of extravagance or sensationalism, of cheap effect or facile appeal. It is not a music with which all hearers can be in sympathy; it covers a comparatively narrow range of emotion; it has little gaiety, little humour; its colouring is often sombre, its texture sometimes heavy and opaque. But for richness of idea, for sheer beauty of melodic outline, and above all for supreme and unerring mastery of structure, it stands, among the compositions of our time, pre-eminent. There has been no musician since Beethoven to whose pages we can so often recur with the certainty of finding fresh cause for love and admiration.

Yet, except on Glazounov and on some of our English composers, the influence of Brahms has been hitherto almost negligible. The Slavonic schools of Bohemia and Russia have principally developed on their own lines, taking departure in the one case from Schubert and in the other from Weber and Glinka; the Norse musicians have, for the most part, found their teachers in Leipzig, and their inspiration in their own folk-songs; the younger generations of Germany, of Italy, and of France have been concerned with problems, now of pure style, now of emotional expression, which have left them comparatively indifferent to the needs of a self-determined architectural scheme. And the reason would seem to be that Brahms, like Bach, stands rather at the end than at the beginning of a period. He has summed up, as fully as our present conditions admit, the pure structural possibilities of symphony and quartet and sonata; he has brought them to a point of organization which, given the musical language of our day, cannot be surpassed. It is only natural that the art should turn aside, as it turned aside in 1750, and follow quests which, for the time, can be more profitably pursued. But, if we may trust the warrant of history, it will be only for a time. After the Viennese school had run its course, Bach came by his own; when music is ready for another stage in its advance it will return to Brahms for counsel.

The period which began with so sharp a contrast has been fertile in contrasts ever since. Through all Europe the field of composition has been broadening; it has been mapped into a thousand routes and traversed by a thousand explorers: Grieg and Dvořák, Cornelius and Hugo Wolf, Bizet's *Carmen* and Borodin's *Prince Igor*, Mascagni's superficial talent and straw-fire reputation, Gounod's insipid sweetness and languorous sentimentalism, Strauss *Isæo torrentior* and the laboured eloquence of Anton Bruckner; at no time has musical activity been wider or more varied, at no time has it offered a more bewildering range of topics to the critic and the historian. To attempt here even a catalogue of its main achievements would be to set an impossible task; to comprise it even under such rough formulae as Classical, or Romantic, or Realist, would be to recall the hospitality of Procrustes: at most we can only sketch a few of its most salient characteristics and illustrate their bearing upon our own English revival.

One such characteristic is a remarkable extension of melodic, and especially of harmonic, idiom. Mill once proved by algebra that musical phraseology was confined within measurable limits, and that it must soon be exhausted; his argument was unworthy of an inductive logician, and it has been discredited by the event. In every age the current shapes of melodic curve have been determined partly by their harmonic basis, partly by their relation to the accepted scale. Almost all the great tunes of Beethoven, for example, imply diatonic harmony (sometimes with a single chromatic point of colour), and in a large number of them the rise and fall is through consecutive diatonic notes. On the other hand, the Hungarian folk-songs derive much of their peculiar character from the augmented intervals which belong to their scale, and to the chromatic chords which these intervals naturally involve. It follows, therefore, that as these develop and interchange, as the use of the scale becomes more flexible, and the range of harmony more extensive, so there will arise in music not only a new idiom, but a new vocabulary. There is no need to complicate the issue by raising the question of rhythm; for rhythm, as Mr. Robert Bridges has said, is infinite, and its resources have always lain open to the hand of genius. But the very language of the art is undergoing a change, by which, for good or ill, its future must be largely determined.

Twenty years ago the typical instance would have been Dvořák, one of whose most remarkable gifts was his power of combining remote tonalities. He was perhaps the first European composer of repute who definitely took the chromatic scale as his unit, who regarded all notes as equally related, all harmonies as equally possible, all modulations as equidistant from the centre. Yet Dvořák was in this matter but the eldest child of his age, and the tendency exemplified in his writing has found fuller and more audacious expression in his younger contemporaries. We find it self-conscious and defiant in Mascagni, declamatory and dramatic in Bruneau; it is half the secret of Strauss's polyphony, it tinges the elusive colouring of Fauré and Loeffler. And in not one of these men is there any trace of Dvořák's influence: they have traversed the frontier for themselves, they have found each his own dialect of a language the range of which is apparently inexhaustible.

Among them the most distinctive and most uncompromising is M. Claude Debussy. His *provenance* is not easy to determine. There are occasional touches in his music which recall César Franck, but its general tone and character are very different from the missals which that cloistered and saintly artist occupied his life in illuminating. Paris has always been the home of experiments, and particularly of experiments in style and treatment; it may well be that we have here but another instance of that keen individual vitality which can transmute as well as absorb the ideas of its generation. In any case he is a true artist, a master of half-lights and delicate shadows, of colours that shift and intertwine and baffle our gaze, of a kind of beauty that is as inexplicable as it is literally beyond question. We may take it or leave it, but we cannot analyse or discuss. The discords—so to call them—of which its texture is mainly composed are such as have no name and no designation: they are so far from being justified by the grammarian that they cannot even be convicted by him; he turns page after page and there is no room for them even as breaches of rule. In the Introduction to *Pelléas et Mélisande* the most familiar passage is one of consecutive fifths balanced by one of consecutive sevenths; the rest is a tangle of semitones falling together in shapes and patterns that own allegiance to no recognized harmonic system. It never modulates, for it is without tonality; it never rests on a cadence, for it is without punctuation; its key-signature is a mere concession to the printer, and in its phraseology the laws of syntax are ignored. Yet the effect of it, as of the whole opera, is indescribably charming. Soft in tone, subtle in workmanship, exquisitely scored, it has all the delicate loveliness of Maeterlinck's play: the silent shadowy lake, the transparent nightfall, the dim castle with its tiny beacon-fire, the gentle hesitating figures that speak in the voices of dreamland. Of the same quality is the music, like floating clouds, which he has written on Mallarmé's *L'Après-midi d'un Faune*, a counterchange of nameless outlines and nameless hues; and still more remarkable, because not dependent on direct poetic suggestion, is the string-quartet which has blurred with iridescent rays the severe contours of chamber composition. The whole thing is sincere, sensitive, refined; it vibrates to a breath, it can be bruised with a touch, it is the direct outcome of a temperament almost too fragile for daily life.

And herein, no doubt, is its chief attendant danger. The style is never robust or vigorous, it does not express the larger and broader aspects of humanity, it does not paint with the great brush or on the great canvas. To impute this as a fault to Debussy would be as absurd as to complain of Maeterlinck because he is not Shakespeare; but it is of some interest to inquire whether in music this limitation depends on the temper of the artist or on the character of his medium. Is it possible, we may ask, that this *genre omnitonique* should be as fit a vehicle for epic ideas as the diatonic scale of Bach and Beethoven? If so, it will in course of time hold the entire field, and the diatonic scale will become as obsolete as the modes ; if not, it will remain for those forms of composition which specially depend on delicacy and refinement and suggestion, and will leave to a simpler speech the direct utterance of more vital truths. The answer, on present evidence, would seem to support the latter side. We do not forget that it must once have seemed unthinkable that the modes should ever be superseded; we do not forget that discords which one age could not tolerate without preparation have given acute pleasure to a later century; the ear has a considerable power of adjusting itself by course of experience, and there is no reason to suppose that it is nearing its limit. But as yet there is nothing to replace tonality except colour, and man cannot live by colour alone. Again, as soon as this hyper-chromatic style becomes insistent it grows, to our present hearing, ugly. Its beauty largely depends on reticence and restraint; it is coarsened by a loud tone or a forcible gesture. The famous violin-sonata in which Herr Max Reger has challenged his critics appears to us merely harsh and strident; there was no need for the rather sorry jest of deriving musical phrases from the words *Schafe* and *Affe*; it is all one torrent of blustering invective, without beauty, without nobility, without moderation. And even as invective it does not sound really spontaneous; it scolds of set purpose, it lashes itself into deliberate fury, it leaves the hearer irritated and unconvinced. Herr Reger is in many respects a person of consequence; he is skilful, ingenious, often incisive; but his sonata has neither the taste nor the self-respect by which the work of a great artist should be characterized.

Indeed it is in these two qualities that the 'advanced' school of German composition is conspicuously lacking. Dr. Strauss is an amazing master of resource; and his symphonic poems are as ostentatious as Trimalchio's banquet. The board groans under a weight of incongruous dainties, luxury follows luxury and surprise surprise, every corner of the empire is ransacked for a new wine or a new flavour; we are sated before the feast is half over and think ourselves fortunate if we escape with our digestions unimpaired. There can be no doubt about the wealth: it cries out to us from every corner, it dazzles us from every piece of plate, it overwhelms us with a hundred marks of lavishness and profusion. And yet when all is done we are at some pains to express our gratitude: we should have been better off with plainer living and higher thinking, with a less urgent host and a less bewildering display.

Now richness and volume of sound are in themselves admirable, and Dr. Strauss often uses them to admirable effect. There are pages in *Heldenleben*, in *Don Juan*, in *Tod und Verklärung* which fill our hearing to the brim with beautiful and recondite tone, and which, if they had been used as points of sensuous or emotional climax, would have triumphantly achieved their aim. But these are precisely the passages on which his lowest light is cast; they are the points of repose, and the climax is too often reserved for splashes of colour which only startle, or for outbursts of sheer noise which only offend. To say that these are determined by the exigencies of a 'poetic' content is not a sufficient answer; it explains them, but it does not justify them. For in the first place the function of music is to beautify and idealize; and not everything can be expressed in terms of beauty, but only those aspects of life and nature which are capable of idealization. In the second place, apart from any question of representative expression, these devices are among the easiest and most obvious that a musician can employ; as pure technique they belong to a lower level of skill than firm outline and harmonious arrangement. Any one can be impressive; any one can surprise and startle and shock; you have but to bid your violins play a quarter of a note sharp to secure the most poignant effect of pain; you have but to introduce into your orchestra the siren and the steam-whistle to arouse the attention of the most apathetic audience. And in the third place all waste is inartistic; one of the essential characteristics of the master is economy and reserve of power. It has been urged against an eminent English novelist that he 'always writes at the top of his voice, and shouts so loud that we cannot hear what he says'; there are many pages of Strauss's music which lay themselves open to the same criticism. The battle-scene in *Heldenleben* is indeed 'with confused noise'; the storms of *Also sprach Zarathustra* beat upon our heads like hurricanes: in *Till Eulenspiegel*, in *Don Quixote*, even in the *Domestic Symphony*, we often struggle amid such deep waters that we would catch at the most jagged discord for safety.

And, what is more serious, the issues are not worth the coil that is raised about them. The accusation of noise is in itself of little account; it was brought successively against Beethoven and Wagner, yet to Wagner's orchestration we have long grown accustomed, and Beethoven's, we are told, is too faint for modern requirements. The really vital point is that Dr. Strauss has transferred the centre of gravity from the end to the means. Of all important composers he is the poorest in thematic invention: his melodies, even that in *Don Juan*, are not of the first order; the characteristic phrases which serve him for *dramatis personæ* are hardly ever adequate to sustain their parts. The result is that he throws the whole of his immense ability into the treatment of themes that cannot properly respond; he heaps up accessories, he covers the stage with furniture, he attempts to supersede plot and character with gorgeous pageantry and with elaborate costume. At every moment our senses are stunned or pampered or stimulated by some explosive device or some voluptuous display; if all else fails he will turn his tragedy to melodrama and his comedy to harlequinade. No doubt his accessories are often very striking: there are forests full of lions and gardens full of peacocks; there are gladiatorial shows and processions of royal state; but the one thing of which we take away no sure impression is the play itself.

All this bears the clear impress of a decadent and sophisticated art. It is the manner, not of Rome and Athens, but of Byzantium and Alexandria; its passion is luxurious, its humour undignified, its workmanship self-conscious and overwrought. It can excite, it can intoxicate, it can dazzle us with coruscations of brilliance and set us tingling with a pleasure that is sometimes very near to pain, but it leaves out of account all the nobler side of human nature; the tenderness that is too deep for tears, the chivalry that is too high to threaten, the indwelling spiritual power with which all great music has held communion. We are in no way concerned with its relation to other forms or methods; art has room for all forms, for all methods, for all languages that can be touched to fine issues. But we are concerned with the essential difference between the love which purifies emotion and the unbridled appetite which degrades it. 'A poem', said Shelley, 'is the very image of life expressed in its eternal truth.' There is no vision of the eternal in this reckless indulgence which lives upon excess and will die of surfeit.

Meanwhile there has been arising in Eastern Europe a school of composition which was destined to infuse the art with new blood and new vitality. Its founder,

Balakirev, came to St. Petersburg at the time when Glinka's career was approaching its end; preached the gospel of nationalism with the fervour of a young enthusiast; and soon gathered round him the remarkable group of artists who called themselves the 'Neo-Russian Innovators'—Cui, Mussorgsky, Rimsky-Korsakov, and Borodin, the greatest of them all. They began with a systematic study of the classics from Bach and Handel onward, they collected folk-songs, they debated ideals, they set themselves in single-hearted earnest to establish a native music on a native foundation. In opera they followed the lead of Dargomijsky, whose *Festin de Pierre* had definitely broken away from the old lyric conventions; in symphony and quartet and song they widened the structural forms and filled them with the picturesque and racy vernacular of the Russian speech. Like all reformers, they met at first with an opposition which they took no pains to conciliate; but little by little their cause prevailed and the circle widened until it reached even the conservatism of Glazounov and the cosmopolitanism of Tchaikovsky. The result of their work has been to develop a music of the highest interest and importance; a music which, we may say advisedly, is not unworthy to rank beside the great names of Russian literature. It has shown itself remarkably divergent in style and mood: saturnine with Mussorgsky, visionary with Rimsky-Korsakov, with Borodin eager, imaginative and romantic; but through all divergencies it reflects, in greater or less degree, the sensitive and impressionable character of its people. Among its principal masters Tchaikovsky is, perhaps, the least central and the least representative; the want of personal force which enfeebled his life renders his music liable to external influences, and allows it sometimes, from very weariness of invention, to sink into triviality and commonplace. But Tchaikovsky, though the most unequal among great composers, reaches at his best an extraordinarily high level of beauty; the first movement of the Fifth Symphony and the march movement of the Sixth are gifts the value of which is beyond dispute; and it is precisely in such numbers as these that he is most characteristic and most national. Of the other men it is more difficult to speak, for opportunities of hearing their work are infrequent and some of it is written in an idiom unfamiliar to Western ears. But there can be no doubt that in Borodin Russia has produced a genius of the first order. The chemistry professor, who joined Balakirev in 1862, equipped with 'a fair proficiency on the violoncello and a great admiration for Mendelssohn's chamber-music', became a national poet by whose melodies the whole achievement of the art has been enriched. He wrote slowly and irregularly, amid the intervals of a scientific occupation; he left barely a dozen completed scores when, in 1887, his career was cut short by a premature death; no musician has ever claimed immortality with so slender an offering. Yet, if there be, indeed, immortalities in music, his claim is incontestable. His symphony in E flat major and his opera *Prince Igor* are masterpieces which the world can never afford to forget; every page is spontaneous, every thought is noble, every incident is alive with the spirit of youth and adventure.

The stimulus which a nationalist revival has afforded to Russian music is the best of auguries for the further progress and development of our own. During the period here under discussion we have been passing through the same phase. When Sullivan came back from Leipzig in 1861 we were at the lowest ebb of artistic reputation to which our country has ever sunk; we were, as Carlyle said, 'a dumb people . . . for Mozart nothing but a Mr. Bishop', and our sole function was to pay our Continental neighbours for puzzling us with problems which we did not understand. The production of the *Tempest* music in 1862, followed a few months later by Bennett's *Paradise and the Peri* overture, aroused some hope that a new era had begun; but neither Bennett nor Sullivan was strong enough to lead the advance. Bennett's delicate and refined talent did much to purify the air, but it so feared vulgarity that it shrank from manliness; Sullivan, after a few unsuccessful essays in the larger forms, devoted the best of his melody and humour to the byways of light opera, and his *Golden Legend* signally confirms the wisdom of his choice. He was not capable of great ideas or of a great style; his strength lay in suppleness, in dexterity of hand, in a natural gift of jest and epigram. His most characteristic work is as good-tempered and diverting as a play of Sheridan; it skims lightly over the surface of things, it is witty and alert and fanciful, and we are but ungrateful critics if we complain of its limitations.

It was about twenty years later that our nationalist movement took definite shape. In 1880 Parry's *Prometheus* was given at Gloucester, in 1882 Stanford's *Elegiac Symphony* was given at Cambridge, and from thenceforward we have never turned back. The advance has been slow and difficult, for no nation ever had so much to unlearn; it has been checked by apathy, it has been hampered by impatience, it has been depreciated by that mock humility in which our pride so frequently masquerades. But in spite of all obstacles and opposition it has won its way. No one can possibly compare the England of the present time with the England of the seventies and doubt that our whole attitude towards music has changed; we are no longer content with pale copies of German or Italian models, we are no longer content with trivial themes and perfunctory workmanship, we have emancipated our native thought, we have rediscovered our native speech, we are beginning once more to resume the place which, ever since the seventeenth century, we had forfeited by our carelessness and indifference. We have not yet attained our end; there is still much to be done before we have finally passed beyond the old errors and prescriptions and have emerged into the open field. But a younger generation is arising, full of talent and promise and enthusiasm; the way lies direct before it, and to its hands the future may safely be entrusted.

The compositions of Parry and Stanford offer an interesting foil and contrast to one another. Parry touches the deeper note; his prevalent mood is one of serious earnest. In the earlier days of his career, in the days of *Prometheus*, of *St. Cecilia*, of the *Lotus-Eaters*, he allowed free play to his sense of colour and romance; in his later writing he has grown reserved, reticent, almost ascetic, deliberately minimizing the appeal to the senses, concentrating his whole force on the intimate expression of religious or philosophic truth. Now and again, in holiday trim, he will set a comedy of Aristophanes and banter, through a few brilliant pages, the sensationalism against which his whole art is a protest; his real message is to reaffirm, in phrase so simple that we may sometimes miss its purport, the awe and mystery which surround the confines of human life. Toward this ideal he has been gradually making his way, accepting first the conventional forms of the oratorio, which not even his genius could revive, and then replacing them by the freer method of ode and cantata which he has chosen for his medium in recent years. And throughout his work he employs an idiom of pure English as distinctly national as that of Purcell himself. He is the spokesman of all that is best in our age and country, its dignity, its manhood, its reverence; in his music the spirit of Milton and Wordsworth may find its counterpart. Stanford's work, on the other hand, is quicker-witted, more skilful, more picturesque; it has less of the prophet, but it has more of the artist. It is filled with the very temper of the Irish folk-songs, their poetry, their humour, their extraordinary beauty of sound. A master of technique, he makes his effects with unerring certainty; his orchestra is a delight to the ear, his songs are vocal, expressive, and often fascinating. But he does not penetrate to the centre, he does not drive to the roots: he stirs us to the emotion of an April day with its counterchange of sun and shower,

all charming, all exquisite, and all transitory. There is nothing in his music so moving as the dirge from the *Purcell* Ode, or the first chorus of *The Love that Casteth out Fear*. His place among great artists has been attained, by other means: by a keen and alert invention, by graciousness of outline and colour, by a natural eloquence which, if not profound, is always interesting and persuasive.

Between these men and their successors of the younger generation there stands one remarkable figure whose influence on English music it must be left to the future to decide. Self-taught, self-centred, self-determined, Elgar may claim, more than any other English composer, that he has been 'his own ancestor'. His position is in some ways comparable with that of Berlioz at the beginning of the last century; there is something of the same audacity, of the same wayward brilliance, of the same desire to push musical expression across the verge of articulate speech. Indeed it is no paradox to say that *Gerontius* offers many points of comparison with *Faust*; the demons are different in language but not different in conception; the song of *Praise to the Holiest* is better written than the *Easter Hymn*, but it is almost as undevotional; the extraordinary skill of orchestration covers in the one case, as in the other, an occasional weakness of idea. And herein is the essential defect of Elgar's music, so far as it has hitherto appeared. Before the highest and noblest conceptions it invariably falters; it can express pain and weariness and impatience and revolt, it can be poignant and bitter and pathetic, and while it moves within this range it is always striking and often exceedingly beautiful. But as yet the large and serene joy of art is closed to it. In *The Apostles* Judas is the central figure; the interest of the whole work gathers round his sneering commentary on the Beatitudes, his temptation, his treachery, his passion of remorse. It is a wonderful piece of characterization, but it throws greater things into the background. And the same want of largeness and serenity often appears in the handling of the music; it is all broken up into little anxious 'motives', which are not blended together but laid like tesserae in a mosaic, each with its own colour and its own shape. No work of equal ability has ever displayed so little mellowness of tone.

He is much more successful in his purely orchestral writings. *Cockaigne* is a vigorous and bustling picture of street-life; the *Alassio* overture, though a little hard, is full of sparkle; the *Enigma* variations are, in their kind, a masterpiece. Here his work is more genial, more evenly rounded, more melodious; he gives a greater impression of ease, he employs to fuller effect his extraordinary power of technical detail. But, if we may hazard a conjecture, we believe that despite his decade of reputation he has not yet found himself. His manner is still somewhat tentative and transitional; it often moves with uncertain step, it often seems to be striving with a thought which it cannot attain. Already he has advanced far beyond the prentice-hand of *King Olaf* and *Caractacus*; it may well be that the coming years will bring a deeper insight and a more mature experience.

Of the new generation it is here unfitting to speak; *non res laudanda sed spes est.* Yet we can find reason for confidence in its talent, its earnestness of purpose, and not less in the wide range and variety of its experiments. Some of these we believe to be on the wrong lines, those in particular which are touched with conscious and exotic artifice, but they are all indications of activity, and in the clash of their conflicting counsels the truth will be established. The chief danger, no doubt, is that we come late into the field, that we are beginning where our neighbours have already achieved, and that some of us are still tempted to regard them not only as teachers but as models for our imitation. To do this is to ignore the qualities no less than the limitations of our national character. We have our own language to speak, we have our own message to deliver, we have our own ideals to maintain; our leaders have arisen to point the road, and it is to them that the younger men will most profitably look for direction and guidance. Every great musician has learned something from foreign schools; not one has ever been absorbed by them. The technical equipment of art is of the common interchange of human society; the truth which it depicts is of the native inheritance of the artist.

SOME ASPECTS OF MODERN MUSIC[1]

1915

WHEN the critic is young he regards every new movement as a sacred cause to be defended, and every man who stands on the old ways as an adversary to be challenged and overthrown. When he grows older he begins to find reason for modifying both these opinions. The claims of novelty if not less attractive become less urgent. Like Browning's Ogniben he has 'seen three and twenty leaders of revolts' and the appearance of a four and twentieth although it rouses him to keen interest no longer thrills him with the sense of adventure. He has exchanged the arena for the laboratory, he has come to see that there are many aspects of truth and that they are all worth studying; he finds himself in sympathy with all forms of original expression, and holds that the only unpardonable sins are imposture and pretentiousness.

It may be said at once that the advantage is not all on the side of age. The quieter temper and the broader outlook are in part compensated by a less quick intelligence and a less ready enthusiasm. A man in middle-life has already fallen to some extent under the dominion of use and custom, his experience has moulded his character in certain directions, his early preferences have tended to harden and stereotype: the very forces that are maturing his judgement are taking their revenge by blunting his sensibility. Not that art means less to him; in many ways it means a great deal more, but the meaning is different, and in the fact of that difference something has been lost. Many of us can remember the stab of physical pleasure with which we first heard the opening of Beethoven's Violin Concerto, or of Bach's B minor Mass, or of the second act of *Tristan*. Much of the new music is charming and admirable and intensely interesting, but it does not reproduce for us those supreme moments of delight.

Hence there is a real difficulty in discussing a phase of

[1] From *The Musical Quarterly*, 1915.

art which is making its appeal primarily to a younger generation. And the difficulty is increased by the extreme rapidity with which the language and idiom of music have altered during the last twenty years. To this it may be doubted whether the whole history of the art can furnish a parallel. We have learned that the Florentine Revolution is an historical myth, and that the first 'opera' followed traditions which had been steadily growing for more than a century. Bach's equal temperament gave a new direction to music, but the splendid harmonic audacity with which he used it had little or no influence on composition until fifty years after his death. Mozart, Beethoven, Schubert, are not so far from each other as the music of 1880 from that of 1914. The Romantic movement was in many ways frankly conservative, and Brahms with greater genius followed it on the conservative side. Wagner broke down the conventions of the drama and gave music a new emotional content, but the considerable changes of idiom which this entailed never really crossed the border into a new language. At the present day it appears as if the whole problem was being restated; as if the very principles of the art were called in question; as if its vocabulary were being written afresh and its most vital distinctions dismissed as obsolete. The first thing then is to inquire whether this is indeed the case, and whether, if so, an art of equal or greater value can be raised on the new foundations.

Here we are met by two rather disheartening obstacles. One of the besetting sins of the present age is its habit of intellectual slovenliness. Everybody wants to be in the movement, everybody is half-educated, there are abundant articles and little hand-books from which you can get up enough for dinner conversation and with that lowly ideal many men seem to be satisfied. It is not easy to discuss recent painting with people who believe that Futurism and Post Impressionism are the same thing; or to discuss recent music with people who ask you 'if you like such composers as Strauss and Debussy'. Criticism is lost in a prevalent fog through which you can hear nothing but the megaphone and see nothing but the electric light. The advertiser strains his voice to the furthest breaking point, and the journalist encourages him with shouting, every opinion is expressed in superlatives, partly to conceal ignorance and partly to attract attention, every shanty is a saloon and every inn a palace, guessing riddles is called a tournament and killing flies a crusade: in all this general welter it is not surprising that distinctions are forgotten, that shades of meaning are confused, and that the power of discrimination is becoming atrophied by disuse. We have many excellent qualities at the present day, but we are losing our sense of scholarship.

The second obstacle, which is, I believe, complementary to the first, is the extreme complexity of much contemporary music. For instance, I am told that Schönberg's *Gurrelieder* is a fine work, and so far as I can make it out I am ready to endorse this opinion. But it is written for five solo voices, besides a 'Sprecher', for two choruses of eight and twelve voices respectively, and for a band which contains one hundred and fourteen orchestral parts. In order to publish it at all it has to be engraved, not printed, on an enormous sheet of paper with notes the size of pin points, directions which are almost unreadable, and leger lines which sometimes require a magnifying glass. The style is that of advanced modern polyphony in which every part is real, no eye can possibly take in a whole page at once, and the chances of hearing the music may perhaps occur twice in a lifetime.

No doubt this is an extreme case, but it is not so extreme as to be outside fair criticism, and it is not unfair to urge that there must be something wrong with a work which, in aiming at its effect, is obliged to use such a suicidal prodigality of means. In the seventeenth century a learned Jesuit named Athanasius Kircher published a treatise on music and quoted as one of his examples a composition which he calls the *Nodus Salomonis*; a canon in 12,200,000 real parts, and capable of further extension.

He does not regard it as practically possible in this world, though he expresses a pious hope that he may hear it in the next; its effect would be that of the chord of G major reiterated for ever and ever; and his account of it ends with the words 'haec ad mirificam Musicae combinationis vim demonstrandam sufficiant'.

Now with all deference we would submit that they can do nothing of the kind. We are not supplicating that music should be starved to the measure of our understanding, but maintaining that when it swells beyond a certain bulk it topples over. No doubt we must allow for the immense improvement in executive skill through which our modern orchestras can play passages which would have been impossible half a century ago: that is all to the good and we may take full advantage of it; but we are pressing executive skill beyond bounds when we use it for compositions which outstrip the capacity of the human ear. A great deal of the most elaborate modern music sounds as if it was all of the same colour: a rich blur of sound in which the different voices are hardly distinguishable, and from which, if current stories are true, they may sometimes absent themselves without detection. It is a far cry from this to the perfect transparence of Debussy's *Pelléas*, where every note tells, and where the full orchestra is used only once throughout the entire work.

We may be told that the ear will adapt itself to the new conditions as it has done many times before, and that the day will come when a symphonic poem of Schönberg is as straightforward as we now find a symphony of Mozart. To this it is a sufficient rejoinder that by that time men will be writing something else, and that these works are therefore in danger of withering before they grow up. But there is a more serious reason for disquietude. One of the clearest lessons in history is that when an artistic school begins to grow luxurious or self-conscious or erudite it is carrying in it the seeds of its own decadence. It was so with the Alexandrine school of Greek literature, it was so with the Roman poetry of the fourth century, it was so with the counterpoint of the Middle Ages, and precisely the same peril confronts the German school of which Schönberg is the greatest exponent. It seems to me not new but old, not adventurous but deliberate, its experiments appear to be the outcome of theories and formulas, rather than the spontaneous impulse of artistic passion. With his early work, derived in some degree from Mahler and influenced in some degree by Strauss, we need not here be concerned: the centre of his mature work is best explained by his own treatise on Harmony. In this admirable work, written with style, distinction, and humour, he sets forth very clearly certain artistic principles of which two seem to be specially significant. In the first place he treats as stable harmonic masses effects which in the older composers were used only as appoggiaturas, or as passing discords: holding, in other words, that anything which the ear can endure for a transitory instant it can equally endure as a point of rest.[1] This drives straight to the roots of the difference between concord and discord, and incidentally, I believe, accounts for many of the more serious experiments in modern harmony. In the second place he sets himself to construct a harmonic scheme on a system of superimposed fourths, now treated melodically, as in the opening theme of his 'Chamber Symphony', now raised in a towering structure across the whole of the great stave. Here he admits some limitations in practice, but it is difficult to see where the line is to be drawn, for he quotes with approval a chord of eleven fourths which contains, in one or other of its forms, every semitone in the chromatic scale. No doubt

[1] In his *Harmonienlehre* (p. 363) he quotes instances from Mozart and Bach, of which the former is an appoggiatura, the latter a dominant seventh cadence with passing notes which are regarded as vital parts of the harmony. I believe that a corollary from this will be the doctrine that if any notes in a chord be chromatically altered, the chord may resolve as though the alteration had not taken place. And this will lead to a considerable extension of harmonic freedom.

the discord may be veiled by differences of orchestral timbre, but even so it is sufficiently striking.[1]

Now this is well enough in a treatise, but as composition it is surely the purest formalism. It is music made according to rule and measure, written by a man of unusual intellect and great receptivity who spoils everything by too obvious an adherence to method. We need not inquire whether the chords in themselves are ugly—there is probably no combination of notes which cannot in its proper context be made to sound beautiful: the primary fault is that they are written to order, that they remind one too much of Leibnitz's definition of music as 'Arithmetic become self-conscious'. And if this is true, the harmony of Schönberg may become a most valuable storehouse and training school, but it will not itself lead far into the art of the future.

Yet when all is said, one remembers the Schönberg of the early songs and the early chamber music, and wonders whether after all this learned and professorial art may not be a transitional stage towards something larger and finer. The little pianoforte pieces, Op. 11 and Op. 19, give me the impression that they mean something to which I have not yet the clue. They start on a different hypothesis from music, like Lobatchevski's geometry which started on the supposition that the triangle contained less than two right angles. And here we come to an alternative on which we may well be content to suspend judgement. If they are spontaneous they will live, and the world will come round to them, though they have little pleasure for us now. If, as I think at present, they are deliberate and artificial, they will go the way of all artificialities and will end their days in the dusty corners of the museum. But in either case, the impression that they give me is that of the end of an old art, not the beginning of a new one.

1 See also the chord from Schönberg's *Erwartung*, quoted in the passage on harmonized instrumentation. It contains thirteen different notes—two enharmonic.

Over against them, arrayed in all the panoply of youth, comes the vigorous and aggressive band of the Futurists. Here again the dispassionate student is confronted with a difficulty, for the very clever young men who surround Signor Marinetti are so peremptory that it is hardly possible to hear them without irritation. 'They raise aloft', says one of them, 'their blood-red banner.' 'They advance', as another tells us, 'with their hearts full of fire, hatred and swiftness.' They wage implacable war upon every known place of instruction. They demand the immediate demolition of every picture more than twenty years old. They write fierce critical volumes to prove the inutility of criticism, and declare in the most egotistical of manifestoes that they have destroyed the egotist from the earth. They have constructed a literature without verbs or particles, they have painted nightmares and built up statues out of cigarettes and lamp-shades: there is no extravagance which they have not committed. And yet there is something in it.

The idea which animates Futurism may be summarized in two propositions. First, that all art is being strangled by tradition, that it is clogged and impeded by the inheritance of the past. We see through the eyes of our forefathers, we hear through their ears, we think through their brains; we have no longer the courage to face nature at first hand, but are dependent on the suggestion of our teachers. Therefore, say the Futurists, if art is to be saved alive, let us sweep away tradition altogether and start afresh. Second, that apart from the essential evils of pupilage, the past has no longer anything relevant to teach us. The conditions of life have so radically altered that they demand an entirely new form of artistic expression. We live in an age of swift movement and dynamic force, of radium and electricity, of the motor and the aeroplane, of a hundred appliances all concentrated on the rapid exercise of power: the characteristics of the new age are force and vigour and lusty youth, impatient of delay, scornful of opposition, annihilating time and space as it flies on its immediate purpose. What have we to do with the suave and leisurely art of the past, with its quiet thoughts and its passive gratifications, its long-drawn problem of style and its logical coherence of structure? The music of old time was an art of peace and luxury, we are for war, 'seule hygiène du monde'.[1]

The conclusions which follow from these principles have been made familiar in more than one manifesto. There is to be no more academic instruction, but every man working out his own salvation in his own way: no more romance—love is too soft for the warrior: no more well-constructed art—when the blood leaps high you have not time to think of style: no more restriction but undisputed liberty of utterance. Melody is to be regarded as a 'synthesis of harmony', based on the chromatic scale as unit and wholly free in rhythm: the old symphonic structures are to go by the board and the form of each composition is to be 'generated by its own motive of passion'; Church music is to be abolished as impotent, and opera (in which the composer must be his own librettist) is to be treated as a symphonic poem where the singers have no pride of place but rank alongside the instruments of the orchestra. Lastly, it is to be the function of the Futurist composer 'to express the soul of factories and trains and steamships . . . and to wed to his central motive the dominion of the machine and the victorious reign of electricity'.[2]

It is plain that we have here much food for contemplation: it is equally plain that there is much with which we are prepared to agree. Every great artist has always stood for freedom, and if the claim is here more strident than usual, that may perhaps be explained by some circumstances of provocation. Again, it is natural that art

[1] Marinetti, *Le Futurisme*, ch. v, p. 53, 'Qui peut affirmer', he says on the preceding page, 'que le mot *homme* et le mot *lutteur* ne soient pas synonymes ?'

[2] Pratella, *Musica Futurista*, pp. 15–16.

should express the ideals and emotions of its own time: its function is to interpret, not to recall, and in every advance of civilized man it has taken its place among the pioneers. But both these points require further consideration before we can understand their meaning. The freedom of the artist means immunity from prescriptive rule: the indefeasible right to see beauty in his own way and to express it in his own terms. But art is not something separate and distinct from human nature, it is an essential aspect of humanity itself; and one measure of the artist's genuineness is that what he sees now the world, through his interpretation, will come to see later. And because the artist is a man born of men his vision will not be out of relation to that which was seen by his fathers before him. He will speak parables, but he will not speak them in an unknown tongue. Hence, any attempt to break violently with the past is foreign to the real nature of art. The sense of beauty may develop more rapidly in one period than another: it has developed with exceptional rapidity in our own generation; but in proportion as it is living it will draw sustenance from the roots of its mother earth.

Free rhythm, free harmony, free use of the chromatic scale, free treatment of structural forms: all these are the colours on the artist's palette which he may employ as he will. It is not about these that there should be any contest, but about the question what he does with them. Does he equally avoid monotony and incoherence, does he express noble feeling, does he use his medium with such reserve as to throw his light upon special points of colour, has he melody and passion and the power of climax? If so, he may go where he pleases, secure that we are ready to follow him. The types of artistic beauty are not one but many, and each type is inexhaustible.

A word should be added on the worship of Mechanism, which seems to be an essential part of the Futurist creed. It is no doubt intelligible that a group of men who derive their inspiration from power and swiftness should be attracted by the marvels of mechanical science and should even come, like the engineer in Mr. Wells's story, to attach religious significance to a dynamo. This exactly fits with the revolt from formal beauty which is at the other side of their minds, and is liable to precisely the same danger. Force and speed are pre-eminent in their own sphere: to be made subjects of art they need to be transfigured and irradiated by something more than their own light. And the same insensibility which accepts them as artistic ideals is apparent in the poetry and the music which these men have offered as the first outcome of their school. Marinetti's poem on the Balkan war is extraordinarily vivid and direct: it carries the reader forward with almost the force of personal experience; but it is entirely without any delight except that of swift motion. Pratella's example of composition, printed at the end of *Musica Futurista*, has some vigorous and swinging rhythm; but there is little in it to arrest the attention, and the greater part of it seems to me either trivial or monotonous.[1] The territory which the Futurists claim may be theirs by right, but they have not yet shown that they can administer it.

Traditionalism closes a chapter, revolt attempts to tear the pages out of the book. A wiser and more progressive art recognizes the value of what has been written and begins its new chapter at the point where the last concluded. Of this we have, in the music of the present day, many instances from many lands: the native wood-notes of Sibelius, the delicate and tender art of Ravel, Stravinsky's melody and humour and amazing gift of orchestral colour, all in their way breaking new ground, all taking their points of departure from past achievement. Among these is one man who may specially be taken as typical: an artist who as yet attempted few fields of composition, but in those has shown remarkable genius and a rapid and continuous advance. Scriabin is still a

[1] It is fair to say that I am judging by the pianoforte score. But it is this which Pratella quotes as his illustration.

young man, and of his published works, which have now passed the seventieth opus-number, more than half have been produced during the last six years. A large majority of them are written for pianoforte solo, among the others are a piano concerto (Op. 20), three symphonies (Op. 26, 29, 43), and two very striking symphonic poems of which *Prometheus* (Op. 60) has done more than anything else to establish his reputation. It is worth adding that ten of his pianoforte works are sonatas and that the latest of these is Op. 70.

So far it would seem as though he were merely a 'conservative' musician, content to accept the traditional forms and little concerned with their extension or development. But when we study the music we find that the reverse is the case. In his hands the sonata widens and enlarges until it becomes a new means of expression. Each symphony is more adventurous than its predecessor, and the symphonic poems are triumphs of successful audacity. Here is no timid and laggard art: every step is planted firmly and every movement is onward. His early work shows traces of Chopin's influence, yet always with a distinctive note: by the time that he has reached Op. 25 (a set of nine dainty mazurkas) the period of studentship is definitely over and from thenceforward he speaks with his own voice. As his work proceeds it grows more sonorous, more impetuous, more passionate: the formal restraints fall away, not by violence but by natural expansion from within: it is music as free as thought and as vigorous as life which has won strength through discipline and liberty through reverence for law. Among technical points may be noted the variety and flexibility of his rhythm, the fullness and richness of his harmonization, and his gradual acceptance of the chromatic scale as basis, an acceptance so frankly given in the end that two of his latest sonatas have no key-signature. But these speak only of the grammar and vocabulary of his art, they are the dry bones upon which he has breathed the spirit of romance. Amid the younger composers of Europe there is none whose present achievement holds out greater promise for the future.

A few years, then, have sufficed to develop a genius which starts from Chopin and has already all the neologisms of music at its command. In its development the stages are as clearly traceable as in that of any other composer—not of course in unbroken line, but in general trend and direction.[1]

And this progress is the reaction of a vivid and powerful mind on resources and materials which had long been in preparation. Take for instance the use of the chromatic scale. As far back as 1840 Chopin was employing half-tones with a freedom which brought upon him the wrath of conservative critics: then came Liszt with his dream of a *genre omnitonique*, then a number of masters who helped each in his way to bring that dream nearer to realization. Wagner treated the appoggiatura as no man had treated it before him, wove his orchestral texture out of a new and often chromatic polyphony, and made his actors follow as nearly as possible the cadences of the speaking voice. Dvořák showed wonderful ingenuity in the combination and succession of remote tonalities, and in one of his smaller works (*Poetische Stimmungsbilder*, No. 12) tried the experiment of such continuous and rapid modulation that the music could bear no key-signature. Grieg devised a scheme of harmonic colour which unquestionably influenced Debussy on one side—César Franck another and richer scheme which influenced not only Debussy but all subsequent French music. Strauss in the first two numbers of *Heldenleben* broke down all distinctions together and treated all notes in the scale as equally related. Meanwhile, the Russian composers

[1] e.g. in the Pianoforte works, the Mazurkas (Op. 25), the Fantasie (Op. 28), the two *Poèmes* (Op. 32), the *Preludes* (Op. 35), the *Poème Satanique* (Op. 36), and the seventh and tenth sonatas. The first symphony (Op. 26) is more or less on customary lines, the third (Op. 43) is virtually a symphonic poem, and after that come *Le poème de l'extase* (Op. 54), and *Prometheus* (Op. 60).

from Mussorgsky onward were bringing their own solution of the problem; one can trace it in Cui, and still more in Rimsky-Korsakov, and so onward to the younger school of which Scriabin and Stravinsky are among the most conspicuous masters. There is no doubt that the whole texture of music has in this way been greatly enriched, its vocabulary widened, its possibility of expression enlarged. But there are two attendant dangers. One that all this opulence and splendour may be gained at some expense of purity, and that the ear overcharged with sound may lose its nicety and cleanness of judgement: one that in employing for common use the whole range of musical language there may be nothing left for moments of emphasis. The effect of harmony depends more than anything else in music on its context: a dominant seventh in Mozart, an augmented sixth in Schubert, may strike us with incomparable pleasure because they stand as supreme points of colour in a phrase that has been specially toned down to prepare for them. Nowadays it is not unusual to see on the printed page an apparently recondite modulation which, when we hear it, leaves us cold because we are already surfeited. In other words, one kind of climax—that which comes from sheer reserve and reticence in colour—appears to be less at the disposal of modern music than it was at that of the great classics.

It is for this reason, among others, that design is becoming more and more dependent upon expression. The balance, held perfectly by Beethoven, is now swinging definitely over to the poetic side, and 'Sonate, que veux-tu?' is no longer an intelligible question. This again is only the continuation of a process which has been going on ever since the beginning of the art: the work of every period has seemed formal to its successor and we are in this matter also the inheritors of past ages. But the insistence on expression and even representation in music is now more urgent and more prevalent than it has ever been. Our favourite forms are dramas and ballets of action, songs in which melody is pushed to the point of declamation, symphonic poems and descriptive overtures; even our chamber-works are beginning to look from their window at the street or the landscape. Now it is a commonplace that all true music is expressive—the outcome of a vital impulse which speaks because it cannot keep silence. Music which has no emotion behind it is a mere academic puzzle: the merriest of Haydn's scherzos, the lightest rondo of Mozart, has its own feeling as truly as the slow movement of the Choral symphony. But to make expression the sole measure of form is an artistic blunder. For one thing, if it is to build a climax wholly out of emotion it is in danger of piling Pelion upon Ossa until it culminates in mere wildness and extravagance; for another, if it entirely disregards formal beauty it will soon dispense with beauty of sound and replace the orchestra, as indeed Signor Marinetti has already done, by a babel of noise-machines. And for those of us who think that the first business of music is to be beautiful these extremes are a little disheartening. By all means, we say, carry your emotion as far as is consistent with loveliness, by all means 'let the idea create its own form', provided that the form be intelligible. But mere intensity is not sufficient in itself—otherwise the most artistic things in the world would be blind rage and inarticulate passion. It is not only that if we abrogate objective law we give up all hopes of a standard and place ourselves at the mercy of any young gentleman who crashes his fist on the piano and calls that a 'Mood' or an 'Impression'. Even if the feeling be genuine it is but the raw material of art, and the finished work must be such as gives us joy in the hearing.

At all times there have been pedants who would check advance and hot-headed revolutionaries who would misdirect it. At all times there have been musicians who sang for profit and musicians who sang for popularity and musicians who, like Dryden's rustic,

> whistled as they went for want of thought.

But at all times, and at the present no less than any there, have been artists of high aim and noble purpose who recognize that the greatest genius is he to whom the world means most, and that if a man is strong enough to create he is also receptive enough to learn. The present age is neither exceptional nor anomalous. Some of the new music is the conscious readjustment of old materials—the sounds are strange, but they have no fresh idea to convey. Some is merely the trick of a mischievous child who will learn better when he grows up; some the natural but passing anger of a revolt against prettiness or pedantry. And through all these the great stream of music continues its appointed course, not unconscious of the swirls and eddies at the bank-sides, but recognizing that some of them are flowing backward, and some are spinning round and round, and yet all will ultimately find their way into the volume of its waters. In art the good that men do lives after them, and all true effort is absorbed in a common immortality.

WILLIAM BYRD, 1623–1923[1]

IN the year 1516 Erasmus published his commentary on the New Testament. After the fashion of the time he illustrated many of his points by contemporary events, and so took the opportunity of a text in Corinthians[2] to censure in drastic terms the Church music of the early sixteenth century.

'St. Paul says that he would rather speak five words with a reasonable meaning than ten thousand in an unknown tongue. They chant nowadays in Churches in what is an unknown tongue and nothing else, while you will not hear a sermon once in six months telling people to amend their lives. Modern Church music is so constructed that the congregation cannot hear one distinct word. The Choristers themselves do not understand what they are singing, yet according to priests and monks it constitutes the whole of Religion. Why will they not listen to St. Paul? In Colleges and monasteries it is still the same: music and nothing but music. There was no music in St. Paul's time. Words were then pronounced plainly. Words nowadays mean nothing: they are mere sounds striking upon the ear, and men are to leave their work and go to Church to listen to worse noises than were ever heard in a Greek or Roman theatre. Money is raised to buy organs and train boys to squeal and to learn no other thing that is good for them. The laity are burdened to support miserable, poisonous corybantes, while poor starving creatures might be fed at the cost of them.

'They have so much of it in England that the monks attend to nothing else. A set of creatures who ought to be lamenting their sins fancy they can please God by gurgling in their throats. Boys are kept in the English Benedictine Colleges solely and simply to sing hymns to the Virgin. If they want music let them sing Psalms like rational beings, and not too many of them.'

A good deal of this may be due to the longstanding quarrel—the *παλαιά τις διαφορά*—between scholar and musician; but two points stand out with special prominence, one the writer's condemnation of polyphonic music, second his selection of England as the chief culprit.

1 Annual Lecture on 'Aspects of Art' (Henriette Hertz Trust), read before the British Academy on 27th April, 1923.

2 1 Cor. xiv. 19. See Froude's *Erasmus*, pp. 130–1.

They constitute, indeed, evidence of the highest value. Words spoken to our praise may be empty or exaggerated compliments; we may at least take all the credit implied in words spoken to our blame.

Now whether or not it be true that all Arts converge on a common sensibility, and this is in any case extremely questionable, there can be no doubt that each has certain special qualities and modes of appeal which are not shared by any of the others. One of these distinctive qualities in Music is polyphony: the conjunction of different voices singing simultaneously different melodic parts. Literature has nothing comparable with this: a fugue expressed not in notes but in words would be only a succession of unmannerly interruptions throughout which the hearer could make nothing of what was said by any of the disputants. But the musical texture consists of these interwoven strands; they do not interrupt but enhance and corroborate; it is their concurrent variety which gives colour and substance and volume to the whole. Even the plainest harmony, note against note, which allows the meaning of the text to come through unimpaired—such harmony as Erasmus would have approved for the Psalms—derives the greater part of its musical beauty from the fact that the voices which are uttering the same words are setting them on different notes.

The world was slow to discover and adapt the loom at which this texture was woven. Greece knew nothing of it; only the redoubling of men's voices by women and boys at the octave, and Aristotle gives the most convincing reasons for holding that no other succession of intervals would be tolerable. The Early Medieval Church, driven perforce by the necessity of having tenors as well as basses in the choir, developed the crude system of organum and diaphony, the two voices singing the same melody a fifth apart, or one holding desperately to a single note while the other pursued the plain-chant. Then began a progress towards independent polyphony in which England was unquestionably a pioneer. We may doubt about our actual achievement in the twelfth century—the well-known descriptions of Giraldus Cambrensis are too vague to be conclusive, and it may well be, as Wooldridge suggests,[1] that so far we were working level with France—but there is no doubt at all about the *rota* 'Sumer is y-cumen in', which at the latest is dated about 1240. That the form in which it is written was already current we know from a punning epigram of Walter Map, that it presupposes a background of great skill and invention is obvious, and so far as our present evidence attests it outstrips the achievement of any continental nation by over a hundred years. Our record, woefully broken and imperfect, is resumed in the fifteenth century when we find John Dunstable acclaimed not only as the greatest of living composers, but as the Master to whom the most notable of musicians from overseas came for instruction. After Dunstable came a breathing-space in which we clearly yielded the palm to the Flemings: in the reign of Henry VII we began to recover our ground, and by the time of Erasmus's commentary we were once more resuming our position in the foremost rank.

But this gradual discovery of polyphonic resource brought its own danger. The device was so attractive that everything else was sacrificed to its display: the music became not only an end in itself but an end too often conceived in terms of mere skill and ingenuity. Three examples may be given. If the words of the sacred text were insufficient to last through a composition, the difficulty was often met by prolonging a syllable over tendrils and streams of melody until it had become inarticulate. Thus in the Conductus *Pater noster commiserans*, quoted by Wooldridge,[2] the first syllable of

[1] *Oxford History of Music*, i. 161 seq.

[2] In the best of these examples the words of the popular song are not used, and the melody is contrapuntally distributed between the voices. It must be remembered in all fairness that there was less difference then than now between the idioms of secular and of sacred song.

Pater lasts for thirty-nine of what we should call bars, and the first syllable of *fragilitatis* for no less than eighty. Secondly, it became customary to take as the staple melody of the Mass some popular or even profane song, and, for its better recognition, to let one of the choir sing it, while his fellow choristers were busy weaving it with descants and counterpoints on the text of the Kyrie or the Agnus Dei. The statement that the words of the secular song were used as well as the tune has been challenged, and it is probable that the first line alone was used, as a sort of title, and that the tune itself was taken in successive portions, as Palestrina, for example, divided that of the hymn 'Aeterna Christi munera'. But in any case the practice was indecorous and gave great offence to the more serious-minded of the worshippers. Thirdly, because composers in such an atmosphere came to have less and less reverence for the service, they took to filling the part-books with puzzles and enigmas which still further distracted the singers' attention. The tenor, for instance, who found that his part jarred at every note with the rest of the choir, was warned by the marginal note 'more Hebraeorum' that he was to sing it backwards. The inscription 'Iustitia et Pax osculatae sunt' showed, to those who could understand, that the same line of music served for two singers beginning at opposite ends and meeting in the middle: *βάτραχος ἐκ Σερίφου* on a blank page signified not that the part had been mislaid but that, according to Aelian, the frogs in the island of Seriphos do not croak. The astonishing thing is that in spite of all this degradation some really fine music was written: there are Masses on 'L'homme armé' and 'Western Wynde' which show true inspiration, and Josquin des Prés, one of the most irreverent of humorists, could show on occasion a sense of tenderness and pathos which has still power to touch the heart; but of the majority, and especially of the rank and file, we may say, with Holophernes, 'Here are only numbers ratified'. Indeed, the condition of affairs grew so serious that the very existence of Church music was in Italy threatened by the Council of Trent; in England closely restricted by Cranmer's Preface to the Litany. In the one country it was saved by the genius of Palestrina, in the other by that constellation of Tudor composers in which the brightest particular star was William Byrd.

The materials for his biography, despite the researches of Dr. Fellowes and Mr. Barclay Squire,[1] are still very imperfect. But it may be taken as certain that the year of his birth was 1543, and as very probable that the place was the village of Epworth in Lincolnshire. There is a strong tradition that he was Lincolnshire-born: the surname Byrd was common at Epworth in the sixteenth century, and, as the parish registers attest, the most prevalent Christian names in the genealogy were those borne by himself and his children. By a piece of ill fortune the register for 1543, which would have settled the question, is missing from its place in the Church records.

He must have had some sound general education, for we find him in later life teaching mathematics to Morley and writing his dedicatory epistles in good fluent Latin. That he was 'bred up to music under Thomas Tallis' is definitely asserted by Wood (Bodleian MS. 19 D (4) no. 106) and corroborated by a laudatory poem prefixed to the *Cantiones Sacrae* of 1575:

> Tallisius, magno dignus honore senex,
> Et Birdus tantum natus decorare magistrum.

As Tallis was at that time organist of the Chapel Royal we may accept without undue misgiving the current view that Byrd had his schooling in London, probably at St. Paul's Choir School, of which he is said to have been head boy, and that he stayed on for a time as Tallis's pupil. Among the most recently discovered of his compositions is a Song on the death of Queen Mary, which took place

1 This address was delivered before the publication of Mr. Howes's excellent monograph.

when he was fifteen years old, and his growing reputation is attested not only by his securing as teacher the doyen of Elizabethan Music, but by his appointment before he was twenty to the organistship of Lincoln Cathedral.

Of his first few years at Lincoln we have no record. Then came two events of great importance. In 1568 he married a Lincoln girl named Ellen or Julian Birley; in 1569, on the death of Robert Parsons, he was sworn in as a Gentleman of the Chapel Royal, and so resumed a close personal relationship with his old master. At first he seems to have retained his post in the Cathedral and to have divided his time between his two spheres of duty; his eldest child Elizabeth was baptized at Lincoln in January 1571–2: but in December of the same year Mr. William Butler is appointed there as his successor; and from thenceforward he and his family resided first at Harlington in Middlesex, then at Stondon in Essex, within easy reach of his London work. For some years he seems to have had a prophet's chamber in the London house of that eminent Catholic peer the Earl of Worcester.

It is worth pausing here for a moment to comment on a rather remarkable fact. Byrd was continuously in the service of the Chapel Royal from 1569, when he was appointed at the age of twenty-six, until 1623, when he died at the age of eighty: first as joint-organist with Tallis, after Tallis's death as sole organist. Yet there can be no doubt that through all that time he was a convinced Roman Catholic, that he composed Masses and other services for the Roman ritual, that he was fined for his wife's non-attendance at Stondon Parish Church, that he was frequently cited before the Archdeacon's Court as a 'Popish recusant', that he dedicated several of his works to well-known Romanist peers, and that he died, as is explicitly stated in his will, a loyal adherent of the faith in which he was born. Yet not only did he suffer no serious molestation—the fine was only a shilling—but he was retained for half a century as a Court official, and was granted in addition special marks of royal favour. No doubt Father Weston, the Jesuit, has left in his autobiography a pathetic account of Byrd's having 'sacrificed everything' for his religion[1]; but it would appear on investigation of the facts that Father Weston was misinformed. There is no reason to believe that Byrd ever sacrificed anything for this cause: the cheque-books of the Chapel Royal are conclusive evidence that he retained his appointment.

We are all familiar with the Abbé Migne's sentence, immortalized by Matthew Arnold, that 'the religious persecutions, which defaced the reign of Henry VIII and Edward VI, ceased for a time under Mary to break out with renewed virulence under Elizabeth'. It is not the view customarily held by English historians, and indeed the whole question of religious persecution in the Tudor period is difficult, partly because heresy was so often entwined with political intrigue, partly because it was not always easy to determine what opinions were heretical. But one point at any rate is clear, that in the reigns of Henry and Elizabeth a special immunity was accorded to eminent composers. At first this may have been partly disdainful: Taverner, accused of Lollardry at Oxford, was acquitted because he was 'only a musitian'; but it soon became evidence of genuine favour and admiration. Marbeck was cited, with two other members of the Windsor Choir, for impiety towards the Mass: the other two were executed, Marbeck let off with a caution on the ground that he was too good an artist to be spared. Tye, 'a peevish and humoursome man', was allowed by the Queen freedoms on which very few of her subjects would have ventured: Sebastian Westcote, organist of

1 'We met there also Mr. Byrd, the most celebrated musician and organist of the English nation, who had been formerly in the Queen's Chapel, and held in the highest estimation; but for his religion he sacrificed everything, both his office and the Court and all those hopes which are nurtured by such persons as pretend to similar places in the dwellings of princes, as steps towards the increasing of their fortunes.' Quoted by Mr. W. B. Squire, Grove's *Dictionary*, i. 430. It is dated 1586.

St. Paul's, was, although an open Papist, confirmed in his office because 'tam charus Elizabethae fuit'; Tallis himself, before his appointment at the Chapel Royal, was organist to the Roman Catholic community at Waltham Abbey. Byrd's security of tenure had plenty of precedent in an age when monarchs were themselves artists and allowed to genius its time-honoured privilege of revolt.

In 1575 the Queen gave her two organists a twenty-one years' patent for the printing of music and the ruling and selling of music-paper; part of which they sublet to Vautrollier and other publishers, the rest they kept in their own hands. Commercially speaking, their venture was not successful: musicians are seldom good men of business, and within two years we find Byrd complaining that the firm had already lost 200 marks in clear deficit. But it gave them the opportunity of publishing their own work, in the accustomed part-books, and of this the first-fruits appeared forthwith in the collection of *Cantiones Sacrae*, to which Tallis contributed sixteen motets and Byrd eighteen. Tallis, who was then about fifty years of age (the exact year of his birth is unknown), had already taken his place in the first rank of English composition: Byrd, who was thirty-two, had not yet published a note of music. The immediate effect of this collaboration was to set the younger man by the side of the elder, whom in a few more years he surpassed as unquestionably as Mozart surpassed Haydn.

There follows another of the 'eremi et vastitates' which are too frequent in the chronology of Byrd's life; and the desert is not traversed until 1588 when he is made the recipient of a very notable honour. An amateur named Nicholas Yonge, whose house had long been the resort of madrigal singers, was in the habit of procuring from Italy the best examples of an art in which she particularly excelled. In 1588 he published, under the title of *Musica Transalpina*, a selection which included specimens of Ferrabosco, Marenzio, Palestrina, Filippo di Monte, and other masters, and among them, as the highest compliment that he could pay to our native art, two settings by Byrd of Ariosto's 'La Verginella'. Historians have incorrectly described these as the first English madrigals—Englishmen had been writing madrigals for over half a century[1]—but they were the first which publicly claimed equality with the best of Italian music.

In the same year Byrd published the first collection which consisted entirely of his own work. This was the book of 'Psalms, Sonets, and Songs of Sadnes and Pietie'—thirty-five miscellaneous compositions, sacred and secular, which range from penitential Psalms to the well-known 'Amaryllis' madrigal, and end with two elegies on the death of Sir Philip Sidney. They are dedicated to Sir Christopher Hatton and prefaced by eight reasons 'to perswade euery one to learne to singe', which run as follows:

First it is a knowledge easely taught, and quickly learned where there is a good Master, and an apt Scoller.

2. The exercise of singing is delightfull to Nature & good to preserve the health of Man.

3. It doth strengthen all the parts of the brest, & doth open the pipes.

4. It is a singular good remedie for a stutting & stammering in the speech.

5. It is the best meanes to procure a perfect pronunciation & to make a good Orator.

6. It is the onely way to know where Nature hath bestowed the benefit of a good voyce: which guift is so rare, as there is not one among a thousand, that hath it: and in many, that excellent guift is lost, because they want Art to expresse Nature.

7. There is not any Musicke of Instruments whatsoever, comparable to that which is made of the voyces of Men, where the voyces are good, and the same well sorted and ordered.

8. The better the voyce is, the meeter it is to honour and serve

[1] Counting the set printed by Wynkyn de Worde in 1530. Edwards's delightful 'In going to my naked bed', a true madrigal if ever there was one, can be dated with fair certainty at 1564. Whythorne's 'Songs of three fower and five voices' were published in 1571. See Fellowes, *English Madrigal Composers*, ch. iv, pp. 33–4.

God there-with: and the voyce of man is chiefely to be imployed to that ende. *omnis spiritus laudet Dominum*

Since singing is so good a thing
I wish all men would learne to sing.

The period with which we are at present dealing was, indeed, one of the most prolific of Byrd's whole career. In 1589 he published *Songs of Sundry Natures*: forty-seven compositions for three, four, five, and six voices, and between then and 1591 produced the two volumes of *Cantiones Sacrae* which, if he had written nothing else, would suffice to rank him among the greatest of composers. Mr. Squire, who speaks in this matter with high authority, assigns the three Masses to the year 1588, though no doubt their composition spread over a longer period, and if the evidence for this is not entirely conclusive we may agree that they are not earlier than this stage in Byrd's career.[1] The problem of dating his work, with any exactitude, in cases where we have no external testimony to guide us, has not yet been completely solved. Scholars who remember the controversies that have ranged round the chronology of the Pauline Epistles or the Platonic dialogues or the works of Chaucer or Shakespeare will sympathize with the difficulty of accurate determination in compositions which fall within a comparatively narrow range of style, and many of which have been too recently discovered for an extended and systematic study. The future will no doubt bring its own answer; for the present we must be satisfied with general principles and flexible frontier-lines.

Meanwhile he was winning abundant laurels in another field of composition. As a player on the virginals he was by all repute unrivalled, as supreme among contemporaries as was Bach later on the organ or Beethoven

[1] Dr. Rimbault, in his edition of Byrd's 5-part Mass, suggested that they were written before 1558, a view which enables us to dispense with the rest of his criticisms. It is like saying that Shakespeare wrote *Macbeth* during his boyhood at Stratford. Mr. Collins believes that the 5-part Mass was published in 1590 and the other two in 1610. See Fellowes.

on the pianoforte, and during these years of strength and maturity he wrote a vast number of pieces—dance-measures, airs, fantasies, variations—for his favourite instrument. Many manuscript collections of them are still extant,[1] among others Lady Nevill's book (1591), transcribed by John Baldwin of Windsor, who at the seventeenth piece has broken out into a spontaneous cry of admiration, unusual in a copyist, 'Mr. W. Birde, homo memorabilis'. Some characteristics of the music will be considered later, but we may here draw attention to the amazing dexterity of hand to which these pieces attest. The exaggerated fame which rewards a virtuoso in his lifetime is usually compensated by undeserved oblivion after his death, and it is well therefore that we should have a permanent record of the skill which Byrd evidently possessed and some of which he must have transmitted to his pupils. It is the more astonishing because the virginal players and organists of the sixteenth century were required, by the position of the keyboard, to dispense almost entirely in rapid passages with the use of the thumb and the little finger. Praetorius, who wrote in 1619, has a significant passage:

'Many think it a matter of great importance and despise such organists as do not use this or that particular fingering, which in my opinion is not worth the talk: for let a player run up and down with either first, middle, or third finger, aye even with his nose if that could help him, provided everything is done clearly, correctly, and gracefully, it does not much matter how or in what manner it is accomplished.'

Praetorius, it will be seen, contemplates the clear, correct, and graceful use of the nose in clavier playing, but restricts the hand to the three middle fingers. And the system which continued in use as late as Purcell allows the thumb and little finger only at the beginning and end of a two-octave scale.[2] All the other notes are

[1] Typical examples in all forms have been published under the very competent editorship of Mr. Fuller Maitland and Mr. Barclay Squire.

[2] See the article on Fingering in Grove's *Dictionary*, vol. ii, pp. 43–5, Mr. Barclay Squire has found some exceptions in the clavier music of Bull.

struck by the third and fourth fingers in ascending movement and in descending by the third and second. Even our masters of technical proficiency might look upon these restrictions with some misgiving.

Byrd was now forty-eight. Apart from the three Masses, he had published, in part-books, over a hundred and fifty concerted vocal compositions, both sacred and secular, and had written some scores of pieces for the virginals. Since the death of Tallis in 1585 he had become beyond all challenge the first composer in England, unrivalled even by the great Madrigalian school which grew up round him. He was in high favour with patrons, with colleagues, and with pupils, as much beloved for his character as revered for his genius; never, we may say, had any artist opened more widely the door of opportunity. Yet this was, so far as we know, the moment which he chose to retire from publication: no printed page of his can be dated between 1591 and 1605. And what is more surprising, it was within this period that the *Triumphs of Oriana* appeared: the collection of madrigals in honour of Queen Elizabeth, prepared and edited by Byrd's pupil and lifelong friend Thomas Morley, as a monument of our native genius; and the name which we should most expect to find is absent from the list of contributors. No satisfactory explanation of this silence has yet been found. It is clear that during this period he continued to write, for he published at its close a volume of over sixty compositions: we do not know why, at the zenith of his reputation, he withdrew for fourteen years from the arena in which it had been won.

The chapter, otherwise uneventful, records a few facts of biographical interest. In 1593 Byrd removed with his wife and children from Harlington and took possession of Stondon Place, near Ongar: an estate sequestrated from the recusant family of the Shelleys, and in 1595 leased by the Crown to the equally recusant organist of the Chapel Royal. It has been suggested that the anxieties consequent upon this change of scene may have been in some degree accountable for his silence; that he may have been preoccupied with personal troubles or dangers and have thought it politic to lie for a time in concealment. But this is on the whole improbable. For one reason the policy would have defeated its own end: his light was too brilliant to be veiled without exciting remark; for another, although he was from the beginning involved in some disputes with the outgoing occupant—the circumstances lent themselves to controversy—yet the tedious litigation with the Shelleys, and the personal distractions which it entailed, came to a head only in later years.

In 1603 James I ascended the Protestant throne, and Byrd, who had been recently excommunicated by his Archdeacon, took part in the Coronation Service and celebrated the occasion by preparing for the press that magnificent collection of compositions for the Roman Liturgy which is known as the First Book of the *Gradualia*. This appeared in 1605 with a dedication to the Earl of Northampton 'in afflictis familiae meae rebus benignissimum patronum', from which we may gather that Byrd had benefited by the protection of a powerful house. A second set of *Gradualia*, equally beautiful, followed in 1607, making up the total of separate numbers to over 100. Assuredly Byrd had returned to public life bringing his sheaves with him.

Meantime he continued his instrumental work, collaborated with Bull and Gibbons in *Parthenia*, and wrote many of the pieces which were afterwards collected in the Fitzwilliam Virginal Book. This direction of his genius was yet more strikingly illustrated when in 1611 he included among his 'Psalmes, Songs, and Sonets' two Fantasies, in six and four parts respectively, for viols alone: the earliest printed compositions for concerted strings which we possess. Three years later he contributed four anthems to Sir William Leighton's 'Teares or Lamentacions of a Sorrowfull Soule'; and these were his last published compositions. On 4 July, 1623, he died. Of his six children one son, Thomas, inherited some measure of his spirit; the others are no more to us than names in a genealogy.

With the exception of Mrs. Shelley, who complains of his 'bitter words', he seems to have had no personal enmities, and the contemporary references to his name indicate not only admiration but affection. Some of them have already been quoted: there are others not less significant. The record of his death, in the Chapel Royal, speaks of him as 'a father of Musicke'. Morley in his *Plaine and Easie Introduction* says that he is 'never without reverence to be named of the Musitians': Baldwin, who copied out Lady Nevill's virginal pieces, sets him above all other composers English or foreign; the anonymous possessor of a MS. of Cicero's *Letters*, now in the Christ Church Library, marks the passage (*ad Atticum*, iv. 16) which states that the Britons are devoid of letters or music with the indignant comment 'Unus Birdus omnes Anglos ab hoc convicio prorsus liberat'. But there is no need of any further witness. It is beyond question that at the time of his death he was regarded with a veneration hardly surpassed by that which was paid to Shakespeare.

> Expende Hannibalem: quot libros in duce summo
> Invenies?

What has become of all this music and this reputation? Why is it that a man who was acclaimed by his contemporaries as a supreme example of creative genius has left a name which sounds at the present day so faint and so unfamiliar? It was not slenderness of achievement, for more than five hundred of his compositions have now been discovered. It was not easy acceptance of a low standard: the Elizabethan age was the most musical in our history. Some very convincing explanation must be found before these contradictions can be reconciled.

We are celebrating this year a greater tercentenary than Byrd's: that of the First Folio. Imagine for a moment that there had been no First Folio: that there had been no

Quartos: that no single play of Shakespeare's had survived otherwise than in separate parts, and that of these parts some were in manuscript copies at his death and the others in ill-printed scripts without division of acts or scenes and without cues. This is precisely the fate which befell the music of Byrd. Of his known compositions less than half were printed in any form during his lifetime, and this moiety only in part-books restricted in use to the singer and easily mislaid. Shortly after his death about twenty of his services and anthems were reprinted by Barnard (1641), but these also were entrusted to the hazard of the part-books, and of Barnard's collection no complete copy is now in existence. There was nothing distinctive about this, it was the common usage of the time, but no better way could be devised of preparing 'alms for oblivion'.

Another equally powerful reason may be added. No doubt it is incorrect to say that the Puritans were hostile to music—Cromwell and Milton are examples to the contrary—but they were eminently hostile to certain kinds of music; and it was not to be expected that they would go far to honour a composer all of whose work was in a style which they disapproved, and more than half of it for a Church which they detested. Nor did the Restoration mend matters, for by the time that it came the whole course and current of musical taste had been deflected. The change wrought by the monodic movement may roughly be compared with that which Caravaggio introduced into painting: instead of the old diffused light flowing equally through all parts of the picture came luminous concentration on a single point, and, as its natural result, the enhancement of romantic or dramatic effect. The parallel must not be pressed into detail, for the monodic composers were far greater than Caravaggio, but it is true in principle. The growth of dramatic and romantic music largely depended on this method of concentration, and helped to render obsolete the old contrapuntal equality which it superseded.

William Byrd, 1623–1923

The eighteenth century treated Byrd with neglect: it was reserved for the nineteenth to treat him with contumely. In 1840 the Musical Antiquarian Society was formed in London and proceeded to publish, for the first time in score, the five-part Mass, entrusted to Dr. Rimbault, and the first book of *Cantiones Sacrae*, entrusted to Mr. William Horsley. The results were lamentable. We may at any rate give Dr. Rimbault credit for good intentions: he seems to have admired Byrd after his fashion; but he knew nothing about the Elizabethan idiom and he was one of the most inaccurate and unscholarly of editors. Byrd's text is emended where it was obviously correct before, his style is smoothed out of recognition: worst of all, his beautiful luxuriant phrases, admirably suited to the declamation of the words, are crammed into a Procrustean bed of regular bars: a bed upon which Byrd never dreamed that he would be made to lie. This is distressing enough, but Mr. Horsley is worse. There is a pseudo-science called 'Strict Counterpoint' which is set forth in the grammatical treatises of Fux and Marpurg and Cherubini and Rockstro: a set of rules and prohibitions, the latter predominating, illustrations of which may be found in the text-books but not in the works of the great composers.[1] As a discipline it may conceivably have some small use: as a basis for criticism it is an insolent pedantry. Mr. Horsley, whose musical exertions had raised him to the dignity of a Bachelor's degree, prefaces his reluctant edition with a diatribe censuring Byrd for disregard of regulations which have no inherent validity and of which he would never for a moment have recognized the jurisdiction. To match this example of assurance we must turn to the eighteenth-century critics who attacked Shakespeare's plays for not being regular.

[1] Mr. Rockstro confesses that in despair of finding any examples from the classics he has been obliged to write his own. See a complete exposure of the whole system in Mr. R. O. Morris's admirable book, *Contrapuntal Technique in the Sixteenth Century*.

William Byrd, 1623–1923

Is it surprising that by the middle of the nineteenth century the name of Byrd had almost vanished from the memory of mankind? A few services and anthems—'Bow thine ear', for instance—still held place in our Cathedral services: an occasional madrigal might very rarely appear on the concert platform: the rest of the treasure lay hidden in its royal tomb unvalued, unexplored, and for the most part unknown. But towards the end of the century the work of excavation began. Dr. Nagel's excellent *Geschichte der Musik in England* aroused a general interest, and before it appeared some of our scholars were in the field, Mr. Fuller Maitland, Mr. Barclay Squire, Mr. Godfrey Arkwright, and others, to be followed later by the Tudor Music Committee and the independent researches of Dr. Fellowes and Mr. Collins. The world has often assigned to its great composers a period of oblivion: the interest in Palestrina was certainly revived by the nineteenth-century scholars at Ratisbon: the first performance of Bach's B minor Mass took place ninety-five years after its composition; when Sir George Grove paid his famous visit to Vienna, nine-tenths of Schubert's music was still unpublished. In the case of Byrd the period of neglect has been longer, but his time has at last arrived.

It remains to set forth briefly the grounds on which a place is claimed for him in the company of the 'di maiorum gentium': not only among the great composers but among the very few who stand at the summit of the art. And first we may observe that he had not only covered but notably extended the whole range of musical composition. The bare catalogue of his work is astonishing: three Masses, over two hundred motets and gradualia, a setting of the Passion according to St. John, a great number of Psalms and anthems, services for the Protestant ritual, one of which is on the largest scale ever attempted, madrigals, songs, instrumental pieces for strings and for virginals; in any period of musical history this abundance would be exceptional, in these early years it was almost unparalleled. In some directions, too, he was an adventurous pioneer. He was one of the first composers to recognize the value of balance between voice and accompaniment, to write solos with independent organ-part, to divide his madrigals between singers and players, and so to enrich their texture with new combinations of colour and design. The variation-form in which he excelled was so supremely his own that historians have accredited him with its invention: most important of all, the string pieces of 1611 are not reduplications of madrigalian music, 'apt for viols or voyces', but genuine concerted works for instruments the structure of which clearly anticipates the cyclic forms of the symphony and the string quartet. To his complete mastery of polyphonic resource there is no need to draw attention: that is an achievement which he shares with lesser men, and it is enough to say that his draughtsmanship is worthy of his inspiration. It is of more moment to consider the character of his musical thought: the kind and degree of beauty which it embodies and expresses: premising always that in music more than in any other art, conception and expression are like the convex and concave 'two in word but one in reality'.

To deal exhaustively with this topic would involve a complete survey of all Byrd's compositions, and that for many reasons is here impossible. But three points may be selected for special elucidation. The first is the magnificent breadth and sweep of his melodic curve; not only in range of compass but in exact propriety of declamation. The latter aspect has been grievously obscured in later times by our habit of printing Elizabethan music in schemes of regular and uniform barring, a method which is entirely destructive of their true prosody. Byrd and his contemporaries wrote before the use of bars had come to supersede the old free rhythm, and their melody flows among triple and quadruple measures according to the requirements of the text. Indeed, one of the reasons why Byrd fell into neglect was because the critics applied to him the wrong metrical footrule and then complained that he would not scan. As a matter of fact his scansion is perfect but it is not that of Bach or Handel. The well-known madrigal 'Though Amaryllis dance in green' is a crucial instance: it was never intended to be performed with a single time-signature.

Secondly, we may note the vividness and significance of his themes. The serene purity of style which was one of the beauties of vocal music in the sixteenth century was sometimes protected by a comparatively narrow range of subject: the melodic phrases, admirably suited for contrapuntal treatment, were not always in themselves very fruitful or characteristic. But Byrd's phrases are often as vigorous as those of Bach or Beethoven or Wagner. Such, for instance, is the opening of the five-part 'Haec Dies':

or the bass entry in the three-part 'Regina Caeli':

or the Alleluias in the second of the *Gradualia*:

1st TREBLE.
2nd TREBLE.

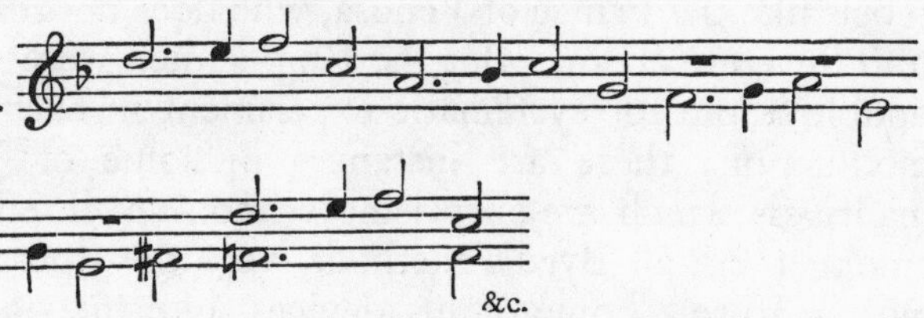

and instances as salient as these can be found over the whole range of his work. This force and vitality give him at the same time a wide and human sympathy with every true form of emotional expression. His Church music, always devout and dignified, can range from the sheer jubilation of 'Laetentur caeli' [1] to the deep and poignant grief of 'Civitas Sancti Tui' [2] or 'Plorans plorabit' [3]:

[1] *Cantiones Sacrae*, i. 28. [2] *Cantiones Sacrae*, i. 21.
[3] *Gradualia*, i. 27.

his madrigals can be gay or humorous or pathetic; even in his instrumental music, with all the necessary limitations of its time, there is sincere feeling behind the courtly reticence of viols and virginals. And throughout it all there breathes an air of certainty and conviction which is one of the distinguishing marks of genius. 'If I were asked', says Mr. Steuart Wilson, 'why I believe that "the sea is His and He made it", I should answer "because Byrd tells me so".'

The third characteristic is the originality and audacity of his harmonic experiments. We may recall, without undue technicality, that a strict adherence to the modal system was incompatible either with change of tonal centres or with variety of harmonic colour and substance. But by the end of the sixteenth century the modes had been reduced, in practical currency, to two, and the balance of usage was gradually swinging towards the employment of the modern scale, for which the conventions of *musica ficta* had long been preparing.

In this matter the English composers had made the farthest advance. In Italy the modes were still in the ascendant and their supremacy was challenged only by rebels like the Prince of Venosa, who does not really come into the comparison. But the Englishmen were using the double idiom for systematic experiment in harmony and modulation: there are instances in some of Weelkes' madrigals which are surprisingly 'modern' in effect; and among them all Byrd's methods were the ripest and the most mature. Some of his devices, like the unprepared dominant seventh, are so familiar to us now that they need no comment; but it is difficult to believe that, even as late as 1611, a madrigalist of the old school could write as follows [1]:

[1] From 'Come woeful Orpheus', from Psalms, Songs, and Sonnets. The words of this particular passage are 'Of sourest sharps and uncouth flats make choice'; so that the music is evidently intended to be partly descriptive: but even so it is sufficiently remarkable. Special attention is drawn to it by Mr. R. O. Morris, *Contrapuntal Technique*, p. 66, and also p. 43 of the illustrations.

(*a*)

The whole scheme is perfectly clear and logical, but it was a 'new music' at the beginning of the seventeenth century. A striking instance of this harmonic freedom is to be found in Byrd's famous 'false relations': the device by which he uses the sharpened and natural form of the same note successively in different parts or even simultaneously in one clashing discord. It was evidently intentional, for Byrd in one passage warns the singers not to suppose that the parts are misprinted—a supposition which, two hundred years later, was attached on the same issue to one of Mozart's finest string quartets. It has been subjected to the most absurd criticism,[1] and even now there are some editors who are inclined to speak of it apologetically. There is not the least need for apology. Apart from an

[1] See Horsley's edition of the *Cantiones*.

extended use of the *Tierce de Picardie*, which is too obvious for discussion, all the examples so far as I know fall into two categories and are covered by two explanations: the double form of what we should call the ascending and descending minor scale, and the fact that in the sixteenth century augmented intervals were not included in the vocabulary of music. Two examples may be given, one of the successive, one of the simultaneous employment of these notes:

(*b*) From the 'Gloria' of the Mass in four parts.

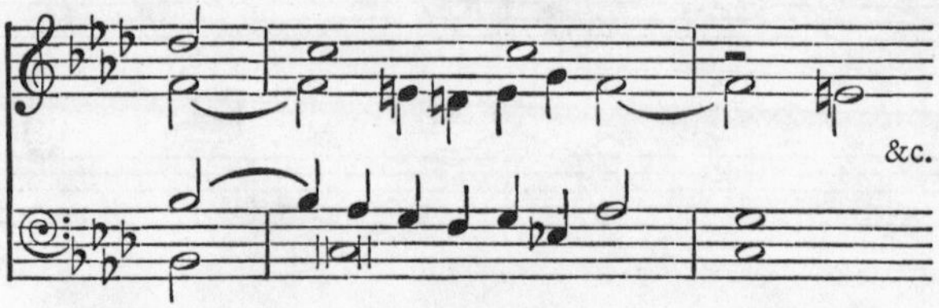

(*c*) From 'Aspice domine': *Cantiones Sacrae*, Bk. I, no. 13.

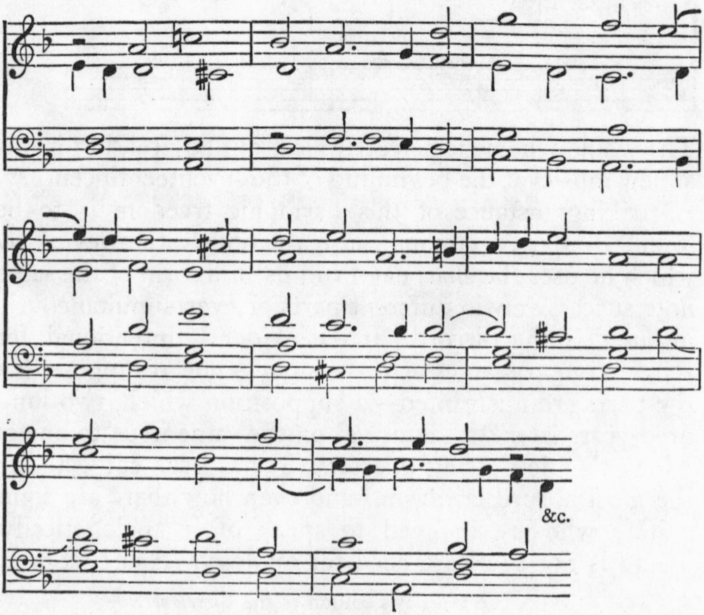

In the former of these it is clear that the exigencies of drawing require the alto to sing E natural and the tenor E flat. In the latter the dissonances of the first and sixth measures are very expressive, that of the fifth is extraordinarily beautiful as well. And we are not likely to quarrel at the present day with an artist who, on wholly intelligible grounds, extended the use of passing discords.

The technique of Byrd's composition for viols and for virginals is naturally affected by the particular qualities and limitations of the instruments. The virginals were incapable either of sustained tone or of graduation of touch; it followed that the music written for them made considerable use of grace notes, and arpeggios, and running passages which were often treated as constituent parts of the melody. The forms which Byrd most commonly used were those of dance measures: the Pavan and Galliard often in collocation, the others usually separate: or of 'ayres', with or without variations, or of 'fantasies', which first applied to the keyboard the fugal style which had been gradually elaborated for voices. In all alike, even to the point of elaborately ornamental melody, he was one of the earliest and worthiest forerunners of the clavier writing of J. S. Bach.

String music was still held by a self-imposed restriction. Though Andrea Amati was born in 1520, the modern stringed instruments had not yet found their way into favour: they were regarded as harsh and intrusive; in the middle of the seventeenth century Mace can still talk of the 'scoulding violins'. Hence all through Byrd's lifetime the 'Consort' was still composed of viols, treble, tenor, and bass, which had far less agility and resonance, but compensated for this, at least in part, by a reedy sweetness of tone which fitted their music and partly no doubt inspired it. As an example of Byrd's composition for strings we may take the sestet of 1611, to which allusion has already been made. It is in three movements: the first broad and dignified, treating in close imitation a series of short well-defined themes, the second a lilting allegro, with great variety of key, the third a charming and delicate minuet which shows already a remarkable sense of thematic development. The whole work has far more than an historic interest: it is a real and valuable contribution to the literature of chamber-music.

Yet in all this analysis we are but emulating the hero of the Greek story who, wishing to sell his house, carried round a brick by way of sample. No amount of illustration, short of a complete programme, can give any idea of Byrd's fertility of invention, of his strength and vigour, of his skill, his humanity, his high and noble seriousness of purpose. He has been compared to Palestrina, with whom indeed he had one curious point of contact,[1] but the comparison is not more fruitful than would be one between the abundance of Shakespeare and the faultless perfection of Dante. This at any rate may with confidence be maintained, that in him the music of our country achieved its highest and fullest expression, and that future ages will set him in the company of the greatest masters, and will grant him equality of renown.

NOTE

A catalogue of Byrd's compositions, so far as they have yet been discovered, is printed in Dr. Fellowes' biography. It comprises:

For the Latin Service: 3 Masses and 219 Motets, Graduals, and other choral works.

For the English Service: 2 sets of Preces and Psalms, 1 of Preces and Responses, 1 Litany, 2 complete Services, 2 Evening Services, 1 Morning Service (fragment), and 85 anthems.

Madrigals and other Secular Songs: 112.

Concerted pieces for Viols: 19.

Pieces for Virginals: 111.

Pieces for Lute: 3.

Miscellaneous instrumental pieces: 21.

[1] The Canon 'Non nobis, Domine', a copy of which engraved on a golden plate is said to have been deposited in the Vatican, has been attributed to both composers. The theme is to be found in the first *Agnus* of Palestrina's *Missa Brevis*, but from this no argument can be drawn, and contemporary testimony is in favour of Byrd.

A CROATIAN COMPOSER[1]

THE study of Human Nature contains few problems more difficult or more important than those which deal with distinctions of national character. In most countries the original race, itself not always pure, has been affected and modified by a hundred causes: by conquest, by immigration, by intermarriage with neighbours, by all the circumstances and conditions of historical development; and the result is commonly a web of many diverse threads, in which we are fortunate if we can explain the prevailing colour and the prevailing pattern. Sometimes, as in our Indian Empire, the threads lie comparatively free, and puzzle us more by their number and variety than by actual closeness of texture. Sometimes, as in the Kingdom of Hungary, the interplay is so thorough and so complex as almost to baffle analysis at the outset. And when to this is added the influence of climate, of government, of religion, of all that is implied in past record and traditional usage, it will be seen that the question of causality is one which may well tax to their utmost limit the skill and patience of the ethnologist.

But if the reasons are hard to trace, the fact is no longer open to intelligible doubt. Physiology tells us that it manifests itself at birth; history, that it has formed a channel for the whole course and current of events. There is no crisis so great, there is no occurrence so trivial, as not to exhibit in some degree its presence and efficacy in the life of man. Nations at peace do not follow the same policy; nations in conflict do not fight with the same weapons; the contrast of laws and customs is so vivid that it has led some impatient philosophers to consider all morality relative. And what is true of the life as a whole is equally true of its specialization in art and literature. For these are pre-eminently the expression of the national voice, as intimate as its language, as vital as the breath

1 Reprinted from *A Croatian Composer* (1897), by kind permission of Messrs. Seeley, Service & Co.

that it draws, and every artist who has compelled the attention of the world at large has done so by addressing it as the spokesman of his own people.

No doubt there are other factors in the case, the personal idiosyncrasy that separates a man from his fellows, and again the general principles, fewer perhaps than is commonly supposed, that underlie all sense of rhythm and all appreciation of style. But to say this is only to say that the artist is himself, and that he belongs to our common humanity. In everything, from the conception of a poem to the structure of a sentence, the national element bears its part with the other two: it colours the personal temperament, it gives a standpoint from which principles of style are approached, and wherever its influence is faint or inconsiderable the work of the artist will be found to suffer in proportion. It is hardly necessary to add that the law holds equally good whether the race in question be pure or mixed. If the former, it will move along a single line: if the latter, it will mark the converging point of many; but in either case its operation is a sure test of genuineness both in feeling and expression. Occasionally, it may be, a careless public has been deceived by some trick of imitation—by the Spanish comedies of Clara Gazul or the Persian Lyrics of Mirza Schaffy; but such instances of deception no more traverse the law than the Ireland forgeries or the pictures of Cariani. Some men are born with a talent of mimicry: none have ever by its means attained to greatness.

It may at once be admitted that this rule of national influence is at present less firmly established in music than in poetry or painting. In the two latter arts we have certain obvious externals to aid investigation—broad and salient contrasts of language, wide differences of scene and subject—with which music as such has little or nothing to do. Her subject is usually vague and indeterminate, her vocabulary is made up of a few scales, and for the rest we are told that her genius is limited to the common emotions of mankind and the common inheritance of pure form. But it is wholly false to infer that music is independent of nationality. The composer bears the mark of his race not less surely than the poet or the painter, and there is no music with true blood in its veins and true passion in its heart that has not drawn inspiration from the breast of the mother country.

Two main causes have retarded the acceptance of this truth. First, the belief that national melody is entirely an affair of artifices and mannerisms, that it is constituted by special turns of phrase and figure—as though you could make a rose tree by tying roses to a Scotch fir, or turn *Rule Britannia* into a Hungarian tune by ending it with a Hungarian cadence. This, it may be said, simply misunderstands the nature of the law which it criticizes. No doubt a certain range of expression belongs to each type of folk-song. No doubt these accidents of figure and phrase appear upon the surface, and are often useful as indications, but it makes all the difference whether they grow naturally in their place or lie there as mere lifeless appendages. Even the foreign idioms which a great composer may occasionally employ are only a graft let into the parent stock; the new growth is at once modified by the influence of the old, and alters its character to match its change of condition. And apart from these rare grafts the phrase of a true master will always be found conformable to the spirit that animates it, not because it constitutes the spirit, but because it emanates as property from essence. The second error springs from our loose and inaccurate methods of classification. That Mozart was an Italian composer seems now to be taken as an accredited jest; but it is more serious when we show our gratitude for the splendid work that Germany has done by scoring to her account all that has been accomplished by her neighbours. Schumann claims Chopin as a fellow-countryman; we are so far from protesting that we add Liszt, for whom 'the great German master' was long a newspaper synonym, and even hesitate about Smetana and Dvořák. It is true that classification is often extremely difficult—records are imperfect, names are misleading, histories are marred by want of ethnological knowledge; but the admission of ignorance is not a very strong basis for dogmatic denial. Critics who traverse a law, because they cannot see its applicability to the facts, would do well to make sure at the outset that the facts have been correctly observed.

The subject of the present essay is one of the most remarkable instances of such misattribution. From the time of Carpani to that of Dr. Nohl, Haydn's biographers have been unanimous in describing him as a German, born, as everybody knows, in Lower Austria, speaking German as his native language, Teutonic in race, in character, in surroundings. Yet the more we study him the more impossible it becomes to regard his music as the work of a Teuton. It is undoubtedly affected by his education and circumstances, by the early study of Emmanuel Bach, and the subsequent intercourse with Mozart, but when we penetrate to the essential spirit of the man himself we find that its inherent characteristics are no more German than they are Italian or French. Haydn's sentiment is of a kind without analogue among German composers—mobile, nervous, sensitive, a little shallow it may be, but as pure and transparent as a mountain stream. His humour is a quality in which he stands almost alone; it differs totally from the wit of Mozart, or the grim jesting of Beethoven; it is quaint and playful, rippling over the whole surface of the page, and equally removed from satire and epigram. Again, he has less breadth and stateliness than belong to the German temper, but he has far more versatility. He was the most daring of pioneers, the most hazardous of experimentalists, and, what is more noticeable, his experiments are rather the natural outcome of a restless and vivid imagination than the efforts of a deliberate and conscious reform. From the external side, too, the same contrast is apparent. The shapes of his melodic phrases are not those of the German folk-song; his rhythms are far more numerous and varied; his metres are often strange and unfamiliar. Throughout Western Europe the four-bar line has almost uniformly been taken as the unit of measurement, carrying with it the corresponding stanza of eight or sixteen or thirty-two. In a hundred German or English folk-songs it will be strange if a single exception can be found: in a hundred melodies from Haydn's quartets it will be strange if the exceptions are not as frequent as the instances. In a word, his range of stanza is far wider than that known to the Germany of his day, and many of his most characteristic tunes belong to another language and another scheme of versification.

The evidence here briefly epitomized can only point to one of two conclusions: either that the law of nationality is inapplicable to Haydn, or that his assignment to the German race is an ethnological error. The former alternative is unsatisfactory enough; the latter was for many years put out of court by our inability to sustain the *onus probandi*. But in 1878 Dr. Kuhač began to publish his great collection of South-Slavonic melodies,[1] and in 1880 he supplemented it by a special pamphlet on Haydn's relation to them.[2] The main points of the thesis are three in number: first, that the Croatian folk-tunes possess all the characteristics which have been noted as distinctive in the melodies of Haydn; second, that many of them are actually employed by him; and third, that the facts of his birth and parentage afford strong presumptive proof that he was a Croatian by race. If this contention can be established it strengthens an important law with valuable and unexpected support, and it remains therefore that we should bring forward a critical statement of the case, beginning, for clearness' sake, with the historical and biographical testimony, and so bringing into prominence the special character of the compositions themselves.

First, then, we must consider whether the character of

1 *Južno-slovjenske Narodne Popievke*: Zagreb, 1878–81.

2 *Josip Haydn i Hrvatske Narodne Popievke*; reprinted from the *Vienac*, Zagreb, 1880.

the Croatian people is such as to render its claim to Haydn reasonable and intelligible. It would be poor logic to illustrate our law by deriving a great artist from an inartistic nation. And the question becomes more pressing when we remember that Haydn's whole family was musical, that he learned his first lessons from his father and mother, that his brother Michael long enjoyed a repute little inferior to his own. But to answer it in the affirmative is to run counter to an established belief. From Mrs. Western in *Tom Jones* to Barto Rizzo in *Vittoria* everybody has had a fling at the Croats. The associations that we used to connect with their name are those of war and pillage, of fierce onslaught and misused victory, of lives bartered for gain or spilled in mere wantonness. Their art is a matter into which we never dream of inquiring, and we should as soon have thought of learning their language as of accrediting them with a literature. To dispel this superstition it is only needful that we should study the country. Few towns are more charming than Agram, few regions more delightful than the long fertile valley of the Save in which it lies. In the remoter districts there is still much ignorance and much poverty, but civilization is spreading from the centre, and eliciting, not creating, the signs of progress. The strongest impulse of the national life is loyalty to race and Church. Recent events have shown us that outbreaks may readily be provoked in religious and patriotic causes, but the temper that will fight for them is not ignoble, and is not infrequently conjoined with the inspiration that will make songs in their honour. And throughout the country the love of music prevails.[1] The men sing at their plough, the girls sing as they fill their water-pots at the fountain; by every village inn you may hear the jingle of the tambura, and watch the dancers footing it on the green. Grant that the music is not always of a high order, that

[1] Dr. Kuhač (*Josip Haydn*, p. 5) declares that one in every three of the population 'either sings, plays, or composes'. And there is a significant Croatian proverb to the effect that 'an age is known by its music'.

the tunes are often primitive and the voices rude and uncouth, still the impetus is there, and it only needs guidance and direction. Certainly the present condition of the race does not disqualify it to be the parent of a great composer.

It will be objected that this is only a present impression, and that it tells us nothing of those days when, apparently, the whole *raison d'être* of the population was to furnish fighting-men for the army of Maria Theresa. In answer to this, two points must be made clear: first, the state of Croatia proper during the past two centuries; second, the position occupied at the same period by other members of the Croatian race.[1] The argument 'e nihilo nihil' need hardly be stated here, though it will be seen later that nothing has been added to the Croats except opportunity.

Throughout the eighteenth century the policy of the Austrian Government was to repress as far as possible the Slavonic peoples that lay under its rule. Bohemia, which had lost its independence at the Thirty Years' War, was intellectually the 'desert' which the Emperor Ferdinand had wished to make it; and the same drastic measures, though for somewhat different reasons, were applied to the subject races that fringed the southern border. Croatia in particular was used merely as an outpost against Turkish invasion: 'purchased', as Dr. Kuhač says, 'with a few empty political concessions', but kept in reality under the close discipline of a barrack-state. 'We were not allowed', he continues, 'to provide for our people the advantages of a real city, we had no centre of intellectual life and progress, and it was considered a sufficient

[1] For the sake of clearness, it may be well to say that Croatia proper means that district across the Save of which Agram (i.e. Zagreb) is the capital; and that the same race occupies the entire territory from the Drave to the Lake of Scutari; and from the Roumanian frontier to the Adriatic. There is some Italian population in the extreme west, e.g. at Zara; but most of this region is exclusively Slavonic, and the Servo-Croatian language prevails with certain modifications over the whole of it. There is also a considerable Croat population in Istria, Carniola, Lower Austria, and the adjoining parts of Hungary.

privilege if the name of capital was bestowed upon one or other of our towns.' [1]

Naturally, the Croatian nobles spent as little time as possible in their own country. It was much more amusing to stay at Pressburg or Vienna, where there were balls and theatres and pageants, and a man could see life. And so it happened that even the chance of patronage was denied, and the people sank to a state of apathy, their gifts forgotten, their voice starved into silence. But about 1835 the poet Ljudevit Gaj began, as Tyl was doing in Bohemia, to restore from its suspended animation the intellectual life of his countrymen. He settled their alphabet. He made their grammar. He collected the folk-songs from every village and hamlet, and enriched them with lyrics of his own. He sowed dragon's teeth over the length and breadth of the country, and there sprang up as if by magic a crop of artists. Of course they were not of any great European importance. Lisinski and Franz von Suppé are the most famous among their musicians—but the whole lesson had to be learned anew, and these men were the first pupils. And when the revolutions of 1848 gave fresh impulse to national life, a second chapter opened in the Croatian renascence, and, under the patronage of Bishop Strossmayer, there rose into being a new artistic generation. Here, again, the musicians rather lag behind the poets and the men of letters; there was no conservatorium, there was no satisfactory method of training, and the young talent was generally too poor to embrace the opportunities which foreign lands afforded. But, if as yet the quality of the work is slight and trivial, something at least should be said about its extraordinary volume and facility. And it should be added that the leaders of the present generation—Zajac, Vilhar, Faller, Dr. Kuhač himself—are all making large use of the national melodies as material.

Meantime, while the fortunes of Croatia were at their lowest, an event of earlier occurrence was producing

[1] *Josip Haydn*, p. 3.

important consequences. The Southern Slavs had always been a migratory people. As early as 595 they occupied the Tyrolean Pusterthal, where they have left their mark, not only in the character of the inhabitants but in a large number of local names [1]; later, under stress of Turkish invasion, they colonized Montenegro; and in the fifteenth or sixteenth century a body of Eastern Croats—Bosnen or Wasser-Kroaten, as the Germans called them—settled in the district of Central Austria which extends from Lake Balaton north-west to the Danube. The new home was eminently suited to the development of the race. It was rich and fertile, with vine-clad hills and broad stretches of alluvial plain, it was well wooded and well watered, it extended to Pressburg, the second city in the empire, and contained at least one other town of considerable note; it was within easy reach of the great intellectual and artistic movements. There is little wonder that this region soon came to be regarded as the focus of Croatian life, and that the wealth which sought it for entertainment attracted in due course the talent which sought it for livelihood.

The number of the original immigrants is unknown, but by the eighteenth century they unquestionably formed the larger part of the population. In 1780 Pressburg contained rather less than 28,000 inhabitants, of whom about half are noted in the official census as Croats or Slavonians; while the smaller towns and villages in the neighbourhood were mainly occupied by the new-comers, and are still, despite German and Magyar influence, largely affected by Slavonic traditions. One curious and rather bewildering consequence is that almost every place in the region has possessed two names, one the German, used for official purposes; the other, Slavonic, for the benefit of the population. And when we add that east of the Leitha the Slavonic name is being ousted by the Hungarian, it will be seen that the unsophisticated traveller may now and again be at some difficulty to ascertain his route.

1 Compare Dr. Mitterrutzer's *Slavisches aus dem Oestlichen Pusterthal in Tirol*, quoted by Dr. Kuhač, *Josip Haydn*, p. 12.

A Croatian Composer

It is something more than a coincidence that among all districts of Austria this area of Croatian settlement has been the most fruitful in great musicians. Veit Bach, the grandfather of John Sebastian, was born at Pressburg; so was Chopin's great hero, Johann Nepomuk Hummel. The Haydns came from a neighbouring village, the proper name of which—Trstnik—was despairingly translated by the Germans into Rohrau. Joseph Weigl was a native of Eisenstadt, so was Ivan Fuchs, who succeeded Hummel as Prince Esterházy's Kapellmeister. Liszt was born at Rustnik, near Oedenburg, Joachim at Kitsee, Ludwig Strauss at Pressburg, Carl Goldmark at Keszthely. And round this constellation there gathers a whole nebula of lesser stars, names unfamiliar, it may be, to English readers, but in their own country accepted and recognized. Of course it is not claimed that all these artists are of Croatian blood. Some unquestionably are not; but there is at least an *a priori* likelihood that some of them belonged to the race which was numerically dominant, especially as that race was Slavonic and therefore musical, and on this general point a word may perhaps be said before we proceed to particularize in the case of Haydn.

Now, apart from his, it should be noted that none of the names given above are distinctively Slavonic in character. For this fact a simple reason suffices. There had long been spreading through the world of music a practice, originated in Europe by scholars and divines, of taking a *nom de guerre* which should either represent the sound or translate the meaning of the family name. Erasmus, Melanchthon, Stephanus are familiar instances in the world of letters, and following these august models Grobstimm became Baryphonus; Schneider, Sartorius; Glareau, Loritius; and the like. Musicians for the most part seem to have avoided Latin and taken in its place whatever language lay ready to hand for display or convenience. Thus two famous Bohemians called themselves Dussek and Gyrowetz; Beethoven's father occasionally appeared as Bethoff; and the list may be extended even to such grotesques as Gionesi and Coperario. This device was specially necessary to the Croatian who was aiming at a career. We know with what diligence poor Abel, fresh from the German vowel sounds, endeavoured to adapt his name to the requirements of a British public.[1] The need of adaptation is still greater when the language is one which hardly any foreigner can hope to pronounce. Thus it was that the Croatian words tended to drop out altogether, and to be replaced by some rough German or Italian equivalent; and so complete was the transformation that we have to look twice before recognizing Beethoven's first violin in Župančić, or finding in Trtić the composer of the *Trillo del diavolo*. In cases where evidence depends on translation it is so slight as to be of very little value: the case is much stronger when the two variants of the name are transliterations of the same word or sound. There can be no reasonable doubt as to the Slavonic origin of Tartini, Dragonetti, Giornovichi, Zingarelli, and many other of Haydn's contemporaries. There may have been in them some intermixture of race, but the parent stock was Croatian.

We cannot, then, assert that there is any antecedent improbability in assigning Haydn to the Croats. They are a musical people, they formed the chief population of the district where he was born, they have a fair claim to other great musicians of his time. It follows that we should discuss the biographical evidence, and see what is to be made out of the record of Haydn's family.

And here attention should be called to three points. First, that the name Hajden or Hajdin (with its derivative Hajdenić, Hajdinović, &c.) is of common occurrence throughout Croatia, and, in days when spelling was roughly phonetic, may easily have appeared in Austrian official documents as Haiden or Hayden, forms by which

[1] He called himself successively Abel, Ebel, Ibel, and Eibel. But his patrons also moved a stage in advance, even completing the circle by pronouncing the diphthong as it is pronounced in the word 'eight'.

its pronunciation is exactly represented. Now among all the variants assumed by the name of the composer's family,[1] these two are the most frequent and the most authoritative. His great-grandfather—the first member of the house who can be traced—appears in the Hainburg register as Caspar Haiden; his grandfather, once by obvious error called Thomas Hayrn, is usually Hayden elsewhere; the contemporary monuments at Rohrau give Mathias Haiden as the name of his father and Josephus Haiden as his own. He himself seems to have used the dissyllabic form up to January 1762, when he signs for salary at Eisenstadt 'Giuseppe Hayden'; in the February of the same year he changes to the signature 'Joseph Haydn', which he afterwards habitually adopted. Even then the majority of documents relating to him are conservative enough to retain the earlier orthography, and the monument in Count Harrach's park, which bears the name Josephus Hayden, was erected as late as 1794. Indeed, there can be little doubt that Haiden or Hayden was the family name, shortened to suit the Viennese convention, as for the same reason Händel used to be shortened to Händl.[2] Secondly, the name, in one or other of its variants, is widely spread over the whole district from Wiener-Neustadt to Oedenburg. Dr. Pohl found it in some ten or a dozen villages, many of which are claimed by Dr. Kuhač as Croatian, and in the country towns like Hainburg or Eisenstadt it is of course more frequent still. There is no need to remind the reader that this is precisely the region occupied, since the sixteenth century, by the Slavonic immigrants. Thirdly, the home of the entire Haydn family is situated at the centre of the district in question. Caspar was born within sight of the Hainburg walls, Thomas lived and died as a burgher of

[1] Dr. Pohl gives fourteen variants, and even his list is not exhaustive. There are at least six in documents relating to the composer himself. See Appendix.

[2] See the announcement of *Alexander's Feast* (Vienna, 1812) preserved in the Gesellschaft Library. Carpani spells the name Hendl.

that town, Mathias, after a brief period of travel, settled at Rohrau some ten miles away, and the most adventurous of his brothers wandered no farther afield than Frankenmarkt or Ungarisch-Altenburg. It fits well enough with this home-keeping temper that Joseph Haydn should have spent more than three-score and ten years of his life inside a thirty miles radius from his native place.

On the father's side, then, Haydn would seem to belong to the Slavonic race among whom he lived and worked.[1] Again, his mother was a native of Rohrau, in her day a distinctively Croatian village,[2] and her maiden name of Koller—a *vox nihili* in German—is plausibly regarded by Dr. Kuhač as a phonetic variant of the Croatian Kolar, 'wheelwright'.[3] Everything that we know about his look and character favour the supposition of Slavonic descent. The lean, ugly, kindly face with high cheek-bones, long nose, and broad prominent under lip, the keen grey eyes softened by a twinkle of humour, the thin wiry figure, the strong nervous hands; all these and their analogues may be seen to-day in any village where Slavonic blood is still pure; and though of course they afford no argument in themselves, they add a touch of corroborative evidence which is worth noting. To the same cause may be traced that intense love of sport which has left his name as a proverb at Eisenstadt[4]; and something, too, of the conviviality which made him say that his

1 It is fair to state that some etymologists derive the name Haiden from the district 'Auf der Haid' near Hainburg. But this is very unlikely. The district is a narrow stretch of moorland, and could not account for the prevalence of the name through the whole country-side, to say nothing of the frequent occurrence in Croatia proper.

2 Its second title, 'Trstnik', is significant enough. And at the present day it contains a good many Croats, especially among the poorer inhabitants.

3 In like manner Pilar has been Germanized into Piller, Solar into Soller, Kresar into Kresser, and so on. See a list of such changes in Kuhač's *Josip Haydn*, pp. 17, 18.

4 To je lovac i ribar kao Haydn; i.e. as good a shot and fisherman as Haydn.

best evenings were those spent with his comrades at the 'Engel'. His talk, like his music, was full of that obvious fun which raises a laugh by a sudden touch of the unexpected; so are hundreds of Croatian ballads and aphorisms.[1] The humour is sometimes primitive, as when a Croat will tell you, 'It is as true as that two and two make seven'; sometimes it reaches a more respectable level, as the gibe at the Bosnian Brethren, 'who were ordered to abstain from something in Lent, and therefore took no water in their wine'. But good, bad, or indifferent, it marks a distinctive type of peasant character; and in remembering that Haydn was a genius we need not forget that he was a peasant. The same holds good, too, of his religious feeling. It is not without significance that we may turn from one of his scores, with its 'In Nomine Domini' at the beginning, and its 'Laus Deo' at the end, to read in our newspaper that another Croatian village has risen in revolt upon the bare report of an ecclesiastical change. His temper, it may be, had grown more equable than that of his uneducated countrymen; it had not lost anything of their loyalty.

The reasons which have led to this indication of detail may easily be misunderstood. It is not, of course, contended that any race has the monopoly of these characteristics, or that it differs ethically from its neighbours except by the very important fact of the proportion in which they are blended. But when it appears that the more we study Haydn, and the more we study the Slavonic character, the closer becomes the accord between them, when every feature of the one finds its parallel in the prevailing qualities of the other, then we may surely infer that to the antecedent probability some weight is added by this estimate of internal evidence. And probability will strengthen to certitude if we realize that Haydn's music is saturated with Croatian melody, that the resemblances are beyond question, beyond attribu-

[1] See instances quoted by Dr. Kuhač, *Josip Haydn*, pp. 27–9.

tion of coincidence, beyond any explanation but that of natural growth. Some of his tunes are folk-songs in their simplest form, some are folk-songs altered and improved, the vast majority are original, but display the same general characteristics. He would stand wholly outside the practice of the great composers if he wrote, by habitual preference, in an idiom that was not his own.

His acquaintance with these folk-tunes must have begun from his earliest years. His father, we know, was a good musician who used, of an evening, to sit by the cottage door at Rohrau, singing to the children until they plucked up their courage and joined in. And when Frankh carried off the boy for his first experience of schooling, it was only to Hainburg, the earlier home of the family, where he may well have heard the same ballads breaking the quiet of the market-place, or echoing under the great arch of the Wiener Thor. Then, no doubt, came a change; the splendid apparition of George Reutter, the halo of Imperial patronage, the ten years in the choir at St. Stephen's, the sharp struggle for existence when the boy's voice broke and he was turned into the streets of Vienna to shift for himself. It is in every way natural that his first composition should show little direct trace of national influence. He was in his student period; like all students he was dominated by the authority of his models, and for a time his chief ambition was to master the form of Emmanuel Bach, and emulate the counterpoint of the Gradus ad Parnassum. But from the days when he began to speak in his own voice the Slavonic qualities unmistakably appear. There is the same general shape of melody, the same repetition of phrases, the same oddity of rhythm and metre, the same fineness and sensitiveness of feeling; and that not once or twice in a composition, but throughout its entire length. The common employment of folk-songs dates from the Symphony in D major (1762) to the Salomon Symphonies of 1795; they find their way into everything—hymns, quartets, divertimenti; not, of course, because Haydn had any need to take them, but because he loved them too well to leave them out. It will be remembered that for thirty years, from 1761 to 1790, he worked as Prince Esterházy's Kapellmeister in the very centre of the Croatian colony. He must have heard these songs every day, he must have set his life to their lilt and cadence; they were the melodies of his own people, the echoes of his own thought. No one is surprised that Burns should have gathered the Ayrshire peasant songs and transmuted them into gold by the fire of his genius; it is not more wonderful that Haydn should have enriched the treasures of Eisenstadt with metal from his native mines, and as Heine pertinently puts it, the Temple is built by the architect, not by the stone-cutters who supply him with his materials.

Among the numerous illustrations collected by Dr. Kuhač, the following deserve special attention.

(1) The Cassation in G major (1765)[1] begins as follows:

a melody noticeable for the breaking of the four-quaver rhythm by alternate bars of six. It can hardly be doubted that when Haydn wrote this he had in his mind the old Slavonic drinking song, *Nikaj na svetu*—

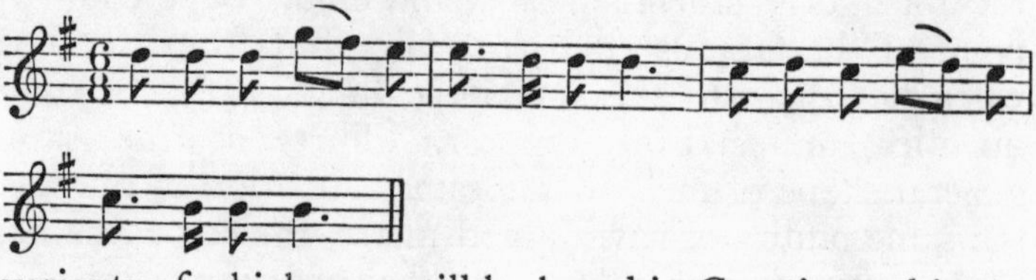

variants of which may still be heard in Croatia, and in the Carinthian Zillerthal. Similar instances of slight adaptation may be traced from the spring song, *Proljeće*—

[1] Dr. Kuhač gives 1754 as the date of this work. If so, it is the earliest known instance. The above date, which is more probably correct, is that given by Dr. Pohl.

which appears at the beginning of the D major Quartet (Op. 17, No. 6) as—

and from the dance-song *Hajde malo dere*—

which is thus altered by Haydn—

(2) The curious and characteristic finale of the D major

Symphony (Salomon, No. 7) is founded on the following theme:

This is simply an amended version of the popular ballad, *Oj Jelena*, which belongs to the district of Kolnov, near Oedenburg, and is specially noted by Dr. Kuhač as being commonly sung in Eisenstadt. Its tune, essentially Slavonic in rhythm and cadence, runs thus:

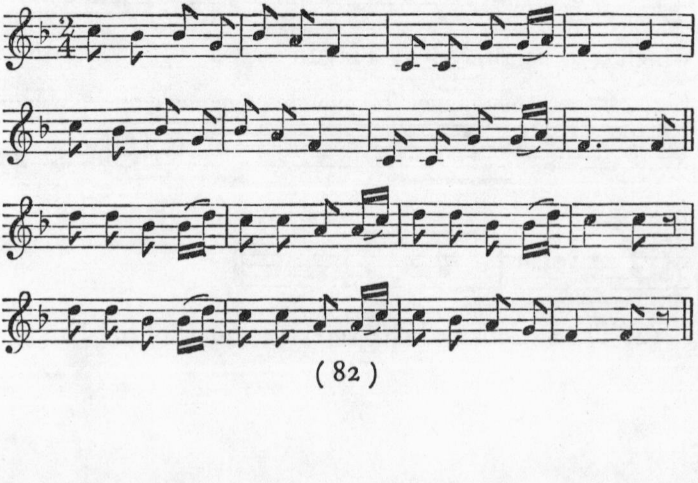

Variants of this melody are found in Croatia proper, Servia, and Carniola.[1]

It is probable that the other movements of this symphony are equally influenced by folk-songs; in any case, no doubt can exist as to the Symphony in E♭, *Mit dem Paukenwirbel.* The opening theme of the Allegro—

is noted by Dr. Kuhač as Croatian.[2] The Andante is founded on two themes, the first minor—

the second major—

[1] See Kuhač, *South-Slavonic Popular Songs*, vol. iii, pp. 98–100.
[2] See Kuhač, *South-Slavonic Popular Songs*, vol. iii, p. 92.

both of which are taken, and considerably improved, from two folk-songs of the Oedenburg district, (*a*) *Na Travniku*:

and (*b*) *Jur Postaje*—

while the principal tune of the Finale—

is that of the song *Divojčica potok gazi*—

&c.

which is common among the Croats, especially those of Haydn's district.[1] Again, the Trio of the A major Symphony (No. 11 in Haydn's Catalogue) contains a Slavonic melody—

and the first movement of its successor (D major, No. 12) suggests another—

&c.

(3) There are several cases in which, without direct adaptation, Haydn has shown the same tendency of thought or phrase as the Slavonic folk-songs. A favourite 'curve' of his may be illustrated by the opening of the B♭ Symphony (Salomon, No. 9)—

as well as by the Dalmatian Overture of Franz von Suppé and the tunes (from Zara and Borištov) on which it was founded—e.g. the ballad *Na placi sem stal*—

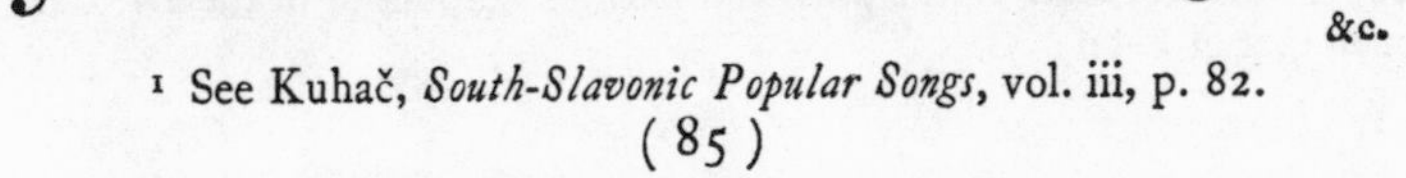

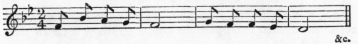

&c.

[1] See Kuhač, *South-Slavonic Popular Songs*, vol. iii, p. 82.

Another, even more beautiful, ends the opening strain in the Adagio of the G major Quartet (Op. 77, No. 1)—

and appears also in the Croatian *Čuješ doro dobro moje*—

while the use of the unprepared dominant ninth, constructed out of a dominant seventh by shifting the melody a third higher, was not so common in Haydn's day that we can afford to neglect the resemblance of—

quoted by Dr. Kuhač from a Quartet in B♭,[1] to—

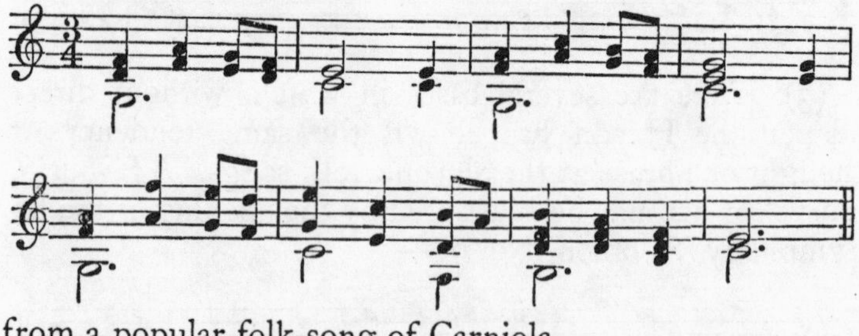

from a popular folk-song of Carniola.

(4) These latter examples do not imply reminiscences, but at most a general sympathy of temper. A good deal more, however, is involved in the treatment of Slavonic dance-tunes. It is hardly too much to say that what the

[1] Dr. Kuhač calls it the Sixth Quartet (*u Allegru šestoga četverogudja*), but it is not the sixth in the Paris and London edition, or in the Dresden, or in that of Peters.

Csardas was to Liszt the Kolo was to Haydn; with this difference—that the earlier and greater musician has throughout made a finer use of his materials. The Kolo is a Slavonic measure, which I have seen the children dance at Agram and the men at Sarajevo, bright and cheery of movement, its tune in two-four time ingeniously varied by patterns of quaver and semiquaver figures. Here, for instance, is an example well known in Bosnia and Dalmatia:

and used with an amended cadence in the Finale of the C major Quartet (Op. 33, No. 3):

Here, again, is a similar dance-tune from Serbia, which opens the Symphony in D major (Haydn's Catalogue, No. 4):

and here another in the Finale of the G major Quartet (Op. 77, No. 1):

in which so wonderful an effect is produced by the alternation of cold unison and glowing harmonies.

Many of Haydn's characteristic melodies follow one or other of these types: e.g., this from the Finale of the F major Quartet (Op. 74, No. 2)—

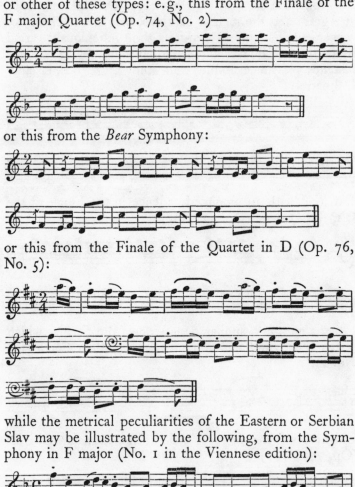

or this from the *Bear* Symphony:

or this from the Finale of the Quartet in D (Op. 76, No. 5):

while the metrical peculiarities of the Eastern or Serbian Slav may be illustrated by the following, from the Symphony in F major (No. 1 in the Viennese edition):

as they may, apart from the Kolo measure, in a hundred of his minuets and finales. Again, the early Pianoforte Concerto in D major ends with an oddly named *Rondo à l'Hongrie*, the principal subject of which is as follows:

This melody, which contains no Magyar characteristics, either of figure, scale, or stanza, is compressed from that of the Siri Kolo, as commonly danced in Bosnia and Dalmatia. The complete tune runs:

A Croatian Composer

a typical rustic dance, which in Haydn's hands has gained not only by compression, but by a more artistic accompaniment.

(5) In addition to the dance measure, Haydn has adopted other instrumental forms, e.g. marches, bagpipe melodies, and the like. Here is one, with a strange rhythm, from the Pianoforte Scherzando in F major:

and here, from the Finale of the B♭ Symphony (Salomon, No. 9), is the march which is commonly played in Turopol at rustic weddings:

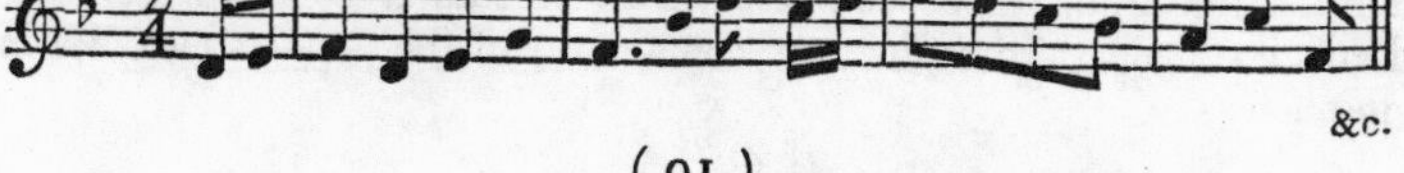

Another Croatian march beginning—

has been identified by Dr. Kuhač from an unpublished Symphony in A major, and there is a further example from the Allegro of the B♭ Quartet (Op. 71, No. 1)—

(6) The two most remarkable instances are yet to come. According to a well-known story, Prince Esterházy once discussed with his Kapellmeister the question whether Church music could not be made 'at the same time religious and popular'. It is hard to realize that Haydn's Masses were ever regarded as too severe; in any case, the Prince felt dissatisfied and wanted a change. He had recently returned from his annual pilgrimage to Maria-Zell. He had heard there music which pleased him, and he seems to have suggested that in the Eisenstadt chapel there was too much counterpoint and too little melody. Haydn listened, sent to Maria-Zell for information, bided his time, and, when next year the day of the pilgrimage was approaching, wrote a 'Mass' or Service to German words,[1] dispatched it to the famous church, had it secretly practised, and finally found an excuse for slipping off on a holiday. The Prince came back more dissatisfied than ever. 'I have heard', he said, 'a service of Church music composed and played in a style which

[1] This story is sometimes told of the Mariazeller Mass in C major (Novello, No. 15). But first, the Mariazeller Mass was written by commission for Anton Liebe von Kreutzner; second, it is set to the usual Latin text; and third, it does not contain any of the popular melodies in question.

you will never equal.' 'Your Highness,' answered Haydn, 'the composition was mine, and I was the organist.'

From this 'Mass', of which at present no other trace seems to be discoverable, Dr. Kuhač quotes seven melodies on the authority of the Dominican Alois Russwurm, who was a personal friend of Haydn, and by whom the story was originally recorded. The first, *Hier liegt vor Deiner Majestät*, is the opening theme of the first number:

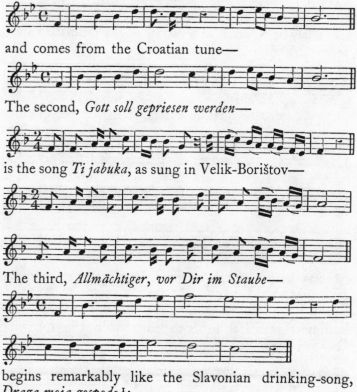

and comes from the Croatian tune—

The second, *Gott soll gepriesen werden*—

is the song *Ti jabuka*, as sung in Velik-Borištov—

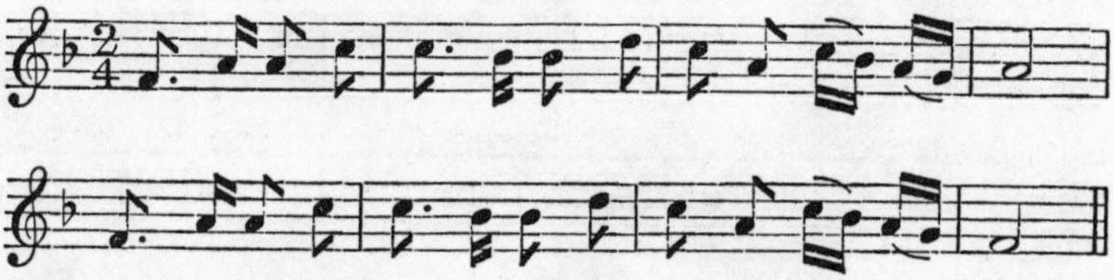

The third, *Allmächtiger, vor Dir im Staube*—

begins remarkably like the Slavonian drinking-song, *Draga moja gospodo* [1]:

[1] The three-bar phrase is a common feature of early Slavonic melodies, especially when conjoined with a second phrase of four bars in irregular balance.

The fourth, *O Vater, sieh vor Deinem Throne*—

may fairly be regarded as a variant of the Dalmatian song, *Jedna Ciganka*—

The fifth, *Betrachtet ihn in Schmerzen*—

&c.

is almost identical in both parts with the following Croatian melody:

The sixth, *Nun ist das Lamm geschlachtet*—

is derived partly from two separate strains in the Croatian and Slavonian versions of a convivial chorus, *Vivla compagnija*—

(*a*)—

(*b*)—

partly from a Croatian sacred song, *Stani gori gospodar*.—

The seventh, *Dich wahres Osterlamm*—which is the concluding phrase of the canticle for the Celebration—

borrows its exact sequence and its curious halting rhythm from the Croatian *Miši prave svatove*—

Clearly, in Haydn's vocabulary 'popular' meant Slavonic.

It may be objected that this example proves nothing. Grant that Haydn was living in a certain district, and that he was asked for once to write in a popular style; what more natural than that he should adapt himself to his surroundings, and use the idioms that he found in common currency? A man readily drops into dialect when he is addressing a rural audience, and does not become a countryman by seasoning his discourse with a few country proverbs and metaphors. This rejoinder would be of more effect if the 'Mass' were an isolated phenomenon: it somewhat loses weight when we remember that the music only turns to Church use the tendencies that have already been noted in symphony and quartet. Still, our case would undoubtedly be stronger if we could find Haydn appealing, in the same tongue, to the Austrian Empire at large, and using the native Slavonic for some great political or ceremonial occasion. Here, at any rate, is a test which we may reasonably regard as crucial, and which, if successfully applied, should go some way towards settling the question.

Unfortunately, the Croatian melodies are not, as a rule, well suited for such a purpose. They are bright, sensitive, piquant, but they seldom rise to any high level of dignity or earnestness. They belong to a temper which is marked rather by feeling and imagination than by any sustained breadth of thought, and hence, while they enrich their own field of art with great beauty, there are certain frontiers which they rarely cross, and from which, if once crossed, they soon return. One limitation in particular will have been observed by every student. It frequently happens that a Croatian or Serbian tune will begin with a fine phrase, and then fall to an anti-climax—either losing sight of its tonality, or wavering in its rhythm, or ending with a weak or commonplace cadence. In almost all the examples quoted above it is the opening of the tune which Haydn has borrowed; its conclusion he has nearly always improved or re-written.[1] And the reasons that impelled him to this practice may be illustrated by the following variants, in all of which are apparent the same touch of inspiration, and the same weakness of development.

(*a*) The song *Stal se jesem*, as sung in Marija Bistric [2]—

Stal se je - sem ra - no ju - tro, Stal se je - sem
ra-no ju-tro Ma-lo pred zor - jum, Ma-lo pred zor - jum.

(*b*) The same song as it appears in the district of S. Ivan Zeline—

[1] See in particular the song *Na travniku* (p. 84), and the first Kolo tune (p. 87).

[2] The musical stanza, in this song, goes to half-stanza of the words. The first is :

Stal se jesem rano jutro	i. e.,	In the early morning stood I
Malo pred zorjum.		Close upon the dawn.

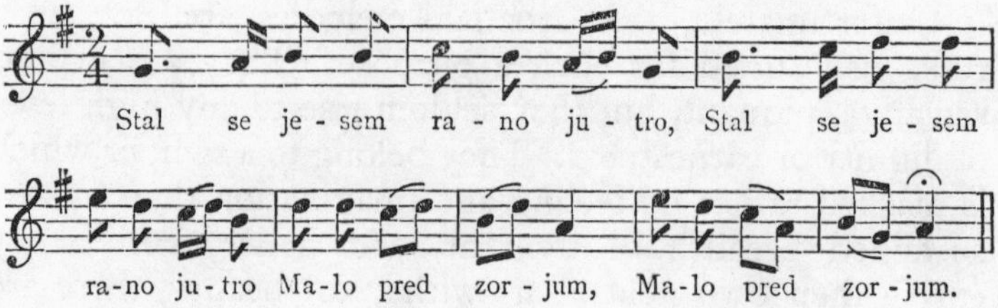
Stal se je - sem ra - no ju - tro, Stal se je - sem
ra-no ju - tro Ma-lo pred zor - jum, Ma-lo pred zor - jum.

(*c*) The same as it appears at Medjumur (Murinsel)—

Stal sem se ja vju - tro ra - no, Stal sem se ja
vju-tro ra - no Ma-lo pred zor - jum, Ma - lo pred zor - jum.

In these versions the last four bars appear to have been loosely attached to the rest of tune; at any rate, they are often found, apart from the first phrase, in Croatian carols and drinking songs. Again, among other districts there has been some rearrangement of the words, with corresponding changes in the music. Either the opening line is not repeated, which leads to the excision of the third bar, and a consequent alteration of cadence; e.g.—

(*d*) Variant from Kolnov (near Oedenburg)—

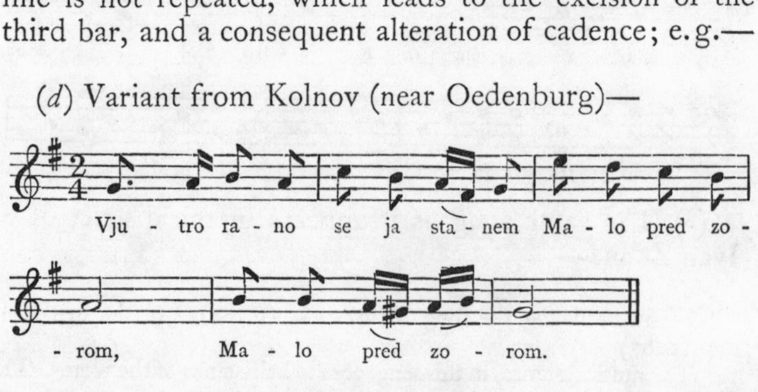
Vju - tro ra - no se ja sta - nem Ma - lo pred zo -
- rom, Ma - lo pred zo - rom.

or it is inserted again after the second, so as to give the stanza an alternation of masculine and feminine endings; e.g.—

(*e*) Variant from Čembe—

Vju - tro ra - no se ja sta-nem Ma-lo pred zo - rom;
Vju - tro ra - no se ja sta-nem Ma- lo pred zo - rom.

The rest is easily divined. When in 1797 Haydn was commissioned to set the National Anthem, he must have had this tune before his eye, and have determined to use it as the pedestal of the *monumentum ære perennius* which his loyalty erected.[1] And here a word may be said as to the manner in which the great tune appears to have been written. It was no momentary inspiration, no sudden impromptu that should come into existence at full growth; like most of Beethoven's music, it was made carefully, and by deliberate weighing of alternatives. By a piece of singular good fortune, we are for once admitted to the master's workshop, and allowed to take our lesson in melody by the observation of his practice.

Now the second strain of the folk-tune is too short to fit the second line of the poem; accordingly, Haydn began by extending its cadence, and instead of—

wrote—

following it with repeat-marks, after the common method of primary form. Two other changes explain themselves.

[1] There is no need to discuss here the question of Telemann's Rondo. If its resemblance to Haydn's tune be anything more than fortuitous, it is probably referable to the same source. See *Josip Haydn*, p. 81.

The measure is dignified by the broader time-signature, and the accent shifted from arsis to thesis by the rearrangement of the bars. Otherwise, in the first half of the stanza the folk-tune remains unaltered.

But for the second half it was manifestly insufficient. Both the possible variants are too trivial, and one too brief, to afford the requisite climax. As a natural consequence, Haydn discarded both, and proceeded to supply their place with two original strains, which in the autograph sketch [1] run as follows:

[1] Preserved in the Museum of the Gesellschaft Library at Vienna. It is a small oblong sheet, similar to those on which Haydn wrote his *Canons*, and contains, first, the complete sketch of the melody:

and below it the third strain amended:

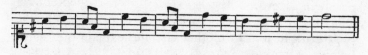

The improved version of the fourth strain is not there, but, curiously enough, Pohl notes an anticipation of it in the Mariazeller Mass. See Pohl's *Haydn*, vol. ii, p. 333.

Still, he was dissatisfied with the result, and it is easy to suggest the reason. In the former of these two strains there is a passage which carries tonic harmony—out of place at this stage of the tune—and its cadence, moreover, rhymes awkwardly with that of the half-stanza. The latter of the two comes down from its point of stress with a fine sweeping movement, but, three bars from the end, breaks its melodic curve into two distinct pieces, and so loses continuity of line. Both were accordingly corrected, one on the same page, the bottom stave of which bears, in hasty manuscript, the amended form—

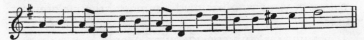

the other, with a few more minute alterations, at a later period of the work.

It is to be hoped that these examples will not encourage any reader to pursue Haydn with the cry of plagiarist. No accusation could be more unfounded or more unreasonable. He poached upon no man's preserve, he robbed no brother-artist, he simply ennobled those peasant-tunes with the thought and expression of which he was most nearly in accord. The whole extent of his indebtedness is at most an occasional melody, and is often but a single phrase; the treatment, the setting, the workmanship belong as truly to him as *Faust* to Goethe, or *Cymbeline* to Shakespeare. The master who has written a hundred and twenty first-rate symphonies, and eighty-three first-rate quartets, may surely claim the right to take his wealth where he finds it; and if we are churlish enough to deny this, at least we may allow him the privilege of speaking in his native tongue. To Haydn, the folk-tunes were little more than the words of his accustomed speech, hardly obscured when the Church asserted her contrapuntal dignity, and reappearing in full significance when he returned to the untrammelled orchestra and the freedom of the four magic strings. It is more important to note how closely his special melodic gift is in sympathy with that of his people. Many of the tunes quoted above are among those which a critic would select as especially characteristic: there are literally hundreds of his invention by which, in a more or less degree, the same qualities are exhibited. No doubt he was not only the child of his nation, he had his own personality, his own imaginative force, his own message to deliver in the ears of the world. But through all these the national element runs as a determining thread. That 'les grands artistes n'ont pas de patrie' is a sentence abundantly refuted by its very author; it assuredly finds no support in the life of the Croatian peasant who has made immortal the melodies of his race.

It is right that full consideration should here be given to a criticism which, on the publication of this essay, appeared in some of the German and Italian newspapers, and which has more recently been revived by the very accomplished musical historian who wrote under the name of Michael Brenet. Its main contention is that the evidence so far as concerns the Croatian folk-songs should be reversed; that the inference to be drawn from these similarities is not that Haydn borrowed from them, but the melodies were of his composition and passed from him into the currency of the people. It is further contended that the argument here maintained requires for its full confirmation that some collections of South-Slavonic folk-songs should be produced which are of earlier date than Haydn. So, and so only, say the critics, can we maintain that they were already in existence when he wrote.

The latter contention has all the appearance of reasonableness and none of the reality. It would, of course, be a very strong witness if it were forthcoming, but this is obviously impossible. To ask for a collection of South-Slavonic folk-songs dated earlier than the middle of the eighteenth century shows as great a want of historical imagination as to suppose that the *March of the Men of Harlech* was written in the reign of Edward IV, or that John Dunstable was the same person as St. Dunstan. Until the beginning of the nineteenth century the country in question had no literature, no art, no printing-press, and hardly even an alphabet. There was no one to collect folk-songs, and no means of publishing them if they had been collected. The witnesses, in short, whose testimony is demanded had, as a matter of common knowledge, never been born. We are bound, therefore, to questions of probability and of internal evidence, and in these, as it seems to me, the testimony is overwhelmingly on the one side. Take, for instance, the popular Mass which has already been quoted. Every one of its numbers has the melody of a folk-song. Which is the more likely, that Haydn composed these tunes for a *pièce d'occasion*, that the villagers memorized them on one hearing and spread them abroad, all six of them, through the countryside; or that Haydn, who was himself a villager hearing folk music on almost every day of his life, should have gathered these wild flowers from the hedgerow and served them up for the discomfiture of his patron? Of the two hypotheses one seems to me entirely impossible, the other so simple and natural that it needs no emphasis. Again, it must be remembered that the resemblances are far more extensive than the critics are willing to admit. They are not confined to a few phrases or to the work of a few years. They run through nearly half a century; they vary from a few characteristic notes to a complete stanza; and when to all this is added the ethnological evidence which makes out that Haydn was of the same race and of the same country, that he held for thirty years an office which gave him constant access to village life and village merry-making, and that, like every other great composer, he was ready to take his good where he found it, there does not require any special pleading to support the view which is here maintained.

The case is strengthened by all evidence of musical history. The same hand which made Germany a people enriched her with the *Marseillaise of the Reformation*, and so founded the long dynasty of her great composers. Art in France was at its lowest, when the chief occupation of Paris was to dispute between the claims of the Bavarian Gluck and the Italian Piccini. Italy herself declined as she lost her national character, the Slavonic peoples have advanced as they have reasserted theirs. And what is true of nations is equally true of their leaders. 'The greatest genius', says Emerson, 'is the most indebted man'; the man, that is, who can turn to the most noble and enduring use the traditions of his age and country. So it was with Haydn. Nothing can be more false than to regard him as merely a Court musician, writing with ready and facile talent the *pièces d'occasion* that were needed for the theatre or the reception-room. His life at Eisenstadt gave him opportunity such as no composer had ever before enjoyed, but the patronage was too enlightened and the character too strong to be satisfied with work that was mannered or artificial. Under the famous 'livery of blue and silver' there beat the heart of a rustic poet, full of kindliness, of drollery, of good-fellowship, of the love of children and animals. His genius, trained by years of assiduous labour, gave him a complete mastery over the inherited resources of his art, his imagination extended them with fresh discoveries and inventions. But throughout the whole his favourite themes are pastoral, songs of the shepherd and the harvester, songs of country courtship, songs of the vintage feast and the jovial holiday. It is little wonder that he should speak in the language of his people, or recall the phrases that had been familiar from his childhood.

Yet it is no patois that he uses, but the speech of a

whole nation; a living force that spreads wide and reaches to distant boundaries. Nor is he great because he has chosen this or that topic, this or that form of utterance; it is because he is great that there was no choice in the matter. He could not have written of set habit in the German idiom; he was Slav by race and Slav by temper, and his music is too genuine to present itself in foreign guise. It is from this point of view that we should understand him; not by loosely classifying him among a people with whom he had little in common, but by regarding him as the true embodiment of his own national spirit. The Greek proverb condemns a man of two tongues: through the world of art the condemnation is still in force, and at least some measure of it should fall on the ingenious critics who call patriotism parochial, and justify their epithet by obliterating frontiers.

APPENDIX

Variants of the Name 'Haydn' within the Limits of the Composer's Family.

(*a*) *Haiden:* Register of Caspar Haiden's marriage, Hainburg, 1657.

Register of Joseph Haiden's death, Hainburg, 19 April 1715.

Register of the composer's baptism, Rohrau, 1 April 1732 (the father's name is given as Mathias Haiden).

Register of his mother's death, Rohrau, 25 February 1754.

(*b*) *Hayden:* Register of Thomas Hayden's death, Hainburg, 4 September 1701, and of his widow's re-marriage, Hainburg, 8 January 1702.

Register of the composer's marriage (St. Stephen's, Vienna, 26 November 1760).

The composer's signature (quittance for salary) Eisenstadt, January 1762.

Register of Mathias Hayden's death, Rohrau, 14 September 1763, and the monument to him now in Rohrau Churchyard.

Frequent concert notices, both of the composer and his brother Michael, the latter at Salzburg.

Habitual signature for many years of Michael Hayden.
The composer's monument in Count Harrach's Park at Rohrau.

(*c*) *Haidin :* The name of the composer's mother is so given on the monument in Rohrau Churchyard.

(*d*) *Heyden :* The composer's name is so written throughout the 'Convention und Verhaltungs-Norma' under which he held his appointment at Eisenstadt.

(*e*) *Heiden :* Register of Thomas Heiden's baptism, Hainburg, 1655.

(*f*) *Hayd'n :*
(*g*) *Haydtn :* } Occasionally, though rarely, in concert programmes.

(*h*) *Haydn :* Register of Mathias Haydn's baptism, Hainburg, 31 January 1699.
The composer's habitual signature after February 1762.
Register of his wife's death, Baden, 20 March 1800.
Diploma of the Freedom of Vienna, 1 April 1804.
Many notices and concert programmes.
Monument to the composer in the Einsiedeln Church at Eisenstadt.

(*i*) *Haidn :* Register of Barbara Haidn's baptism, Hainburg, 2 January 1658.
Frequent notices and concert programmes.
Letter of Beethoven, 1822.

(*k*) *Hayrn :* Register of Thomas Hayrn's marriage, Hainburg, 23 November 1687—his father's name is also given as Caspar Hayrn; see letters (*a*), (*b*), and (*c*).

(*l*) *Hein :* Register of Mathias Hein's marriage, Rohrau, 24 November 1728.

(*m*) *Haden :*
(*n*) *Hädn :*
(*o*) *Hayn :*
(*p*) *Hain :*
(*q*) *Heim :* } Occasional variants in registers and documents at Hainburg, Rohrau, &c., noted by Dr. Pohl.

BEETHOVEN [1]

IT is strange that a nation so fond of music as our own should be so little inclined to allow it the rights of intellectual citizenship. For nearly three centuries we have treated it as the Athenians treated their resident aliens; granting it domicile and protection and freedom to exercise its craft, generous in material rewards and in praise sincere if not always discriminating, but holding it aloof as a remote and picturesque stranger whose purpose we did not know, whose claims to equality we did not admit, and whose language we could not hope to understand. To learn music, with us, means generally to learn how to play or sing; to train for a professional career or to add a pleasant accomplishment to the amenities of life. We do not, at the present day, realize that the appreciation of music can be made, and ought to be made, as essential a part of our equipment, as an appreciation of poetry or painting, of oratory or drama, of the marvels of Science or the meditations of philosophy, of all that can teach us 'to find our pleasures and pains aright', to strengthen our reason and to purify our spirit.

Now here we are certainly in error. We do music a grave injustice when we regard it as an Arabian Nights' banquet spread by the hands of unaccountable magic and offered for the passing delectation of the sense. It is as natural a mode of expression as speech itself, and to ignore this is to stunt and curtail our common humanity. It is as capable of noble use or ignoble misuse as any other of the arts, we are traitors to the law of beauty if we sacrifice this distinction to trivial enjoyment or pass it by through indolence or inattention. It is as truly a language as any tongue that man has ever spoken: infinitely subtle and delicate, capable of infinite extension and development, but none the less based on profound psychological laws and on enduring principles of style and construction. In

[1] Annual Master-mind Lecture (Henriette Hertz Trust), read before the British Academy, 20th June 1917.

a perfect melody the notes follow as inevitably as the words in a perfect sentence or the measures in a perfect verse: the whole is vital, organic, growing as if by necessity of its own nature and filled with the utmost significance that it can bear. And precisely the same is true of the larger and more complex forms; they imply the same kind of creative power in the artist and offer the same kinds of problem to the critic. For the two temporal arts, poetry and music, are essentially one: differing in the media which they employ, and in all that this difference involves, unified in the sources from which they spring and the needs to which they minister. It was no idle fancy which led Beethoven to call himself by preference a tone-poet; he is of the company of Shakespeare and Goethe not less than of Palestrina or Bach or Mozart. And if we are inclined to disallow this it is because here again we have chosen to place music at a needless and arbitrary disadvantage. Imagine what would be our conception of Shakespeare if we knew him only through public representation on the stage; if we had not the volume to read and re-read, to perpend and study, to assimilate until the thought and cadence of it run in our blood. At most we may see a given play twice or thrice in a year, and by seeing it may be stimulated to fuller knowledge and understanding: what if, to carry us from one occasion to the next, we had no better resource than imperfect and indistinct recollection? But with a Beethoven Symphony our acquaintance begins and ends in the concert-room; we may perhaps recall it through a pianoforte version as we may place on our writing-table the photograph of an absent friend, but we never think of using the score except as accessory to the performance. And in this way we shut ourselves out from that intimate and personal communion with the work which is the source of nearly all our love and admiration of great poetry. We can never fully understand music until (and it is no hard task) we learn to read it in silence with our feet on the hob, following at our leisure the development of the composer's idea, stopping to savour some turn of melody or modulation or cadence, looking back to remind ourselves how cunningly the untwisted knot has been tied, entering step by step into the soul of the master, and so comprehending, to the limit of our capacity, the secret which has been given to him to reveal. I do not, of course, depreciate the value of public performance in either art: its value is incontestable and may be paramount; but I am convinced that, under the conditions in which we live, public performance alone is insufficient, and that a more personal and intimate study will often lead us to discover beauties of which we had hitherto been wholly unaware.[1]

Music, then, is poetry expressed through tones instead of words. It follows to consider briefly and summarily what are the actual distinctions here implied and on what basis of unity they are superimposed. In this way we can most directly approach the work of that composer by whom their unification has been most completely vindicated. Now in point of pure form, if we may for a moment use that abstraction, the pre-eminence clearly rests with music. The highest praise of sound that can be given to a language is that it is musical; that it approximates to a standard which music itself has set. No doubt there are some ears to which this ordered sweetness is cloying or even painful—we may remember one over-sensitive man of letters who avenged himself with an epigram about 'le plus désagréable de tous les sons'—but Gautier was contemporary with the beginnings of modern orchestration and to him much may be forgiven. Again in rhythm, the very pulse and heart-beat of both artistic forms, the balance is incomparably on the same side. The greatest

[1] I find the following in a gossiping literary Diary, attributed to one Thomas Green, and published at Ipswich in 1810. 'It is a lamentable drawback on musical composition that the author cannot exhibit his conceptions directly to the public; but must trust for this purpose to the agency of others. The Painter, the Architect, and the Poet address themselves at once and without any intervention to the senses and feelings of mankind: an inestimable advantage.'

masters of verbal rhythm, Virgil for instance, or Racine, or Coleridge cannot match the musician, their most exquisite measures move heavily beside the Overture to *Figaro*, or the opening of the Fifth Symphony or of Schubert's A minor Quartet. Musical prosody is literally illimitable: it not only contains every conceivable metre in a hundred different shapes, but it can vary and combine and divide and syncopate, it can break into a thousand shoots and blossoms and tendrils, until the poet's measure stands amazed at its own luxuriance:

Miraturque novas frondes et non sua poma.

Thirdly, the poet can offer no analogue at all to the beauty of musical texture—the twining blending voices that enrich and reinforce and ennoble one another, each maintaining its own personality yet all serving a common purpose, so ordered that their simultaneous converse is not an interruption but an added grace. Set four poets to speak at once, you have chaos: four musicians to sing at once, you have creation.

Against this must be set, no doubt, the greater definiteness of poetry, and its far greater power of evoking images and ideas of human experience. I do not propose here to discuss a couple of current propositions, that the value of poetry is independent or even exclusive of its meaning, and the still more tiresome paradox that music is the more determinate art of the two. Music in this relation is clearly indeterminate: it can describe nothing, it can depict nothing, it can prove nothing. When we call a melodic phrase 'significant' we are, I think, using the word in a fuller sense than when it is applied to a line in a picture, but a sense far less definite than as applied to a line in a poem. It is true that, as Tennyson said, words are only half-revealing. It may be true, as a greater critic than Tennyson has said, that they owe much of their meaning to use and association, so that when we read familiar poetry—Shakespeare for instance, or Wordsworth—we are not consciously impressed by the unitary force of each word, but by a general flow of significance in which the sound plays a very important part. Yet even so the distance between poetry and music is not obliterated: it is hardly even lessened. Contrast for instance any landscape in the *Excursion* with the first two movements of Beethoven's *Pastoral* Symphony. Wordsworth sets before us his Cumberland dales: it is they that we see through his eyes, and interpret through his thoughts. Beethoven sets before us no scene at all. The first movement of the symphony is no more like a landscape than it is like anything else that is large and simple and open: no brook in the world ever meandered like the violins in the adagio. And this is not because Beethoven tried to do something and failed; but because, like all supreme artists, he recognized the limitations of his medium and forbore. The warning which he wrote on the manuscript contains, in this regard, his entire confession of faith. Music to him was always 'mehr Ausdruck der Empfindung als Malerei'.

Yet there is one direction, and that the highest, in which this limitation itself is transcended. Plato tells us that beyond the transitory world of phenomena is a real world, real because ideal; in which exist the eternal archetypes of those qualities whose interplay covers and constitutes the range of our human experience. It is this ideal world which is the ultimate source of all beauty and the ultimate object of all art. We apprehend it in proportion as we withdraw ourselves from the phenomenal world as such, in proportion as we can penetrate through the avenues of sense perception to the divine spiritual reality that lies behind them. Beauty, truth, goodness are the three folds of the garment by which we see God, and in their essential being these three are one.

For the service of this ideal every art has its own means of approach, its own ritual of worship. The great picture is a window into Heaven, the great poem catches the inspiration of a Divine message. But herein music stands on a different ground from all the so-called representative arts, and if in comparison with them it loses on the one hand it assuredly has its gain in compensation. It cannot, so intimately as they, associate itself with the wonders of nature or the achievements of human life—those 'effluences from noble action' of which Plato speaks; but its very remoteness from human experience means that it is nearer to the ideal world. The poet, the painter, the sculptor are bound to a greater or less degree by the facts of life and nature; if they disown this obligation they produce what is at best an amusing artifice and at worst a deformity. The musician is bound by no laws except those of the human soul, his work stands in no necessary relation to the phenomenal world but has already passed beyond. In one word, the painter manifests his idea through representation; the musician, without it. Poetry clothes its thought in the imagery of sense-perception, and expresses it through a speech that has been chiefly framed for the empirical world: music is 'an inarticulate unfathomable speech which leads to the edge of the infinite and lets us for moments gaze into that'.

Yet this inarticulate unfathomable speech has within it differences of race, perhaps even of dialect. It is an entirely false inference that because music is infinite it is therefore cosmopolitan: one might as well argue that all great poetry is written in Esperanto. The work of every true artist largely reflects the formative influences that have gone to make up his character, and among these race and environment are obviously the two most powerful. Sometimes, as in the French poets and composers, the racial element is extremely pure, and the environment usually corroborates and confirms it: sometimes, as in Heine, the two run counter one to the other: sometimes, as in English music of the bad period, a native style may be temporarily overlaid by slavish adherence to foreign methods. But this means that the causal activities are complex, not that they are inoperative. We need not be afraid of the spectral name of Nationalism: that word, with some others of like structure, is but a penalty which outraged civilization is imposing on us for our complacent and disdainful ignorance of Greek.[1] Surely it is plain common sense that if a man writes sincerely he will write out of the fullness of a heart that has been enriched both by his inheritance and by his surroundings.

It is therefore of interest that we should note the stock from which Beethoven sprang and the conditions under which his work was accomplished. His family, on the father's side, was Flemish: compatriot, that is, of the first madrigalian school, and of a roll of great painters from the Van Eycks and Memling[2] to Rubens and Vandyke. The ancestral home was near Louvain: a younger branch settled at Antwerp in 1650, and there, at the beginning of the eighteenth century, was born the composer's grandfather, Ludwig van Beethoven the elder. He began his career as bass singer in the church of St. Peter at Louvain, and was thence transferred to the Archiepiscopal service at Bonn, where he sang the solos in Mass and Opera, rose to be the Director of the Music, and, in all the glamour of success, gathered round him a colony of Flemish friends and neighbours. We have a pleasant picture of him in old age—small, bird-like, bright-eyed, trenchant in speech, a great martinet with his choir and orchestra, and much beloved by the little grandson who, in later years, carried his portrait to Vienna as one of the few family heirlooms worth preserving! His son, Johann, was a tenor-singer in the same Capelle, who married a German girl from Ehrenbreitstein, and settled down into the careless, slovenly, intemperate life which was not uncommon among operatic artists at the time. Of this pair Beethoven was born on 16 December 1770.

Bonn was then a typical 'little town' such as Heine

[1] It would be good for our language and still better for our controversies if all words in '-ism' were prohibited by law: Socialism, Capitalism, Imperialism—in each of them a question begged, or rather demanded at the pistol's mouth.

[2] It may be worth recalling the fact that Memling, who painted the St. Ursula coffer at Bruges, was contemporary with Josquin, the earliest composer whose work still speaks to us in the language of human passion.

describes in his *Book of Ideas*: less than 10,000 inhabitants, quiet, orderly, somnolent, contentedly dominated by the palace in which for some four centuries the Archbishop of Cologne had held his court, and, according to a jest which it shared with other towns of more pretension, 'fed by the bakemeats of the Electoral kitchen'. There the child grew up with a few scraps of general education, a fairly solid grounding in violin and organ, and a complete training in the clavier; and learning in a harder school than the pedagogue's, those lessons of self-reliance and responsibility which his father's idle and dissolute habits made it necessary for him to acquire. At twelve years old he was already deputy organist in the Electoral Chapel; at sixteen he had shown so much promise that he was sent on a visit to Vienna, where Mozart heard him improvise and foretold a great future for him; at twenty-one he presented a Cantata to Haydn, who was passing through Bonn on his way back from England, and who was so much impressed that he offered at once to adopt him as a pupil. There was some delay, for the Archbishop was at Frankfort, taking part in the Election of the Emperor: on his return the requisite leave was obtained, and by the end of November 1792 Beethoven was settled in Vienna with virtually the whole of his career before him.

It is true that he had written a certain number of compositions at Bonn—the Serenade Trio, a few boyish exercises in sonata form, a handful of smaller clavier-pieces; but, unless in improvisation, there was nothing as yet which indicated the distinctive character of his genius. Nor need we wonder at this. Almost all musicians have manifested early some power of expressing themselves through their art: very few have written before manhood any work of real depth or significance. Mozart, Schubert, Mendelssohn are three exceptions, and of each of these almost all the best work was written towards the close of a tragically short life. It is no very cynical asperity to say that the world would not be appreciably the poorer if it lost all the music composed by Bach before he went to

Weimar, or by Handel before he came to London, or by Haydn before he accepted the memorable invitation of Count von Fürnberg.[1] Indeed, if we may venture upon any generalization, it would be that the gift of musical invention usually begins to ripen in early manhood, and that it comes to a fuller maturity as the whole character strengthens and develops.

This may help to explain the fact that Beethoven at Vienna proved to be a most refractory pupil. He learned nothing, as he says, from Haydn, he learned less than nothing from Albrechtsberger, his debt to Salieri began and ended with a few lessons in Italian declamation. The truth is that he had passed beyond the stage of tuition. Rugged, obstinate, intensely sincere, he revolted from any suspicion of patronage or prescriptive right: rigorous in self-criticism, he was wholly intolerant of external rule or injunction: he had his own message to deliver, his own path to tread, and his technical equipment was fully sufficient for him to advance with certainty and confidence. That he learned much from the study of Mozart is incontestable—Milton in like manner 'acknowledged that Mr. Spenser was his original', Shakespeare in like manner modelled some of his early versification on Marlowe—but even in the earliest of his Viennese compositions there rose a note which no music before had sounded, and which no tradition had power to restrain or modify.

Yet throughout his career his main interest was centred on a structural form which at first sight may seem specially amenable to the influence of tradition: the form which serves as ground plan to the sonata, the quartet, and the symphony. The first fifty-three of his published works were all based on one or other of its variants; in his total list the number is almost exactly doubled; at the close of his life he could find the general scheme as fit a vehicle for

[1] Byrd published his first known composition at the age of thirty-eight, and his last at the age of seventy-six. Gluck was forty-eight when he produced *Orfeo*: Rameau fifty when he produced *Hippolyte et Aricie*. There are many other examples.

his thought as he had found it at the beginning. But this no more hampers the poet's freedom than do the five acts of Elizabethan tragedy: if it be a convention it is so wide and flexible as to admit within its limits an almost endless variety of treatment. And herein Beethoven was unquestionably *felix opportunitate vitae*. The forms in question, after a long period of slow and gradual development, had in the last half of the eighteenth century been brought to a fuller organization by C. P. E. Bach and Haydn and Mozart, with the twofold result that Beethoven not only entered into the inheritance of their labours but could address an audience that had learned to appreciate them. He could thus take for granted a general acquaintance with the principles of structure, and use that acquaintance itself as a *point d'appui*. Knowing the kind of scheme which his hearers expected he could baffle their expectation before he allowed it to be gratified: he could hold attention in suspense, divert it by ingenious misdirection, concentrate it on a moment of sheer surprise, set it guessing between alternative issues, and so bring it at last to a conclusion not less unforeseen than inevitable. The secret of his constructive power is that every one of his great movements gives us the impression of a voyage of discovery, which he permits us to share with him.

It may be said that the effect of this must necessarily weaken as the music becomes familiar. The landscape gardener in Peacock, who enumerates among his aims not only symmetry and proportion but 'a quality which I will venture to call unexpectedness', is, you will remember, silenced by the inquiry, 'Pray, sir, by what name do you designate that quality when a person walks round the grounds for the second time?' But as applied either to literature or to music this criticism is not only untrue: it is the reverse of the truth. The first sense of wonder and expectation is not obliterated but deepened by closer familiarity: the first thrill is itself reproduced by an almost physical act of association, and its content is made all the fuller and richer from the fact that we not only feel but understand it! A mere device may grow wearisome on repetition, we soon tire of the wit which exhausts itself in catchword and paradox, but the variety that springs from the organic life of a poem is of the kind which age cannot wither or custom stale. We cannot imagine an Athenian following the *Agamemnon* with less interest because he was already acquainted with the story: we know from our own experience that the plotting of Iago becomes more sinister and the prowess of Falstaff more delightful every time that we read of them or see them enacted.

Another aspect of this wide human sympathy is Beethoven's astonishing force and vitality of invention. There is no composer who repeats himself so seldom, who makes less use of the formula. His phrases are like living words, his rhythms are like gestures, that wonderful polyphony which he brought to perfection in his last compositions speaks with a voice like the sound of many waters. Even his lightest utterances are extraordinarily free from convention, they express with perfect genuineness the emotions that have aroused them, and are consequently always fresh, and always, in the truest sense of the term, original. The same is true, in a different way, of his schemes of organic structure. For instance, one of the most sensitive places in a 'cyclical' movement is that in which the voyage of adventure begins at last to come into sight of port; the point, in other words, where the skilfully woven plot approaches its *dénouement*. Beethoven always marks this (for our better attention) by some special effect of colour or modulation or melody, something which shall rouse our curiosity and prepare us for the coming event. And in no two of his works is the effect produced by the same means. The unexpected horn entry in the Eroica, the exquisite modulation in the so-called Pastoral Sonata, the ringing challenge in the G major Quartet, are but random examples of a boundless fertility which may be illustrated through the whole course of his compositions. 'Here', in Dryden's phrase, 'is God's plenty'; and it is bestowed on us with a lavish hand.

Many of the great creative artists have been brilliant improvisers, who, like Scott and Shakespeare, never blotted a line. Beethoven's method was entirely different from theirs. At the clavier he could exhibit a power of improvisation which outmatched that of all his contemporaries: in the study he beat his music out in a sort of physical agony, turning it again and again on the anvil, and forcing it by sheer titanic energy into the shape that he desired. The sketch-books, which he always carried with him, are a complete musical autobiography: they show the thought from its first germinal inception to the ultimate form which alone could satisfy him: sometimes there are as many as twelve versions of the same theme—each exhibiting some advance, some more felicitous turn of phrase, some further revelation of meaning, until the melody bursts into full blossom, the more vivid and spontaneous for the successive stages that have brought it to birth. There are famous instances in the slow movement of the Fifth Symphony, at the beginning of the great B♭ Sonata (Op. 106), in the Rondo of the A minor Quartet: they are not afterthoughts—they are hardly even corrections, but rather the slow growth of a living phrase through the innermost principle of its own being.

The whole record of his life at Vienna displays the same tenacity of purpose, and, it may be added, the same obstinacy of temper. He neither accepted patronage like Haydn nor defied it like Mozart, but went his own way, visiting where he pleased, making friendships as occasion arose, and dominating by sheer force of character every assembly in which he took part. His manners, totally devoid of grace or polish, 'imposed themselves', to use his own phrase, by a sort of relentless integrity which drove straight to the root of the matter without arrogance and without affectation. His sense of honour was so keen that the smallest suspicion of insincerity could rouse him to tempestuous anger; not for the personal slight but from a passionate love of truth in all things. A convinced republican, who dedicated a symphony to Napoleon as

First Consul and withdrew the dedication from Napoleon as Emperor, he paid no regard to wealth or station, laughed at Goethe for his courtiership, and was never happier than when he could retire to Baden or Gneixendorf and commune with nature alone or in the company of a few pupils or intimates. Yet within this stubborn nature were unplumbed depths of generosity and tenderness. He was the most loyal of friends, the most appreciative of critics; he taxed his scanty resources to provide for a ne'er-do-weel nephew, whose ingratitude and incompetence he bore without a word of remonstrance; the one great passion of his life was as noble as it was unfortunate, the inspiration of a few golden years which, when it passed away, left no trace of rancour or resentment. He was as incapable of hatred as he was of meanness or jealousy or self-seeking, and the most poignant lamentation to which he ever gave utterance was a cry of sorrow that his deafness was gradually isolating him from human sympathy and companionship.

Many characteristic pictures of him have been left to us by friends and visitors. The portrait of Johnson in Fleet Street is hardly more vivid than that of the short, sturdy, broad-shouldered figure, the large head, the stiff black hair, the swarthy ugly face, grim-mouthed, heavy-jowled, pitted with small-pox, redeemed by the lofty brow and the large luminous brown eyes, the long arms, the rough hairy hands, so stubby-fingered that they could scarcely stretch a tenth on the keyboard; the scrupulous cleanliness of person—one of his landladies gave him notice because he washed so often—and the attire so careless that the street boys mocked at him as he passed. We can see him 'standing in the full glare of the sun' and declaiming on aesthetics to Bettina von Arnim whom he was supposed to be escorting home; or running by Prince Lobkowitz's palace in order to avenge a mistimed criticism by shouting 'Lobkowitzer Esel' through the doorway; or sitting absorbed and foodless in the little vaulted eating-house which he frequented, while Schubert, a few paces off, watched him in silent adoration, too shy to speak. But no story better illustrates the endearing defects, which everybody loved and laughed at, than one told by Paer, the Italian musician, who on a visit to Vienna produced at the Kärnthnerthor an indifferent opera named *Achille*. Beethoven, who had been searching in vain for a libretto that would satisfy at once his literary taste and his stubborn Puritanism, sat next the composer on the first night and followed the plot with increasing pleasure and admiration. 'Ah! que c'est beau,' he repeated; 'ah! que c'est intéressant,' and at last in an uncontrolled outburst of enthusiasm: 'il faut que je compose cela'.

Croce, in one of the most interesting and stimulating of critical essays, has told us that 'we may define beauty as successful expression, or better as expression and nothing more. Consequently', he says, 'the ugly is unsuccessful expression. The paradox is true that in works of art that are failures the beautiful is present as unity and the ugly as multiplicity. Thus with regard to works of art that are more or less failures, we talk of qualities, that is of those parts of them that are beautiful. We do not talk thus of perfect works. It is in fact impossible to enumerate their qualities or to designate those parts of them that are beautiful. In them there is complete fusion: they have but one quality. Life circulates in the whole organism: it is not withdrawn into certain parts.

'The qualities of works that are failures may be of various degrees. They may even be very great. The beautiful does not possess degrees, for there is no conceiving a more beautiful, that is an expressive that is more expressive, an adequate that is more than adequate. Ugliness on the other hand does possess degrees from the rather ugly, or almost beautiful, to the extremely ugly. But if the ugly were complete, that is to say without any element of beauty, it would for that very reason cease to be ugly, because in it would be absent the contradiction which is the reason of its existence. The disvalue would become non-value: activity would give place to passivity with which it is not at war, save when effectively there is war.'[1]

It is from no disrespect to the accomplished author of these paragraphs that I venture to disagree with almost every sentence which they contain. In the first place beauty cannot be defined as 'successful expression': if it could we should have to admit that there was nothing more beautiful than an inarticulate cry of rage. In the second place, though we may agree that the beautiful implies organic unity, yet this unity is so far from excluding multiplicity that in it multiplicity is actually presupposed. Mere unity is not beautiful: a symphony in F, as Whistler protested, does not consist of the note F and nothing else. No doubt at the first presentation of a work of art—especially of some white-hot lyric outburst—we may be so rapt with delight that we cannot yet distinguish between parts and whole: yet it cannot be contested that our sense of its beauty grows more active as our power of discrimination increases. We are all familiar with imperfect compositions which contain, in Rossini's phrase, 'good moments and bad quarters of an hour'; none the less in a perfect work such as a madrigal of Wilbye, or a fugue of Bach, or a quintet movement of Mozart, we are conscious of the succession of themes, of their contrast and interrelation, of what, in a word, Croce calls their qualities. Again, it is partly true that all unsuccessful expression is ugly in so far as it is recognized to be unsuccessful, and we may even go so far as to admit that an essential characteristic of it is incongruity. But to argue from this that if the ugly were complete it would cease to be ugly is either false or unmeaning: false if it asserts that triumphant ugliness would be beautiful, unmeaning if it merely implies that there would then be no beauty left to sin against. And, lastly, it is surely impossible to maintain that the beautiful does not admit of degree. The perfect expression of a light or transitory emotion is unquestionably beautiful, but to hold that there can be no higher reach, no

[1] Croce, *Aesthetic*, ch. x.

fuller content, would be to rank a nocturne of Chopin beside the slow movement of the Choral Symphony. There is here no question of any extraneous standard: no intrusion of ethical or metaphysical judgement: we need not travel beyond the limits of pure aesthetic to reach a conclusion which is ratified by the common experience of mankind. For beauty appeals to us in two ways: partly by the impression that it gives of mastery over a medium always more or less intractable, partly by the chord which it sets vibrating in our own souls. We may gain from a facile triumph the pleasure which bears witness to any successful achievement; but we are far more profoundly stirred as the emotion grows deeper and the problem of expressing it more difficult.

For what is the difference between a fugue of Bach and a fugue of Marpurg? Not the command of counterpoint, for Marpurg's is perfect: an 'adequate' than which, in Croce's phrase, 'there cannot be a more adequate'. It is that Marpurg's theme is an academic text, the meaning of which is exhausted in its adaptability to contrapuntal display, whereas Bach's theme is a quickening spirit, which is not only alive itself but a radiating centre of life through the whole composition. It is the difference between a good copy of Latin verse and a page of Virgil. In like manner, the difference between Beethoven and his famous contemporary Hummel is not a matter of successful expression, but of what there is to express. One cannot sum it up as a distinction of form and content, because these (like life and organism) so react on one another that they cannot be separated: it is rather a comparison between the weaker vitality, with its more uniform manifestation, and the strength that displays itself in an inexhaustible abundance.

Nor is the comparison less fruitful, though in a different way, if we set Beethoven's instrumental music beside that of Mozart. In vitality of invention, in sweetness of melody, in unerring mastery of resource, Mozart touches the outside verge that rounds our faculty. There has never been music of more pure delight than his Symphony in G minor: here if anywhere we might say that Croce's maxim is illustrated and justified. Yet if we pass from this to any typical work of Beethoven's maturity, we enter into a new world; we are initiated into new mysteries. It is not only that his whole scheme is larger in conception, so that his Sonatas are on a level with the symphonies of his predecessors: it is not only that he is the first composer who throws aside altogether the conventions inherited from the Suite, it is that with him there comes into music the element of the incalculable; the figures that he evokes have not only the impress of his creation, but a life and personality of their own. Shakespeare, one remembers, had 'to kill Mercutio or be killed by him': in like manner the thoughts of Beethoven sometimes seem to escape from the control even of the mind that was great enough to conceive them.

Historians have customarily distinguished his music into three periods, a division which is really valuable if we do not insist too closely on lines of demarcation. They cannot be chronologically determined, partly because Beethoven did not master all his media simultaneously, partly because, like all great artists, he occasionally threw back to an earlier idiom or method. Still, allowing for some looseness and elasticity in the use of terms, the distinctions are not only intelligible but illuminating. There can be no doubt that the first two symphonies are essentially different from the Eroica, the first six string quartets from the Rasoumoffskys: the three piano sonatas published as Op. 31 are described by Beethoven himself as 'written in a new style'. An equally unmistakable frontier is crossed by the last pianoforte trio, the last violin sonata, and the F minor Quartet, precursor and herald of the greatest achievements in all chamber-music. It may be observed that the succession corresponds closely to the natural growth and development of Beethoven's character. To the first period belong almost all his experiments in varieties of instrumental combination—experiments which his later judgement modified or discarded—and almost all the works in which either theme or topic recalls, however remotely, his predecessors of the eighteenth century. The second period represents his poetic gift at its full manhood:—the three Rasoumoffsky Quartets, the Violin Concerto, the Piano Concertos in G major and E♭, *Fidelio* with its four overtures, the Mass in C major, *Egmont* and *Coriolan*, the Kreutzer, the Waldstein, the Appassionata, the Symphonies from No. 3 to No. 8—all that amazing wealth of vigour and tenderness and noble beauty which sets upon the stage the whole pageant of man's life as it reveals itself in action, and penetrates to its innermost springs of motive and purpose. And so the third period rises from the active life to the contemplative; from the transfiguration of human joys and sorrows to the awe and rapture of the prophetic vision. Sometimes it speaks in parables too hard for our understanding—there is no music in the world so difficult to estimate and appraise; it may be that sometimes the message is too sublime for utterance, and we can only catch faint echoes and intimations of its inner meaning; but where we have ears to hear, it gives us melody the like of which man has never known and will never know again. In the last pianoforte trio, in the last of the sonatas and quartets, in the slow movement of the Choral Symphony, there is music which seems to come straight from 'some spiritual world beyond the heavens', and the thoughts that it arouses in us are too deep for tears.

It is no easy matter to express these thoughts in any intelligible phrase. The *patrii sermonis egestas*, which presses hardly on poet and critic, is even unjust to the musician, for language has been framed with little reference to his need. But it may be possible by a very rough analogy to indicate the voice with which Beethoven speaks to us. Take three famous passages from three English poets, each inspired by the same subject—a movement or pageant of spirits in the air. The first is the advance of Michael's legions in the sixth book of *Paradise Lost*:

On they move
Indissolubly firm; nor obvious Hill,
Nor strait'ning Vale, nor Wood, nor Stream divides
Their perfect ranks; for high above the ground
Their march was, and the passive Air upbore
Their nimble tread.

That is Bach: every detail, every epithet, every point of colour, not only beautiful in itself, but justly subordinated to the general texture of the whole. No word is chosen for its own sake, but for its bearing on the matter in hand—'obvious' hill, 'strait'ning' vale, 'passive' air, 'nimble' tread;—all the majestic march and dignity of the passage comes not only from the sonority of the language, but from its entire fitness to the scene which it clothes. It is Matthew Arnold's definition of the grand style, 'a noble nature treating with simplicity and severity a serious subject'.

The second is from Shelley's *Prometheus*:

The rocks are cloven, and through the purple night
I see cars drawn by rainbow-winged steeds
Which trample the dim winds: in each there stands
A wild-eyed charioteer urging their flight.
Some look behind, as fiends pursued them there,
And yet I see no shapes but the keen stars:
Others with burning eyes lean forth and drink
With eager lips the wind of their own speed,
As if the thing they loved fled on before,
And now, even now, they clasped it. Their bright locks
Stream like a comet's flashing hair: they all
Sweep onward.

That is Schubert: instinct with the very spirit of romance, full of delight in sheer colour—the 'purple' night, the 'rainbow-winged' steeds—and swift movement with the quickening sense of the unknown and the adventurous. There is little here of simplicity or severity, but pure loveliness of phrase, and within it a pulse which sets our blood tingling.

The third is from *The Tempest*:

These our actors,
As I foretold you, were all spirits, and
Are melted into air, into thin air;
And, like the baseless fabric of this vision,
The cloud-capped towers, the gorgeous palaces,
The solemn temples, the great globe itself,
Yea, all which it inherit, shall dissolve,
And, like this insubstantial pageant faded,
Leave not a wrack behind.

That is Beethoven: a fuller note, a deeper meaning, a vision clad in all the hues of the sunset, and fading away into the solemn stillness of the night.

It has already been said that throughout his career his greatest work was, as a rule, written for instruments alone. One of his odd limitations, due perhaps to his increasing deafness, was a want of sympathy with the human voice; and in his vocal compositions there is sometimes a sense of effort which is not wholly repaid. *Fidelio*, except for one magnificent scene, is not really dramatic; the solo songs, except perhaps the 'Liederkreis', are but the chips of a great workshop; the last movement of the Choral Symphony seems to burst asunder the bounds of human expression. Yet it is from a vocal composition that the spiritual intensity of his later writing may most easily be illustrated: partly because the text may help to focus our understanding of the music, partly because in this he towers even higher than usual above his Viennese predecessors and followers. The work in question is the Mass in D major, the slow-wrought masterpiece of three years' almost incessant toil. At the time when it was written, Mass-music had fallen upon evil days. With the exception of Bach and of some among the great Spanish masters, none of Beethoven's predecessors for a couple of centuries had treated the text with any true reverence or insight: Haydn, though one of the most devout of musicians, carried to an extreme his doctrine that 'God would not grow angry if He were praised with a cheerful heart';

Mozart wrote one superb Mass for his own Wedding Service—his others of the ordinary office are so perfunctory and (apart from a few tunes) so unworthy of him that publishers are still able to include among their number a wretched and palpable forgery. These works are at their best when they have some simple and obvious emotions to express, or when by accepted custom they are allowed opportunities of technical display: they invariably fail when they approach the more intimate and mysterious moments of the rite—the Incarnatus and Crucifixus of the Creed, for instance, and especially that very heart and spirit of the whole Service, the miracle of the Sanctus. In Haydn and Mozart the music of this last number is simply negligible; in Schubert, who at best had little religious feeling though he thought otherwise, it is usually a splash of gorgeous colour, beautiful in itself but wholly inappropriate. Again, the Agnus Dei was almost always ruined by the convention that every sustained piece of music must end on a lilting allegro: so that whereas the first clause was often pathetic and sometimes even penitent, the last completed the petition with a trivial and undignified finale. All these errors Beethoven swept away at a stroke. His Mass—gigantic in scale, terribly exacting in performance—is the closest and most intimate interpretation of the text that has ever been written. Every word has its full weight, its full significance, illumined not by a splendour from outside but by a lamp within the shrine: the emotions of praise and prayer, of glowing faith and passionate entreaty, are here set forth not in their external manifestation but in their essential nature. Well might Beethoven inscribe on the title-page of his score, 'From the heart it has come, to the heart it shall penetrate'. Think of the delicate tender colour of the Incarnatus, and the awe-stricken whisper in which the voices announce the mystery; or the pleading tone of the Agnus Dei, rising to the very height of supplication at the cry 'Dona nobis pacem'. Above all, contrast the Sanctus with the glorious number in Bach's B minor Mass. The one composer surrounds us with the choiring of an infinite heavenly host, where the morning stars sing together and the sons of God shout for joy: the other sets us kneeling with bowed head before the sanctuary, and the still quiet music is the voice of our own adoration.

It is not to be supposed that Beethoven's music, even in its later period, always moves along this level or breathes the pure serene of this atmosphere. To the artist, as to the philosopher, the contemplative life does not exclude but absorbs and transfigures the practical: it has full room for human joys and sorrows, for human love and sympathy, for pathos and laughter and all noble sense of adventure and achievement. Its moments of supreme spiritual ecstasy are rare, and ought to be rare, for the soul of man cannot wholly lose itself in an 'O altitudo'. Indeed, there is nothing more characteristic of Beethoven than the power with which he touches to fine issues every natural and healthy emotion of mankind. Are we in a mood for sadness—there is the C♯ minor Quartet; for gaiety, there is the Quartet in G major; for romance, there is the Emperor Concerto; for drama, there are the Appassionata, the Trio in D major, the Fifth Symphony. It is idle to ask what these mean—they can no more be rendered in another medium than, to use Mr. Tovey's phrase, 'you can translate Rheims Cathedral into Greek prose'; they carry their significance in themselves, and their appeal is the more irresistible because it is direct and immediate.

All this immense mastery of emotional expression might well justify a lavish or even extravagant use of resources. By Beethoven no such justification is claimed or needed. The piano alone, the four strings alone are amply sufficient for his purpose; his orchestra is that of Mozart, and its louder instruments are held in reserve for special moments of emphasis or climax. One of the most miraculous effects in all his music is a single soft chord sustained for some fifteen bars across the throbbing rhythmic beat of the drum. One of the most divine of his melodies is a dance-tune scored for strings and woodwind, and set with harmonies as simple as a nursery tale. The opening of the Fifth Symphony, unforgettable by any one who has ever heard it, is a unison phrase of two notes, one of them thrice repeated: the tempest which breaks upon the Ninth gathers its terrific force from a plain harmony followed by a plain cadence. Much of his strength lies in this quietness and confidence, in the reserve which can hold back its forces until the time has come for their full display. The master of every device of harmony and rhythm, he can weave from three tones in the scale a texture of incomparable beauty; with the whole palette at his command, he can produce an enduring impression with a few strokes in monochrome.

The value of this reserve is twofold. In music, more perhaps than even in poetry, the significance of a phrase depends on its context, on the preparation by which we are led to it and the response which follows, rhymes, and corroborates. If the whole page is set on a low or quiet scheme of colour, it can be suddenly set ablaze by a single point of greater vividness, which would have passed unnoticed if the scheme had been heightened from the beginning. And thus the strength of a self-controlled art is that it always uses its climaxes to their fullest effect, whereas an art that is extravagant or luxurious overstimulates our interest at the outset, and, when it wants to strike, finds that the blow has already been forestalled. In a good deal of modern composition you may find harmonies and modulations which make a brave show on paper, which are all sprinkled over with accidentals and changes of key-signature, but which, when we hear them, produce no real effect, because they involve no real change of colour. And as a further consequence, there are some deliberate and determined composers at the present day who, having no genuine emotion to express, produce their climax by sheer noise and ugliness, because this is the only way in which their overcharged stream of sound can attract attention. Beethoven, who can make an interesting paragraph out of themes which any one else would have discarded as commonplace, has only to hasten his rhythm or enrich his harmony, and we are straightway thrilled and delighted. In the finale of the D major Trio, for instance, there is a modulation from tonic to dominant—the first modulation which children learn in the harmony class—so skilfully placed that it seems to enlarge the whole range of musical expression. Again, this wise economy of resource gives the hearer a wonderfully satisfactory sense of security—a feeling that however much is expended there is an illimitable wealth in reserve. 'The value of art', says a writer in *The Times Literary Supplement*,[1] 'lies in the fact that it communicates the experience and the experiencing power of one man to many. When we hear a symphony of Beethoven we are for the moment Beethoven, and we ourselves are enriched for ever by the fact that we have for the moment been Beethoven.' This seems to me essentially and profoundly true, and its truth is nowhere more evident than in the sense of mastery which is communicated to us by great music. The effort to produce may actually have been toilsome—we know that with Beethoven it often was so; in the finished work all trace of effort has disappeared, and the phrase a dozen times reconsidered sounds as spontaneous as an impromptu. It is the pleasure of sharing this victory over a medium always difficult and often rebellious which gives at least a part of our delight as listeners, and this pleasure is enhanced and intensified by the assurance that such a victory is in the end certain. One of the essential marks of genius is that the power which it puts forth is always proportionate to the issues which it has to confront: with Beethoven we know that however great the problem, the strength will be unfailing and the purpose achieved.

The history of almost every art contains very roughly a series of alternating periods, in which the stress is laid now on perfection and beauty of form, now on wealth of emotional expression. This does not, of course, mean that in any art worthy of the name either of these objects can

[1] 14 June, 1917.

be wholly disregarded: take away beauty of form and there is mere chaos, take away emotional content and there is mere academic precision, each of which is, on its own side, not a kind of art but a denial of art. Yet it remains true that in each period, often through the influence of some special master of genius, the attention of the artist is specially directed either to perfecting the pure melody and texture of his work or to the enlargement of its means of expression, until the period closes on some supreme master who combines the two ideals so far as the resources of his time permit. So in the sixteenth century, the great period of modal counterpoint, after some natural oscillation between the claims of formal and poetic beauty, came to its climax in the work of Palestrina and the English composers by whose genius the two claims were held in just balance and equipoise. So again in the first half of the eighteenth century, the growing development of harmonic form and the growing sense of emotional beauty came to their climax in the two great contemporaries Bach and Handel, so far as the climax could be embodied in the types of musical structure which had then been discovered; and it was because the half-century which followed Bach was specially prolific, both in the further development of musical forms and in the growth of musical drama as a living force, that Beethoven could enter into a fuller inheritance than any of his predecessors, and administer a realm far wider than they had ever known. In his work, the balance of expression and form was brought to the highest perfection. The earliest sonatas, in which he is most nearly influenced by the work of his predecessors, are full of poetic significance. The latest quartets, in which his thought penetrates to the innermost recesses of being, are as impeccable in structure as though his main purpose had been their formal completeness; and just as before his time the balance was slightly on the formal side, so after his time it swung across to that of emotional and romantic expression. Berlioz, who worshipped Beethoven more as a poet than as a musician, and more as a rebel than either, followed him in the intense desire to make music expressive. He fell far behind him in that of making it architectonic. Schumann, a greater musician than Berlioz, had as a matter of temperament comparatively little interest in the development of structural form, and in dealing with it seldom advanced beyond ingenuity. Wagner, who in sheer intellectual force is more comparable to Beethoven than any other musician of the nineteenth century, devoted his whole career to the stage, which enacts its own laws and imposes its own conditions; but it is worth while recalling that, among all his predecessors, Beethoven was the man whom Wagner held in the highest reverence, and from whose work he derived his fullest inspiration.

At the present day we are confronted with two musical problems of great interest and difficulty; and while they are in process of solution it is impossible to judge how far the direct influence of Beethoven's works will remain paramount. The first is the extraordinarily rapid change in the vocabulary and idiom of music which has come about during the last twenty years: a change as important and as fruitful in possibilities as the substitution of the diatonic scale for the ecclesiastical modes. Our ears have grown accustomed to accepting the chromatic interval as the unit, with the result that in melody, and more especially in harmonic texture, we can gain the keenest delight from successions and combinations of notes which would have been unintelligible or excruciating half a century ago. No doubt this new idiom has been turned to account by a certain number of light-hearted and irresponsible composers who have mainly used it for the manufacture of catchwords. But in itself it is an important step in musical progress, and we cannot yet determine how much of past music it will render obsolete and how much by force of genuine sincerity will survive as classic. The other problem is raised by a marked divergence, more clearly defined than ever before, between the two chief aims of musical composition. To one school the ideal is first to set a general pattern of aesthetic beauty and then to fill it with all the emotional content that it will hold. The other, which may be exemplified in many great works by contemporary French composers, aims at reducing the claims of formal beauty to a minimum and allowing the music to follow the course of emotion, expressing it point by point but treating with apparent disregard the structural principles of the whole. And there seems every sign that for some years to come, at any rate, the latter of these two ideals will hold the pre-eminence. The structural ideal in music has fallen into the hands of men like Arnold Schönberg, who are not innovators or discoverers but only very erudite and capable grammarians; and under their manipulation it is hardening into a dry and stony formalism. These men claim the traditions of Beethoven and Bach as the Pharisees claimed the tradition of the Elders, with the result that though the outside of the cup and platter are usually clean, the inside is always empty.

In this war of conflicting schools we may have temporarily lost sight of the influence which Beethoven's music has exercised on the whole subsequent course of the art. Yet the influence is still apparent, not so much in point of theme or method, but rather because his work has become as necessary a part of our artistic life as of our physical life is the atmosphere that we breathe or the nature that we contemplate. Nearly a hundred years have passed away since his death; much of the work of his contemporaries, and still more of his immediate successors, is trembling in the balance or has definitely passed away; but to whatever extent we directly own him as leader, there is no sign of faltering in the adoration which worships him as hero. There will always be preferences amongst his compositions: for one reason we are not equally in tune with all, for another no supreme artist has always written at his best; and we may even admit a few experiments and a few inequalities over which it is no impiety to turn the page. But when we speak of Beethoven it is not of these that we are thinking; it is of the far outnumbering crowd of masterpieces which have given to us more delight than any other music in the world, and which, despite a century of discovery and invention, are as fresh now as when they were first written.

In Mr. Joseph Conrad's last novel there is a ship's captain of whom it is said that he 'enunciated platitudes not with the desire to dazzle but from honest conviction'. I am afraid that during the last hour I have only too often called him to your remembrance! But indeed I am not trying to say something new about Beethoven—no one can say anything about him which his music has not already anticipated—I am advancing under the protection of his shield to contend against the apathy, the indifference, the *incuria*, which has so long refused to open to his art the door of our intellectual life. The poets pay music many notable compliments—

> Music, sister of sunrise, and herald of life to be—

some of which she resents as one hopes that an intelligent woman of the Middle Ages may sometimes have resented the Troubadours, and pleaded for less praise and more comprehension. Here is a great ocean of beauty spreading beside our shores, and because we far over-estimate the difficulties of its navigation we fear to venture beyond its shallows. Here is a language that for centuries has been turned to noble account, and we listen to it as the Northumberland audience listened to Father Gavazzi,[1] thrilled by voice and gesture, but understanding no word except the proper names. The whole career and character of Beethoven is a protest against this attitude of mind. His music is not only a joy of beautiful sound and of emotion nobly felt and nobly communicated: it is also a marvel of intellectual power and of deep spiritual insight; nor is it only as a master of melody, but in very truth as a *Maestro di color che sanno*, that I ask you to place him among the master-minds of all human history.

[1] G. M. Trevelyan, *Garibaldi and the Thousand*, p. 24.

BRAHMS AND THE CLASSICAL TRADITION [1]

THE death of a great artist should affect us with something more than the sense of personal loss. It is doubtless natural that we should feel ourselves the poorer, that we should indulge in vain and unavailing regret, that we should mourn the glory departed and the generous hand now closed to us for ever. But if our first thought be of our bereavement we are soon called from inaction by the march and progress of events; we see our leader still present in the work that he has done, and hear his voice in the orders that he has issued for our guidance. 'Princes are mortal, the State is everlasting'; and we shall pay most honour to the dead if, when we think of him, we are roused to remember our citizenship.

It is true that the work of Brahms is still too near us for any certain or dogmatic estimate of its value. The perspective of criticism needs distance to focus its object; familiarity with a new method can only be attained after long and patient study. Indeed, it is a commonplace that contemporary judgement has usually been astray: Haydn was called extravagant and Mozart obscure, Beethoven censured for lack of form, and Schubert for lack of melody; and though many of these verdicts were due to sheer blindness and incapacity, there are yet some which can be partially excused by the circumstances of their delivery. Men who are in the heat of contest can take no dispassionate views of either comrades or opponents; amid the clash of arms there is little hope that reason should get a hearing. Indeed, as human nature stands, toleration is commonly a mark of deficient interest, and we are often inclined to administer Solon's law and disfranchise the doubter who stands aloof from his party. But, at the same time, the principle which Brahms maintained during the last half-century is of such significance to the general development of music that in whatever terms we appraise it we can hardly misunderstand its

[1] From *the Contemporary Review*, May, 1897.

import. He was the last great representative of the classical tradition in German music, and it is by reference to that tradition that his work can most profitably be discussed.

Art may roughly be said to fulfil two main functions: the first that of communicating some emotional idea, the second that of exhibiting a mastery over some medium or material. By the one it appeals to our sympathy, by the other to our admiration; the former influences us chiefly by choice of theme, the latter chiefly by manner of treatment. The painter no more copies Nature than the dramatist copies life: each finds in certain facts the opportunity for self-expression, and sets before us not a transcript of reality, but the impress which reality makes upon the conceptive temperament. And in music, where the empirical element hardly exists, we may note even more clearly the immediate response of personal feeling. It may be too subtle for analysis, it may elude our clumsy devices of terminology and classification, but it remains among the truest and most vivid experiences of human nature. Melody that is conceived and born of a living soul can stir our hearts as deeply as the passion of Juliet or the courage of Hotspur; it has its own aspects of humour and pathos, of serenity and agitation, and what it lacks in concrete presentment it more than compensates in the directness and concentration of its touch. But to regard this as constituting the character of the art is as grave an error as it would be to criticize a picture or a poem by sole reference to the subject with which it deals. Of far more importance is the question of treatment, the relation to some standard of absolute beauty, the development of a style, the gradual victory over a stubborn or difficult medium. Here we can advance to something further than a mere personal statement of likes and dislikes, here we can follow an intelligible method and apply an intelligible test. And not only is judgement easier on this side, it is also far more valuable. One would hardly ask a painter whether Diderot or Gautier were the better critic; and if in a representative art the difference be crucial, it is surely so in that which claims to be the type and standard of formal perfection.

This, then, explains the meaning of the term *classical*, as distinctively employed in musical history. A classical composer is one who pays the highest regard to his medium, who aims before all things at perfection of phrase and structure, whose ideal is simple beauty, and whose passion the love of style. By some unlucky chance the name seems to have been transferred from architecture at a time when English taste was at an ebb-tide, and it is for this reason often supposed to carry some connotation of formalism and artificiality. But classical writing does not mean 'correct' writing in the sense which Macaulay satirized. It includes many grades of rank and many types of character: the richness of Bach, the lucidity of Mozart, the magnificent strength and dignity of Beethoven; and a pedantic insistence on authoritative rule is not a mark of its true nature, but a sympton of one of its deadliest diseases. Nothing, therefore, is implied by the title as to the particular aspect of style in which the artist happens to be interested. If the interest is paramount, the work is so far on the side of the classics.

In contradistinction to this may be set the method of which an essential characteristic is the desire to communicate at all hazards a more or less definite emotional state. No one who had any feeling for propriety of language could call Wagner a classical composer. In his drama the music is never an end in itself, but is merely a co-operating element in the general stage effect. Its office is to heighten the speech of the actor, to intensify or explain the dramatic situation, to bring the audience into accord with the requirements of the scene. And neither by temperament nor by training was Wagner fitted to combine this ideal with that of pure artistic composition. His melody is not of the first order, his harmonic devices are comparatively few, even his polyphony is often forced and unnatural. At the theatre such things are of little importance; they count for no more than the stage conventions, from which no dramatist is altogether free, or the unconvincing properties which no manager troubles to discard. The centre of Wagner's art is the dramatic illusion, and the music, accessory to this, fulfils its whole office by the emotional illustration of the text. With Berlioz, again, we are listening not so much to a musician as to a poet who speaks in musical sound. His compositions are ostensibly designed to suggest images, pictures, scenes of actual occurrence; they are voluptuous, or stern, or grotesque, according to the theme with which they deal, but they seldom give us the delight which arises from the mere contemplation of a fine thing finely accomplished. Contrast, for a moment, the 'Symphonie Fantastique' with any symphony of Beethoven. The difference is not only one of degree in achievement; it implies, in addition, a wide diversity of aim.

From this conclusion two results would seem to follow. First, that in classical music the range of emotion must be somewhat circumscribed, since not all things can be told in beautiful form. Extremes of passion, extremes of terror, which form the climax of the one school, lie outside the limits of the other; in it everything is chastened, modified, clothed with a certain dignity and reticence that would rather forgo the appeal than make it in unseemly terms. Secondly, the music which is based on emotional conception is never so distinguished as that which arises from the highest appreciation of style and treatment. Schumann, with all his genius, never let us forget that he 'learned his counterpoint from Jean Paul'. His art is always best when he can give free rein to his fancy; it weakens before the very obstacles for surmounting which distinction of style is most needed. The Pianoforte Concerto, for instance, is full of suggestion, but its workmanship looks coarse and clumsy beside Mozart's; the three string quartets have abundance of poetic charm, but now and again they sink into difficulties over which a less preoccupied musician would have triumphed. In short, compared with the great Viennese masters, Schumann seems almost like a highly cultivated amateur; he has been privileged to enrich the art, but theirs is the closer intimacy.

And it was into their family that Brahms was born. By natural temper of mind he was a pure musician, a chosen lover to whom Art revealed her innermost secrets. In music, as in literature, there is a peculiar tact and instinct of style which, though it be difficult to define, is for all that a true and genuine gift. Not only are its possessors incapable of writing what is vulgar or commonplace, not only do they shrink unconsciously from cheapness or sensationalism or imposture, but in their own work the power is manifested by the witness of certain visible qualities, by a special texture, a special colour, a special sense of design, which it is wholly impossible for the outsider to assume or imitate. A waltz of Schubert is as unmistakable as a lyric of Heine; it may consist of a single quatrain, a fugitive thought expressed in a few simple phrases, but there is something in the attitude, or the feeling, or the form of stanza, which proclaims its divinity. And in like manner the lightest melody of Brahms, equally with his most elaborate exhibition of science, is elect of the inner sanctuary and is touched with fire from off the altar. Not, of course, that it all reaches the same level of beauty; there are distinctions in him as there are in Bach and Beethoven, but his poorest tune, his most learned piece of counterpoint, is inspired with that special kind of vitality which we find in the great classics, and which we do not find in the music, considered from the musical standpoint alone, of Wagner and the romantic composers.

Again, he belongs to his order not only by right of birth but by right of education. There is nothing in musical history more remarkable than the difference between the training of the old masters and that of the generation which succeeded them. Haydn worked sixteen hours a day with Fux's Gradus and the sonatas of Emmanuel

Bach; Mozart, the quickest of pupils, was taken by a careful and exacting teacher through the most rigorous course of study that the age permitted; Beethoven spent his boyhood in almost overstrained labour, and at an age when many men would look upon their education as complete, set himself again to write themes for Haydn and counterpoint exercises for Albrechtsberger. But Berlioz, Liszt, Wagner, can hardly be described as educated musicians at all. No doubt the first of them was technically at the Paris Conservatoire, but of his connexion with it the less said the better. Liszt, as a young man, had little inclination to exchange the triumphs of the virtuoso for the drudgery of the student. Wagner was given up as incorrigible by two masters, and by the third sent out as a finished composer after six months. And even the musicians of this period who stand nearer to the classical line—such as Schumann and Chopin—are affected in some degree by the want of balance and completeness in their musical training. In their student days they were brought up on Bach's 'Well-tempered Clavier'; but they knew little of his choral work, certainly not the Passion music or the B minor Mass; they heard some Mozart and Haydn, but little of Beethoven, and of Schubert virtually nothing; they were taught how to write a fugue, but not how to write a sonata or a symphony. No doubt Schumann discovered for himself a great deal more than he ever learned from Kuntzsch; there is the famous story of his training his hand for chamber music by 'shutting himself up with all Beethoven's quartets'; but this is a very different thing from studying the great model at the proper time and under the proper influences. And Chopin, a few years before his death, had never heard of the F minor—the 'most Beethovenish of them all', as Mendelssohn called it—and had to send round to a music-shop in order to procure a copy. Imagine a poet of the present day who should take his friend's advice and order *Lear* or *Hamlet* from the circulating library.

It is therefore significant that at the age of thirteen

Brahms was placed under Eduard Marxsen, the most enlightened and cultivated music-teacher of the time, and that he spent with him seven years of unrelaxed discipline. When he emerged, for his trial flight with Reményi, his equipment was extraordinarily solid and complete; not only everything which could be learned from precepts and familiarized by practice, but all that could be added by a careful and exhaustive study of every classic that was then known to exist. Recent discoveries had increased the store of Bach; Beethoven was resuming his empire after two decades of abeyance; even Schubert was not wholly unknown, thanks to the *Neue Zeitschrift* and its editor, and it was on this foundation of broad eclecticism that the superstructure of the new architect was firmly and steadily established. And since pure music is the most continuous of all the arts, since in course of development every generation must needs take its point of departure from the position which its predecessor has attained, there is little need to point out that the more comprehensive the survey of that position the more sure and confident will be the advance. That the work of Brahms will take higher rank than the work of Schumann or Chopin is hardly to be contested, and of this fact one reason may be found in the contrast of formative conditions.

Again, it was well for Brahms that his life should have been in a pre-eminent degree quiet and eventless. 'Es bildet ein Talent sich in der Stille,' says Goethe, and the words are almost prophetic of this shy, silent, secluded artist. The only offices that he ever held were the post of Kapellmeister at Lippe-Detmold, and, later on, a couple of conductorships at Vienna; he was but once in his life out of hearing of his native language, and that for a short holiday visit; he refused every appointment that would take him away from his adopted home; he was unmarried, he had few near connexions, he left no will. For the last five-and-thirty years the occurrences of his life were the meetings of the Tonkünstler-Verein, the summer trip to Ischl or Carlsbad, the invitation, rarely accepted, to conduct a symphony at Leipzig or an overture at Berlin. To publicity, to notoriety, to fame itself he had the most cordial and unaffected aversion; his work once finished, he took no further interest in its fortunes, and received its failure or success with equal modesty and equal indifference. To this, no doubt, is due some of the contemplative quality by which his music is so frequently characterized. Songs like *Feldeinsamkeit*, movements like the adagio of the Pianoforte Quintet, works like the *Schicksalslied* or the German Requiem, are all the outcome of a mind that is grave, steadfast, earnest in temper, occupied with the deeper mysteries and the more serious issues of life. It is noticeable that Brahms never wrote a line for the theatre, and that when he is at his most passionate—*Verrath*, for instance, or *Meine Liebe ist grün*—he shows much closer analogy with one of Browning's dramatic lyrics than with the more direct and vivid emotions of the stage. But most of all may we thank the conditions of Brahms's life for supplying him with the atmosphere which his genius essentially needed. A style so opulent, so original, so perfect in form and balance, could only have been elaborated in seclusion.

And it is as a master of form that he will live. To no one since Beethoven, and to one other alone beside Beethoven, has there been granted such unerring certainty of phrase, or such wide and comprehensive grasp of structure. True, Mozart has shown once for all that music can be made wholly transparent; his writing has every quality of precision and delicacy, of charm and sweetness; but Mozart at his greatest never attains the broad virile strength which Brahms has inherited from Bach and Beethoven. And it is false criticism to estimate a style merely by the continuity of its triumphs. Much depends on the nature of the enemy against which it was contending, and in this respect a high failure may often overleap the bounds of a low success. And, further, when the music is full and complex we have no right to expect the lucidity which reveals its truth at a single glance; it is enough if we ultimately attain to the meaning, and recognize that it was but our own weakness which obscured it before. A stream is not necessarily turbid because we cannot count the pebbles at the bottom; it may baffle our imperfect eyes by the depth of its waters and the volume of its current. It is thus with a great deal of Brahms's music. At first hearing we are often bewildered by the very complexity of the phrase; our ears are overcharged with excess of sound; we are conscious that the web is of magnificent texture, but we cannot unravel it, or even, as yet, interpret its design. A little further experience, a little closer familiarity, and the difficulties begin to disappear. Gradually the eye acquires power and confidence; the chaos becomes order; the confusion melts into beauty and arrangement; and there emerges a scene of gods and heroes so clear, so vivid, that we look back and marvel at our blindness. There is probably no student of Brahms who has not at some time felt this sense of awakening. The obscurity of which amateurs complain arises not from deficiency of light, but from deficiency of attention.

It may possibly be asked whether the need of such attention is not in itself a sign of artistic weakness; whether it does not belong to self-conscious and recondite days in which music has ceased to be spontaneous and has become reflective and calculating. Plato has told us that the highest beauty is simple in character; and there is more of the true poet in 'dewdrops of celestial melody' than in elaborate monologues and ingenious allegories. There is something painful, industrious, mechanical about an art which involves so much expenditure of labour; better the careless rapture that recks nothing of rule and measure, that sings without thought, without premeditation, unconscious even that it is overheard, oblivious of all except its own need of utterance. But in the first place the complexity of Brahms is not a matter of superfluous lines and unnecessary details; it is the grasp of an artist who can compose a hundred figures as readily as a score; and in the second place the strong intellectual element in his work is to be regarded as constituting not the source of his poetic impulse but its requisite guidance and control. The self-conscious method of composition, the *Kapellmeister-musik* of Wagner's epigram, is always essentially imitative, drawing inspiration from its library and assimilating style from its models. Brahms, though like every great composer he is affected by past tradition, is yet one of the most original of thinkers; he administers a kingdom that he has inherited by right of race, and is not the less a monarch because others have preceded him in the dynasty. That there is sometimes a touch of deliberation in his music we are not concerned to deny; it is a characteristic of the age, and he has adapted it to its noblest use. But to infer from this that the work is dull or academic or artificial is merely to show that perverse ingenuity in paradox which is sometimes mistaken for the critical faculty. We do not call the human body a machine on the ground that it is a highly developed organism directed by a thinking mind.

It is important that some stress should be laid on this aspect of Brahms's writing, at a time when German music seems to be entering on a period of riot and intemperance. It has conquered its empire; it has enjoyed the rewards of victory; its last great legislator is dead; already there begin to appear the signs of corruption which often follow too long a period of prosperity. Excessive sensationalism, excessive stimulation, thought that is often morbid, phrase that is often deliberately harsh and cacophonous—all these are the marks of an art that has passed its prime, and that strives by desperate artifice to stir the jaded senses into a semblance of their lost vigour. Like certain classes of literature, it has left the natural passions and gone off in quest of the monstrous and the horrible; its talents—and there are many men of great talent in its ranks—are misused to evoke some transitory thrill; it has lost all reticence, all purity, all dignity of tone, and has degraded its religion into a corybantic orgy. There is little wonder if beside this the music of Brahms appears cold and self-contained. The 'old blind schoolmaster's tedious poem on the fall of man' seemed a very dull affair to readers who had Sedley and Rochester; the wits of the Parc aux Cerfs preferred their evil and poisonous romances to any more austere embodiment of French genius; but, apart from the ethical question, which we are too ready to disregard, there can never be the smallest doubt as to which is the winning cause. If German music returns from its period of anarchy it may once more resume its high position in the artistic world. If not, the sceptre will pass into other hands.

This is not the place to describe in detail the features that distinguish Brahms's manner of composition. In his early days he started with an almost obstinate force and vigour, lavishing a strength which he had no care to economize, and making perhaps too little concession to the limitations of his auditors. But the year that marked the turning-point in his life marked also the turning-point in his style, and the first two piano quartets which he brought in manuscript to Vienna already indicate that feeling for mellowness and geniality which steadily grew and developed up to the end of his career. We need only instance the D minor Violin Sonata, the second String Quintet, and, better still, the great chamber work for clarinet and strings, all of which were written during the later years, and all of which possess that golden opulence of beauty which his highest work so conspicuously displays. Yet it is easy to overstate the changes that followed from the course of age and experience. The B♭ Sestet is an early work, the Pianoforte Quintet is not much later, the 'Schicksalslied' was written in 1871, and the Second Symphony in 1877. And in all these we shall find the same richness of polyphony, the same love of deep and massive harmonization, the same contrasts of pale transparence and glowing colour, the same broad diatonic melody, the same unerring mastery of chromatic effect. Some of his qualities he shares notoriously with Bach: the moving bass, the independence of part-writing, the balance held between contrapuntal and harmonic ideals; but he adds to these a sense of structure and a power of narration which could only have come after a century of later experience. In his form he is largely influenced by Beethoven, more so, indeed, than any composer of our time, yet he has not failed to gather from the best of the Romantic movement, and to augment the whole with treasure from his own store. The common devices of the composer—syncopation, transference of themes, combination of rhythmic figures, organization of key-system—acquire with him a new value and significance; we can trace their ancestry to the simple methods and practices of a past age, but they are more subtle, more delicate, more civilized than their forerunners. And when to this it is added that for pure charm of tune Brahms has been equalled by no composer since the death of Schubert; that beside his melodies even Chopin seems trivial, and even Schumann ineffective; there need be no further question about his claim to immortality. Had he written nothing but his songs he would be one of the greatest names in musical art, and his songs are but a small portion of his whole achievement.

It is probable that another decade or two will pass before his full influence is felt on the course and progress of composition. At present we only half understand his message, and must attain to a fuller comprehension before we can interpret it in our own practice. And, beside this, there is every indication that a period of Slavonic supremacy is at hand, and we cannot as yet forecast either the limits of its tenure or the character of its administration. Yet changes of dynasty, though they count for more than changes of potentate, have rarely exercised any permanent influence on the direction of events. The principles of historical development lie deeper than the record of kings and conquerors, revolution itself is more often a symptom than a cause, and the true efficient force originates in the fundamental needs of human nature. This is conspicuously so in the history of music. There freedom means order, broadening from precedent to precedent, and willing to take what is best in the heritage of past attainment and to hand on the tradition, amended and revised, for the guidance of the generations to come. And it is in thus maintaining the continuity of the art that Brahms has done it the most signal service. Leaders of mere anarchy and revolt have usually found their reward in swift oblivion; through all ages it is the lawgiver that is had in remembrance.

SIR HUBERT PARRY[1]

THE twin arts of Music and Poetry, the 'sphere-born harmonious sisters, voice and verse', have met with curiously different fortunes in the history of this country. Our poetry has the most continuous, and except for Greece, the most famous record in Europe: apart from our dark century—and that not so dark but that it produced some of the best of our English ballads—the line of succession is virtually unbroken from *Beowulf* to the present day: there is no generation, there is almost no decade, in which Englishmen were not at the forefront of skill and invention. But our musical history contains a lamentable number of what Bacon calls the deserts and waste-places of time—it has one century of lavish fruitfulness, and for the rest has been until now a parched land with a few infrequent oases. There was one lyric outburst in the thirteenth century, it was followed by silence for over a hundred years. John Dunstable was the first musician of his time: at his death the sceptre passed, not to his English imitators, but to his Flemish disciples. Then, no doubt, came our glorious period of Tudor and Elizabethan composers, the period at which English music and English poetry attained side by side to the heights of human achievement; but there was no musical Milton to follow that Elizabethan age, only a Dryden, and he short-lived and without successors. It is of no service to make excuse—to say that Handel was an English musician of German extraction or to complain that his brilliance reduced our native genius to darkness. German art was not obliterated by Haydn, or French by Lulli: they were strong enough to accept the foreigner's music and graft it into the parent-stock. We let Handel overshadow us like a beech tree, under whose spreading and magnificent foliage nothing prosperous can grow.

But of all our dark periods, the blackest was the third decade of the nineteenth century. The talent of Sterndale

[1] From the *Proceedings* of the Musical Association, Session XLV, 1918–19.

Bennett, once as fresh and bright as the mill-stream or the fountain, had lost itself in the sands of official and administrative drudgery; Sullivan had not yet found his collaborator, and the promise of *The Tempest* music was declining upon the anticlimax of the 'Prodigal Son' and the 'In Memoriam' overture: Wesley, a true genius within narrow limits, had virtually given up composition, and beside these there was nothing. The records of our provincial festival give sufficient evidence: the imitations of Mendelssohn, the academic oratorios in which counterpoint took the place of inspiration, the feeble sentiment, the obsolete technique, the official dullness masquerading for its hour upon the stage, and then going back to dust and oblivion.[1] Think of the music that was being written during these years in Germany and Austria and France and Italy and Russia. To that great treasury of Art we, and we alone, made no contribution.

At the very nadir of our fortune, when we had entirely ceased to count among the musical nations of Europe, there appeared at the Gloucester Festival of 1880 a cantata entitled 'Scenes from Shelley's *Prometheus Unbound*'. The personality of the composer excited some local interest. He was a son of Mr. Gambier Parry of Highnam, he had been educated at Eton and Oxford, he had taken a musical degree while still a schoolboy, he had received lessons from Elvey, Bennett, Macfarren, Pierson, and from Mr. Dannreuther, the famous pianist: he seemed to have written a good deal of chamber music and he had recently produced an overture and a pianoforte concerto at the Crystal Palace. Though he was now thirty-two, he had published nothing except his Mus. Bac. exercise, a few anthems and songs and a partita for violin and piano: altogether a difficult man to place, and in those days we liked above all things to know where we stood before delivering judgement. So after all the judgement was misdelivered. The audience, which naturally associated a

[1] Barnby's *Rebekah*, Ouseley's *Hagar*, Cusins's *Gideon*, are fair and typical examples.

festival with the *Messiah* and the *Elijah*, was possibly bewildered by the new idiom: *The Times* paid the composer a formal compliment on his choice of a libretto, and then relapsed into extreme caution; the other papers, led by the worst critic who ever darkened counsel, filled the air with the customary complaints of obscurity, extravagance, and an undue straining of resources. No one seems to have had any idea that, on that evening in the Shire Hall, English music had, after many years, come again to its own, and that it had come with a masterpiece in its hand.

In 1882 Parry produced his first symphony at Birmingham, and in 1883, the year in which he was appointed Professor of Composition and Musical History at the newly founded Royal College of Music, he wrote three important works—the F major Symphony, the incidental music to *The Birds*, and the noble setting of Shirley's 'Glories of our Blood and State', the reception of which at Gloucester made some amends for the error of 1880. It is worth noting that the first two of these were written for Cambridge, at the instance of Sir Charles Stanford, whose generous appreciation of Parry's music was the first authoritative pronouncement in its favour. 'When twain go forth together,' says Diomede, as he chooses his comrade from the heroes of the Greek camp: it was to these twain, and to the unselfish support which each gave to the other, that we owe the strength and certainty of our advance.

The duties and responsibilities of the new Professorship afforded very little leisure for composition, and the next four years saw virtually nothing except the Trio in B minor, the *Suite Moderne*, the fine sets of piano variations, and the first two volumes of *English Lyrics*. It is true that the lyrics mark an epoch in the history of our native song, it is true that the professional work bore fruit in an admirable volume of critical biographies, none the less there was for a while some reason to fear that the cares of office were becoming too heavy a burden, and that the whole-hearted devotion with which he undertook the lightest of his duties would draw him away from the leisure and freedom that were necessary for the practice of his art. 'I can hardly ever compose', he said once in those days, 'until after ten o'clock at night, and there is very little powder left then!' Fortunately, however, these fears proved to be groundless. The difficulties were surmounted partly by his immense energy, partly by his swiftness and certainty of judgement, and from 1887 onwards the stream once more flowed in full volume. In that year came *Blest Pair of Sirens*, of which no higher praise can be given than that the music is worthy of the poem, and then followed, in unbroken succession, *Judith*, the third and fourth symphonies, the *Ode for St. Cecilia's Day*, *L'Allegro ed il Pensieroso*, the *Eton Ode*, the great setting of *De Profundis*, the incidental music to *The Frogs*, the Choric Song from *The Lotus-Eaters*, *Job*, the *Overture to an unwritten Tragedy*: a wonderful outpouring of genius at the very heart and prime of its manhood.

The year 1894, when he succeeded Sir George Grove as director of the Royal College, saw a notable turning-point in his career. It is no coincidence that *King Saul* is the last of his oratorios. One cannot study it without seeing that the oratorio form, which he had always used with considerable freedom, had ceased to be a fit vehicle for his thought. Among all his great works it is the only one which can be called diffuse, which seems to be laboured and to be written *invita Minerva*. At any rate on that page he wrote no more. For the rest of his life his chief choral compositions were, with a few exceptions, either settings of the Latin Liturgy, like the 'Magnificat' and the 'Te Deum', or the Cantatas and *Symphoniae Sacrae*, close-woven, concentrated, simple almost to austerity, in which he found expression for some of the deepest thoughts that have ever penetrated the heart of man.

It is worth noting how this form grew under his hand, resolutely discarding all that is non-essential, turning aside from every external appeal, intent on one thing, and one alone, to interpret the very centre of the vision, and gaining in power and intensity as the years wore on. First came settings of two noble poems by Robert Bridges—the 'Invocation to Music', and the 'Song of Darkness and Light'—in which, though much of the old idiom remains, there is already a fuller tone and a profounder significance: then 'Voces Clamantium' with its double message of rebuke and consolation: then in due succession 'The Love that casteth out Fear', the 'Soul's Ransom', 'Beyond these Voices', the 'Vision of Life', the exquisitely tender setting of Dunbar's 'Ode on the Nativity', until they reach their fulfilment in the last and most wonderful of his choral writings, the 'Songs of Farewell'.

Something of the same tendency may be observed in his instrumental compositions of this period, though he never expressed himself so fully in instrumental music as in vocal. The Symphonic Variations of 1897 belong in spirit to the second stage, the Symphonic Fantasia of 1912 belongs to the third, and the closing word is said in the two volumes of organ preludes which are fit pendants to the 'Songs of Farewell', and which are, and will always remain, in their kind, unsurpassed. Yet it would be wholly wrong to conclude that even in these later days he took an ascetic view of art. No man touched life at more points than he, and music to him, as Dr. Vaughan Williams has well said, was a part of life. To the end of his days he had a boy's high spirits and a boy's sense of enjoyment: his 'Pied Piper' is a bubbling well of humour, and there is no wittier music in the world than that which he wrote for *The Clouds* and *The Acharnians*. But as he himself has told us, 'every great artist is serious at heart', and though his laughter is irresistible yet he never forgot that 'if fun is good, truth is better, and love best of all'.

For purposes of description we may conveniently divide his music into the customary three periods: premising that any such classification is to be accepted only on the pragmatist principle that it is true so far as it works. The frontier dates are roughly 1880 and 1894, and the periods are those of pupilage, adventure, and discovery. Like almost every great musician, Parry began to show his gifts in early childhood. He was taking the services at Highnam when he was eight years old, and composing chants and hymn-tunes for the use of the choir: at his private school near Winchester, he came under the spell of Wesley, from whom he gained 'his first enduring musical impression'. In 1861, at the age of thirteen, he went to Eton, and soon made his mark as an unusual combination of artist and athlete. A few of his schoolboy compositions are still extant: an overture for pianoforte duet in F minor, a couple of anthems written under the direction of Elvey, one or two songs and part-songs (including 'Why does azure deck the sky?'), and the Mus. Bac. exercise which astonished Sir Frederick Ouseley and was triumphantly performed and published in 1867. At Oxford he helped to found the University Musical Club, wrote the *Anacreontic Odes* and a collection of pianoforte pieces, and took more or less desultory lessons in composition, but as yet music was regarded only as an appanage and accomplishment in an extremely full and varied life, and it was not until the fortunate accident of a disaster at Lloyd's, whose office he entered upon taking his degree, that he began to place it in the forefront of his career. From 1874 to 1880 he studied with Edward Dannreuther, wisest and most sympathetic of teachers, who realized at once that his pupil was a man of genius and gave him a free hand. It is noticeable that during these years Parry devoted himself almost entirely to instrumental music. There is an opera 'Guinevere', set, significantly enough, to a German text: there are a few songs which already foreshadow the *English Lyrics*, but the majority of the works were composed for Dannreuther's chamber concerts, performed as they were written, and then, in a large number of instances, lost or destroyed. There still survive, in print or in manuscript, about a dozen compositions, which include a couple of pianoforte trios, a pianoforte quartet, a quartet and quintet for strings, a nonet for wind, the partita for violin and piano, and a few smaller pieces of which the trio in E minor, the partita, and the string quintet, are still occasionally to be heard. All three, indeed, are well worth preserving: the trio strong, vigorous and forthright, the partita breathing a new spirit and a new melody into a bygone form, and the quintet broad and dignified, with a slow movement of remarkable beauty. At the end of the period follow two works on a larger canvas: the overture *Guillem de Cabestanh* and the pianoforte concerto in F♯, which were produced at the Crystal Palace in 1879 and 1880 respectively. Of these, the overture is the less interesting: it seems to move heavily under the trappings of the orchestra, and to show signs of the prentice hand that has not yet mastered its medium: the Concerto, which has some happy audacities of form and colour, is a much finer composition, and might well be restored to the repertory of our concert-room.

It must be remembered that all these are works of discipleship, and that they naturally bear the marks of their environment. The gift of composition does not issue at full growth like Athena from the head of Zeus; it is the reward of long training and steady endeavour. During these early years Parry had already begun to show some of the qualities which he was afterwards to turn to such account: dignity and sincerity of theme, firm intellectual grasp of design and texture, purity of line, beauty of concerted sound: it needed only that all this equipment should find its due occasion for use; that it should be vitalized by an inspiration which should lift it from the heights of perfected craftsmanship to those Olympian peaks where dwell alone the Immortals.

Such an inspiration he found in Shelley's *Prometheus*. Its flame of imagery, its soaring verse, the sublimity of its themes, fired his imagination, the music was written at white heat, and with it he enters, beyond cavil or question, into the company of the great creative artists. In richness of colour, in justness of declamation, in purity and sweetness of melodic line, it is as far above praise as above criticism, and through all these burns a sense of poignant tragedy and an emotional fervour which is of the very spirit of romance. One need only recall the opening monologue, the choruses which seem to etherealize the range of human feeling, the scene in which Zeus celebrates his triumph and meets his destiny: here is indeed a new music, intense, vivid, passionate, and turning passion itself to the service of pure beauty.

Through the choral works of the second period, Parry maintained this high ideal. The symphonies are side issues, and though two of them—the 'Cambridge' and the 'English'—contain slow movements which any man might be proud to have written, they do not really represent his genius. But in *Blest Pair of Sirens* he began to show his power of building up great epic masses of sound—a power which is perhaps seen at its height in the chorus 'Et ipse redimet Israel', from the *De Profundis*—and in *Judith*, *St. Cecilia*, and *Job* he proved still further his gifts of strength and tenderness, of masterly invention and of noble utterance. It is fair to say that throughout these works are traces of mannerism which mar their perfection. One is his fondness for sequences as a form of continuous texture, though this, if it be a defect, he shares with most of the great polyphonic composers: another is his habit of closing his episodes with an instrumental ritornello, like the comments of a Greek chorus, and this practice he presses dangerously near the bounds of convention. But every artist has his conventions: they are only 'the clattering dishes at a royal banquet', and in no way detract from the munificence of the feast.

It is of more account that in all these works are moments of that sheer divine inspiration which is possible only to the highest genius, and which the highest genius does not often attain: the entry of the voices in the finale of *Blest Pair*, the return of Judith to the watching sentinels, the lyre of Orpheus, breaking like a ray of sunlight on the sunless realm, the exquisite tenderness of the cry 'then should I have lain down and been quiet' in *Job*, and the sublime series of pictures which deploy before us through its closing chorus. These are things which, once heard, are never forgotten: they remain with us as a part of our being, and enrich our lives with a sense of personal experience.

Goethe in a fine simile compares poems to the stained-glass windows of a cathedral: if you stand outside, they are dark and unmeaning; if you enter the portal the master's design is made manifest by the light of heaven shining through it. This truth lies at the heart and centre of Parry's later cantatas. We shall wholly misunderstand them unless we realize that their essential purpose is to lead us within the gates, to show us the true meaning of the words which they interpret. Their astonishing technical skill is so entirely subordinated to this end, that we are in danger of overlooking it—as indeed he would have been quite willing that it should be overlooked. Open a choral page at random, it seems but a simple diatonic texture with little inherent quality or character. Look closer and you will see that every voice is so placed and every entry so regulated as to bring out the full significance of the text. Hear it and you will find that poet, prophet, and evangelist have spoken to you with a new depth of meaning. You have passed from the glare and turmoil of the street into the quiet sanctuary, and you listen with bowed head and with heart attuned to worship.

From the two earliest of these I propose to give you illustrations. From the later ones it is impossible to make excerpts, for each must be judged as a whole. Even such supreme moments as the opening plea in *The Love that casteth out Fear*, or the scene of Peter's denial in the same cantata, or the concourse of the people in *Voces Clamantium*, lose much of their force if they are taken apart from the context. And because it would outstrip the limits of my time to describe them all, I will ask leave to take one as typical—the cantata 'Beyond these voices there is peace': not as being greater than the others, but as representing in some measure the general scheme on which they are based.

A short introduction, dark, restless, yet shot through with a golden thread of hope, leads to the opening chorus —'What profit hath man of all his labour? One generation goeth and another generation cometh, and the earth abideth for ever. . . . All things are full of weariness, that which hath been is that which shall be, and there is no new thing under the sun.' The music is full of short broken phrases and unquiet changes of tonality: it is the very voice of weariness and complaining, and behind all and through all, is the steady march of inexorable fate. Then man sets himself to contend with circumstance, to acquire wealth and pleasure and power—'Whatsoever mine eyes desired, I kept not from them, I withheld not my heart from any joy. . . . And behold, all was vanity and vexation of spirit, and there was no profit under the sun.' Hitherto the gloom of the introduction has overspread the entire work, though Parry, with extraordinary insight and sympathy has varied the form and manner of its expression; but at this point there steals across the orchestra one of the most divine of his melodies, and the chorus takes it and fashions into it a hymn of serene resignation. 'To everything there is a season, a time to every purpose under heaven.' Man's discontent is not an arraignment of the order of things: God's purpose is set upon eternal foundations and 'Whatsoever He doeth it shall be for ever'. Yet the reconciliation is only half complete. God's eternity may explain the universe, it is little comfort to man, transitory, short-lived, soon to pass away. And once more the questioning voice begins, though in calmer tones, 'Truly the light is sweet and a pleasant thing it is to behold the sun. Yea, if a man live many years, let him rejoice in them all. Let him remember the days of darkness . . . in that day when the keepers of the home shall tremble . . . because man goeth to his long home and the mourners go about the streets. The dust shall return to earth as it was, and the spirit to God who gave it.' This, then, is the question, the brevity and futility of man's life, how can it be justified in the counsels of the Eternal? For a moment the motive of gloom and despair threatens to return: it breaks off suddenly, and clear and confident sounds the answer, 'Ho, every one that thirsteth, come ye to the waters. . . . Let the wicked forsake his way, and the unrighteous man his thoughts, and let him return unto the Lord, and He will abundantly pardon.' And so the music rises and surges and eddies into a great hymn of praise; the glorious words in which Isaiah celebrates the majesty and loving-kindness of the Almighty. 'It is He that sitteth upon the circle of the earth, that stretcheth out the heavens as a curtain, and spreadeth them out as a tent to dwell in. . . . He fainteth not, neither is weary. . . . He giveth power to the faint, and to him that hath no might He increaseth strength. . . . They that wait upon the Lord shall renew their strength, they shall mount up with wings as eagles, they shall run and not be weary, and they shall walk and not faint.' And at the height and climax of this jubilant outburst, the pageant suddenly ceases, and one quiet voice, with the chorus like an echo at the cadence, tells the conclusion of the whole matter: 'Thou wilt keep him in perfect peace whose mind is stayed on Thee.'

On the aesthetic qualities of the music there is no need here to dwell. I can only say that I never return to it without finding new beauties, new causes of wonder and delight. Its mastery of resources is so complete that one is hardly conscious of the problems which it surmounts: it is a monument at once of noble purpose and of unfailing achievement.

Among Parry's smaller works, a special word should be said about the songs. All his life through he was a song-writer from the days of 'Why does azure', which he wrote at Eton, to the great setting of Blake's 'Jerusalem', which he wrote in the year before his death, and the Sonnets, the *Anacreontic Odes*, and above all the nine volumes of *English Lyrics* contain much of his most characteristic melody. The workmanship is extraordinarily delicate: never an overloaded bar or a superfluous phrase: the emotional range is wide—humour, pathos, meditation, romance—and is restrained with so firm a hand that he has sometimes been unjustly censured for coldness. But there is no coldness in 'When shall the lover rest', or 'When we two parted', or 'There is a lady sweet and kind', or the 'Dirge in Winter', or the two numbers from the Greek anthology, or the Mary Coleridge songs. They are entirely free from extravagance and sensationalism, but they can appear insipid only to critics who mistake sensationalism for eloquence, and extravagance for energy. Parry's music always speaks without gestures and its speech is the weightier for that reason.

This reserve power is one of the characteristics which make him so essentially a spokesman and representative of English music. He stood always for the national ideal and upheld it at a time when it needed asserting against the two erroneous schools of criticism which have done most to obscure the real issue. One holds that a work is national in proportion as it is based on the folk-song; the other roundly denies that nationalism has any place in art, and declares that 'les grands artistes n'ont pas de patrie'. The former of these is nearer the truth, but it has been so overstated that in its extreme form it is clearly untenable: a work is not made national because it weaves a few folk melodies into its texture, nor cosmopolitan because it discards them altogether. The latter, pressed to its defence, can mean only one of two things—that distinctions of national character do not exist, or that they are inexpressible in terms of music; and neither of these propositions can be seriously maintained. Every great artist, painter, poet, or musician is to some extent the child of his time and country, and the genuineness which marks his originality will itself be influenced both by his inheritance and by his surroundings. He will use the style and idiom which come most naturally to his hand: he will express through them the thoughts and feelings which he shares, though more fully and deeply, with the rest of his countrymen. And this is exactly what Parry has done. He represents in music the essential sanity of the English genius: its mixture of strength and tenderness, its breadth, its humour, its entire freedom from vanity and affectation. It is idle to compare his gifts with those of the great Continental composers—'great in their way, not ours nor meant for ours'; one might as well compare the serenity of an English landscape with the glow of sunset on the Apennines or the Aegean.

This brings us to another side of his career: his position as teacher and writer. He lived through one of the most interesting periods of musical history: perhaps the most interesting, except the change from the sixteenth to the seventeenth centuries. When he was born Schumann was still living: Mendelssohn but recently dead: Wagner had not yet written any of his greatest works: Brahms was a boy of fifteen studying the piano at Altona. Before he died there had come about those fundamental changes in musical idiom and expression which we associate respectively with the names of Debussy and Ravel, Strauss and Mahler, Stravinsky and Scriabin. It is worth considering how he faced the problem of reconciling the old and the new.

Briefly his attitude was that of Hans Sachs in *Die Meistersinger*. By temperament, by predilection, by training, he was on the conservative side: he reverenced above all things nobility of thought, cleanness of line, thoroughness of workmanship; he distrusted rhetoric and emotionalism, the overwrought feeling and the overcharged palette. But no man was ever less of a pedant: his sympathy was unbounded even with forms of art most alien from his own; and he was stern only to imposture and insincerity, to the work of the mountebank and of the conscious imitator. It was this combination of breadth and staunchness, of loyalty to his ideal and tolerance of the ideals of others, which set his critical judgement on a basis that stood foursquare: he brought to the task a mind enriched with wide knowledge both of music and of literature, a keen logical faculty, a memory which was never at fault, and a style which clothes his thought in the fittest and most flexible of garments. His Oxford lectures and the addresses which he gave to the Royal College are enduring models of their kind: so in a more technical field are his articles in Grove's *Dictionary*: his contribution to the *Oxford History* gives distinction to the entire series: his volume on Bach is a classic: his *Evolution of the Art of Music* is the best book on the subject that has yet been written, and it is no secret that among the works which mainly occupied his last years is a book dealing not with music, but with the large issues of human life in the light of which he saw, with increasing certainty of vision, the ultimate explanation of art and of beauty. Plato, the most poetic of philosophers, lifted poetry into the realm of pure thought and discarded only those forms and aspects which could be turned to trivial or ignoble use: Parry has learned the Platonic lesson as no Englishman before him but Wordsworth had ever learned it, and by sheer force of his own personal sincerity and goodness has transmuted the service of art into the unalloyed gold of worship and adoration.

As is the man, so has been his influence. I do not speak only of the pupils who have passed under his hand, of the friends who have been privileged to know him, of the struggling musicians whom he has helped and encouraged: there is no side of our musical life in England which is not the better and the nobler because he has lived. Among his contemporaries, old and young, there are many to whose names we point with a just pride, who have helped us to achieve our independence, and to take our due place in the artistic development of mankind: every one of them is glad to acknowledge his leadership and his inspiration. Through him we have learned to speak in our own tongue, to deliver our own message, to bind once more the broken thread, to recall the forgotten tradition. From those of his own time he has won the fullest tribute of veneration and love: his name will be enrolled among the heroes by those who come after.

MUSIC AND DRAMA[1]

A PHILOSOPHER who is seeking for an illustration of the One in the Many will find it ready to his hand in the history of artistic criticism. The problems of art are innumerable; they press round us in such multitude that they often obscure our view of the artist; and yet, when all is said, they are only the transitory versions of one eternal problem—the relation of form and content, of expression and design. Is the main function of art to interpret reality and 'paint man man, whatever the issue', or to create its own reality by presenting, through a chosen medium, some vision of ideal beauty? or may we believe that each of these is but a half-truth, and that the highest achievement is to maintain them both in a due balance and equipoise which shall reconcile their conflicting claims without sacrifice and without concession? The extreme arguments on either side are familiar enough. The artist who fixes his attention on pure design stands in some danger of formalism, and even of conventionality; his work at the best may be coldly perfect, at the worst artificial and unmeaning. The insistence on expression and interpretation may be carried to a point at which beauty itself disappears. Daedalus, as the story goes, carved the legs of his statue with such fidelity to nature that it ran away in the night.

It is probable that in no field of art has the battle been more urgently or persistently fought than in that of the musical drama. At the end of the sixteenth century it raged round the 'Nuove Musiche'; at the end of the seventeenth round Lully; in the latter part of the eighteenth round Gluck; in the latter part of the nineteenth round Wagner. On each occasion the ground of controversy was in all essentials the same. A past tradition had hardened until it was merely an obstruction and a hindrance; a reformer arose to clear it from the path and to

[1] From *The Quarterly Review*, January, 1912.

vindicate for art the utmost freedom to proclaim what it would. The very terms of recrimination repeat themselves. 'Your old music', says the attacking force, 'is so stereotyped that it has no longer any significance; it may give pleasure to the ear but it says nothing to the soul.' 'Your new music', say the defenders, 'is mere violence and anarchy; it may express passions which, perhaps, were better left unexpressed, but it is false to the principles and ideals of its own cause.' Monteverde, Lully, Gluck, were assailed with the same charges of ugliness and bad musicianship which, thirty years ago, were brought against Wagner; they responded by building up a scheme of dramatic music upon which, for our own generation, Wagner has laid the coping-stone.

It is necessary to state this fact at the outset, because criticism, which in every age believes that its verdict is not only final but original, has too readily assumed that the real problem began with the publication of *Oper und Drama*, and with the composition of *The Ring*. Even Wagner himself, it may be said with deference, does insufficient justice to Gluck, and almost ignores the important part played by Lully. That he should do so is entirely natural. He was preoccupied with his own statement of the question; and of necessity the terms in which he stated it were different from those employed by his predecessors. He was in the thick of the arena, and may well have gazed more keenly on opponents than on allies. But now that the battle is over and the smoke has rolled away, it is possible to look back dispassionately on the whole course of events, to trace the ancestry of the Bayreuth idea, and, what is more important, to estimate in some measure its influence on the subsequent course of the musical drama.

Tolstoy, that uncompromising preacher of artistic truth, once declared that the musical drama was an untenable convention, and illustrated this doctrine with a very unsympathetic description of *Siegfried*. If we grant his premiss, the conclusion is unanswerable. Assume that the drama is the direct representation of humanity, the mirror held up to nature, the faithful reflection of life which, if seen through a temperament, is nevertheless seen as it is, then it would seem to follow that a play in which music is the medium of the dialogue must of necessity be untrue. The drama which Plato feared for his Guardians, and would have feared still more if he could have foreseen *The Powers of Darkness*, consists wholly of imitation; in modern terms it gives us human speech and action as we might expect to find them outside the theatre. In *Hedda Gabler* and *Die Weber*, in *Strife* and *Justice*, we are moved by the fidelity with which the dramatist sets living men and women upon the stage; the illusion (if we can call it an illusion) would be shattered by the ordered phraseology of music. But to take this as the type and pattern of dramatic truth is to prove far too much. It would rule out *Faust*, for men do not speak in rhyme, and *Othello*, for they do not speak in blank verse; it would close the doors of the theatre on almost all its greatest masterpieces. Let us examine the assumption from which this conclusion proceeds.

The origin of our drama is to be found in religious service. The Doric word, from which its name is derived, has a definitely ritual meaning; the earliest examples were choric songs and dances with a single episode, in which the poet, who was also the chorus-leader, improvised before the audience a story in honour of the god. These episodes were probably accompanied by mimetic or sympathetic gestures on the part of the chorus; they were wholly rhythmic in form; they were almost certainly in that heightened 'poetic' tone of which recitative and *aria parlante* are our modern equivalents. In course of time the episodes became more numerous, and so led to a rude dialogue between leader and chorus; then, as a later development, came the gradual introduction of actors and of scenic representation. And, long after these had become familiar, the ritual conception remained paramount.

The plays were given at the Dionysiac Festival; the subjects were taken from the mythology of gods and heroes [1]; the altar stood at the centre of the orchestra; more than half the principal seats were reserved for the priests. To this corresponded the whole character of the earlier Greek Tragedy. Aeschylus, as Professor Murray says, carried his theme on a great wave of religious emotion; the characters are of more than human stature; the style and phraseology are raised above the level of common speech. To an audience that felt these stories as an essential part of its religion the whole effect must have been comparable to that produced by the Christian Passion-play at Ober-Ammergau or the Mahommedan at Teheran. When we remember that in all countries music exercises a potent influence on religious emotion, there is little wonder that the very texture and fibre of Aeschylean tragedy should have been saturated with it. The musical drama in short is not a perversion, not even an extension, of the dramatic idea, but the pure essence of its original form.

With Euripides there comes a change of aim which may very roughly be compared with the distinction between music-drama and opera. Whether we regard him as a rationalist or as 'the one religious man in an irreligious age'—and both views have been maintained—there can be no doubt that he humanized tragedy, and that in so doing he considerably modified the orthodox idea of his time. Contrast, for example, the three great presentations of *Electra* in Greek Tragedy. In Aeschylus the human motive is almost ignored; in Euripides it animates the whole play and sets the entire tone of its most dramatic scene. In Sophocles the counsel of the gods is not to be challenged; Euripides not only challenges but condemns—his Orestes obeys the divine voice and is punished with all the bitterness of remorse. Hence in Euripides we are no longer sustained by the feeling of ever-present Godhead working out a divine purpose which we can neither

[1] A few on 'historical' themes. But the only one of these which has survived—the *Persae*—is a sort of *Triumphlied* or *Te Deum* after victory.

judge nor comprehend; that solace is denied us, and we are left face to face with the naked issues of human sin and human suffering. For this reason his tragedy would often be unendurably poignant—it is so, for instance, in *The Trojan Women*—unless he had alleviated it by passages of sheer music, points of repose in which we gain a momentary respite from such pity and such terror. So we have the Euripidean choruses—the 'interpolations', as Aristotle calls them—which carry us far away from the stage, which sing to us the song of Cyprus or the song of the western seas, which bathe our souls in pure melody, and send us back to the scene quieted and refreshed. Music, in short, is here used not to intensify the dramatic note but to relax it; and from this usage important consequences were to follow.

Greek Comedy sat looser to the religious conception, for its purpose was largely a satiric portraiture of current life and current events. But Aristophanes always makes his appeal to patriotism, which at Athens was a second religion, and in more than one play shows himself fully conscious of his religious surroundings. The very licence of the *Frogs* is, so to speak, under ecclesiastical sanction; it is the direct ancestor of the *Messe de l'Âne* and the *Fête des Fous*; and amid all its audacious burlesque this comedy contains two of the most beautiful hymns in the Greek language. Further, as Greek Comedy departs from ritual observance it becomes less musical: in the *Plutus* the chorus is no more than a stage crowd; it is absent from the recovered scenes of Menander.

When, after the dark centuries, drama revived again in western Europe, it passed through very much the same stages of evolution. No doubt there were two convergent streams—that of the folk-drama with its mumming play, its May game and its morris dance; and that of the liturgical drama with the story of the Nativity for Christmas, the 'Quem quaeritis' for Easter, and the cycle of mystery plays for Corpus Christi. But, though divergent, they both alike sprang from religious origins: the one from some primitive memory of nature-worship, the other so directly from the ritual of the Church that historians are unable to date the point of transition; and both were for the most part essentially musical in character. The dances had their rude accompaniment, the choral songs their rude melody; the ecclesiastical chant, already at a high pitch of organization, announced the sacred message in melodic phrase and celebrated it with hymn and canticle. From the former of these sprang the *Maggi* or May songs of the Tuscan peasants, which are at least as old as the fourteenth century. From the latter came, in direct succession, the *Sacre Rappresentazioni* and their kindred forms, which, during the fifteenth and sixteenth centuries, appeared in Florence, in Mantua, and in other Italian cities. The musical importance of these is discussed in an admirable essay by M. Romain Rolland,[1] and in the very interesting volume recently published by Mr. W. J. Henderson. They deserve, indeed, some special consideration, for they anticipate by nearly two hundred years the music-drama which we usually associate with the name of Monteverde.

They were given on great festivals after Vespers. The scene was one of the Florentine churches—notably San Felice in Piazza—and was embellished with every form of decoration and stage device that the best artists and mechanicians could invent. Here is the description of a scene by Brunelleschi[2]:

'Dans la voûte de l'église, un ciel, plein de figures vivantes, tournait; une infinité de lumières luisaient et scintillaient. Douze petits angelots, ailés, aux cheveux d'or, se prenaient par la main, et dansaient, suspendus. Au-dessus de leurs têtes trois guirlandes de lumières, d'en bas, paraissaient des étoiles. On eût dit qu'ils marchaient sur des nuages. Huit enfants groupés autour d'un socle lumineux descendirent ensuite de la voûte. Sur le socle était debout un petit ange d'une quinzaine d'années, solidement attaché par un mécanisme de fer invisible et assez souple pour lui

1 *L'Opéra avant l'Opéra*, in *Musiciens d'Autrefois.*
2 *Musiciens d'Autrefois*, pp. 26–8.

laisser la liberté de ses mouvements. La machine une fois descendue sur la scène, l'ange alla saluer la Vierge et fit l'Annonciation. Puis il remonta au ciel, au milieu de ses compagnons qui chantaient, tandis que les anges du ciel dansaient dans l'air une ronde.'

The stories were taken from Holy Writ, or (occasionally) from the lives of saints, and were represented by dramatic action and by dialogues and speeches which, it would appear, were sometimes recited and sometimes sung. To quote again from M. Rolland:

'Certaines parties de la pièce, d'un caractère traditionnel—Prologues (*Annunziazioni*), Epilogues (*Licenzi*), prières, etc.—étaient sans doute chantées sur une cantilène spéciale. De plus, on intercalait dans la *Sacra Rappresentazione* des morceaux de caractères variés: soit des pages de liturgie régulière ou populaire (des "Te Deum" ou des "Laudi"), soit des chansons profanes et de la musique de danse, comme l'indiquent certains *libretti*: "Tel morceau doit être chanté comme les 'Vaghe montanine' de Sacchetti." Tel autre marqué: "*bel canto*". Ici, "Pilate répond en chantant *alla imperiale*." Là "Abraham tout joyeux dit une *Stanza a ballo*." Il y avait des chants à deux et à trois voix. Le spectacle était précédé d'un prélude instrumental, qui suivait le prologue chanté. On avait donc un petit orchestre; et nous voyons mentionnés, çà et là, des violons, des violes et des luths'.

The intervals between the acts were filled with choruses and ballets of action, chosen apparently not for sheer contrast, as was the practice of eighteenth-century opera, but with some bearing on the main issue. Thus we read of a chorus of huntsmen as intermezzo in the story of St. Margaret; and there would seem to be other instances of a similar kind.

It is difficult to see what element is here lacking. We have prologue and overture, orchestra and singers, the play presented in musical phrase,[1] and with scenic effects so elaborate that they could hardly be surpassed by Munich and Bayreuth. We may smile at the simplicity

[1] M. Rolland goes so far as to speak of 'un récitatif moulé sur la phrase parlée'. If this is correct, little was left for the moderns to invent.

of the directions; we may sometimes wonder at the incongruity of the designs; but we cannot doubt that to the congregations which assembled to witness these dramas the simplicity was natural and the incongruity non-existent. They were religious offices as vivid as the Good Friday procession in a modern Italian town, and at least as intimate as, to an Athenian audience, the representation of *Agamemnon* or *Œdipus*.

In course of time the frank paganism which marked one side of the Renaissance invaded these ecclesiastical dramas and introduced among the most sacred subjects the triumphs of Caesar and Trajan, and even the cars of Neptune and Venus. So, little by little, the scene shifted from church to palace, from Pius II to Beatrice d'Este and Ludovico Moro. About 1472 Politian wrote his *Favola di Orfeo*, which Symonds describes as a true lyric drama, and which Mr. Henderson, who devotes to it nearly a third of his entire volume, places 'at the foundation of modern opera'.

'Poetically' (he says) 'it was the superior of any lyric work except, perhaps, those of Metastasio. Musically it was radically different from the opera as it was from the liturgical drama. But none the less it contained some of the germs of the modern opera. It had its solo, its chorus and its ballet. . . . It was distinctly lyric and secular, and was therefore as near the spirit of the popular music as any new attempt could well approach.' [1]

By the end of the century the change was complete; in 1502 five comedies of Plautus were given at Ferrara with ballets and 'choruses *à l'antique*'; in 1518 came the *Suppositi* of Ariosto with an orchestra of 'fifes, bagpipes, cornetti, viols, and organ', and a flute obbligato 'which gave much delight to the company'. The whole form was growing artificial and courtly; music and spectacular display were gaining the upper hand; a direct way was being paved for the baroque opera of the seventeenth century.[2]

[1] *Some Forerunners of Italian Opera*, pp. 66, 67. See also pp. 90, 91.

[2] See Mr. E. J. Dent's article on the Baroque Opera, *Musical Antiquary*, January 1910.

As so often happens, this clash of ideals struck into existence a form which owed direct allegiance to neither—the Italian pastoral, of which Guarini's *Pastor Fido* is the best-known example, and Tasso's *Aminta* that of the chief historical importance. Indeed, Tasso deserves in this matter more than a passing mention. He was devoted to music, 'the soul of poetry' as he calls it; he deplored its misuse in mere tunefulness and sensual delight; he was the direct precursor of that Florentine revolution the originality of which has been somewhat over-estimated by musical historians. M. Rolland remarks on the significant fact that, at a famous performance of *Aminta* in 1590 Rinuccini and Emilio dei Cavalieri were both present.

Hence followed those meetings at Count Bardi's house in Florence, where Peri, Caccini, Rinuccini, Vincenzo, Galilei and others proceeded to apply to secular art the reform which Cavalieri was furthering at St. Philip Neri's Oratory in Rome. They had two antagonists to meet at the same time. Learned music, as represented by the great contrapuntists, was bound by a system of elaborate and formal rules, admirably adapted to preserve its purity and dignity of utterance, but not sufficiently flexible to allow of its extension into the domain of the theatre; drama, transferred from ritual observance to courtly display, was treating music as a separate independent art which made its own appeal, gave its own pleasure, and year by year was breaking the last threads of connexion that bound it to the requirements of plot and character. The aim of the Florentine reformers was to set on the stage a music which should be wholly expressive and dramatic, should emancipate itself from all formal regulations, and follow without question or hesitation the lead of the poet.

Their method of effecting this was to recover, so far as they could, the principles of Greek Tragedy.[1] They were all scholars; they were all animated by that passion

[1] In comedy they moved with a more tentative step. Vecchi's *Amfiparnasso* (1594), though very expressive and often very amusing, is a

for Greek art which had spread through Italy since Chrysoloras came from Byzantium to lecture in the Florentine schools; in Peri's *Euridice* and in Monteverde's *Orfeo* they once more vindicated that absolute fusion of music and drama which, as tradition attested, had been wrought by the hand of Æschylus. And herein lay at once their strength and their weakness. Greek Tragedy gave them the noblest of models; on that score their choice could not have more happily fallen. But it gave them also a range of themes which had become cold and remote, and which, for at least a generation, had been associated in the public mind with pageantry and scenic display. To ancient Athens Orpheus was a national hero, to medieval Florence he was the centre of a picturesque fairy-tale; and it needed more genius than these men possessed to relight the fire on that old and forgotten altar. They struck a gallant blow in the cause of freedom, and in so doing have earned an honourable place in the history of the art; but they had not the strength to consolidate a permanent victory; and, despite all their endeavours, Italy soon fell back from its new ideals and accepted in their place the artificial pageants of the seventeenth century and the absurd pseudo-classicism of the eighteenth. It is significant that in 1644 Evelyn speaks of having seen at Rome an opera 'given by the architect Bernini'; it is not less significant that, some seventy years later, Addison summed up his experience of the Italian style by roundly asserting that 'music renders us incapable of hearing sense'.

Peri and Monteverde never reached the goal; and the art of their country turned aside from it. But they ran their stage in the race, and, when they ceased, handed the torch undimmed to a more powerful successor. Lully was born at Florence in 1639, was taken in early childhood to France, entered the royal service as violinist, and at the age

curious compromise between the methods of the stage and those of the madrigal.

of twenty-three was made Court composer, an office which he held until his death in 1687. His life in Paris coincided with the most splendid period of French Tragedy. The *Cid* appeared in 1636, *Horace* and *Cinna* in 1640, *Andromaque* in 1667, *Iphigénie* in 1674, *Phèdre* three years later. To a musician of true dramatic instinct there could have been no atmosphere more sustaining or more stimulating. For a time, no doubt, he was occupied with ceremonial duties, writing ballets and *divertissements*, many in collaboration with Molière, composing and arranging incidental music for *M. de Pourceaugnac* and the *Bourgeois Gentilhomme*. Yet even these he inspired with the same vigour with which Ben Jonson inspired the English Masque; indeed, with him they are not mere pageants or episodes, but studies and sketches for the finished picture to come. All this while, too, he was improving his technique, analysing the work of Cavalli the Venetian, borrowing somewhat unscrupulously from his French predecessor Cambert, taking his goods where he found them, and bringing his orchestra to a perfection hitherto unknown in Europe.

Thus, when in 1672 he began with Quinault that series of operas which has made him famous, he came to the work with full equipment—a master of virile melody and of harmony which in his day was considered audacious, a great conductor, a great disciplinarian, and, above all, a dramatist who was determined to give to music, as nearly as possible, the rhythm and inflexion of the spoken word. He chose his opera-singers less for their vocalization than for their power of acting; he filled page after page of his score with free declamatory recitative, keeping the melodic stanza for special effects of lyric emotion. To him belongs in full measure the praise which Wagner bestows upon Gluck, that 'in his music he took pains to speak correctly and intelligibly'. 'Si vous voulez bien chanter ma musique', he said, 'allez entendre la Champmeslé,' naming a famous actress of the Comédie Française who, we are told, had been taught every tone and every phrase by Racine himself.[1] So far, then, as concerns the important matter of a just and expressive recitation, he marks an epoch in the history of the music-drama.

We may here pause for a moment to consider the point that has been reached. The religious impulse has for the time vanished altogether and has taken with it that particular need of dramatic music which it originally fostered and justified. In its place we have a form of secular tragedy, where the spoken voice is heightened by the musical medium, and the action emphasized and in some measure interpreted by musical accompaniment. This tragedy is not yet completely humanized; it still wears the pall and buskin; its characters, though we can recognize their image, are not of our mould and figure. The very titles are significant—*Atys* and *Thésée*, *Proserpine* and *Bellérophon* and *Roland*; the stage is set upon distant heights; the atmosphere is purer and more serene than our lower air. Yet, like Racine, Lully treats his heroes with true psychological insight, with less genius, of course, but with something of the same method and purpose; and the music which he employed as vehicle is no more of an intrusion than the Alexandrine couplet. It was entirely due to him that the French opera of his time 'appartenait', as M. Lanson says, 'à la littérature autant et presque plus qu'à l'art musical'; and in this sentence we may find the explanation of his dramatic ideals.

The direct school of Lully failed through the docility of its scholars. His immediate followers were men of little talent, who copied his forms without a breath of his animating spirit, and soon wearied Parisian taste by mere insipidity. But his own operas continued to hold the

[1] The converse of this statement throws some light on the rhythm of the 'classical' Alexandrine. If Lully's recitatives may be taken as an indication, its basis was far more 'anapaestic' than 'iambic'—more like Byron's *Destruction of Sennacherib* than the last line of a Spenserian stanza. Of course even then there were cross-rhythms; and since Victor Hugo ('J'ai disloqué ce grand niais d'alexandrin') the pattern has been much altered.

stage, and some half-century after his death were uplifted as a party banner against a new and redoubtable antagonist.

Rameau was in many respects the exact opposite of Lully. His main interest lay in pure music, which he may even be said to have approached on its scientific side, for he began his career with a treatise on harmony. He wrote for the theatre by necessity rather than choice; and his first venture was so unsuccessful that he was with difficulty persuaded to continue. To the merits and demerits of his *libretti* he showed the most complete indifference; 'a composer of genius', he said, 'will find all subjects equally suitable—qu'on m'apporte la *Gazette de Hollande*'. His great qualities are all essentially musical—striking effects of harmony and modulation, interesting points of orchestral colour, strength of melody for its own sake. The claims of the drama he held to be subservient; and even in his best opera, *Castor et Pollux*, he treated them with comparative disregard. With him, then, there comes a change of principle, a shifting of the centre of gravity. The dramatist recedes into the background; the stage becomes a concert-platform, adorned with scenery and action, but entirely controlled by the hand of the musician. Paris at once broke into a feud of Lullists and Ramists which lasted through the middle years of the century. On Rameau's side were novelty, some brilliance of invention, and a large and impressive rhetoric which he aided by considerably increasing the resources of chorus and orchestra. The partisans of Lully found valuable allies in the Encyclopaedists and particularly in Rousseau, who has left an amusing account of the Académie de Musique under his enemy's directorship—the whole stage overwhelmed in a flood of musical grandiloquence, singers and orchestra straining in perpetual rivalry, and the conductor, from sheer despair, belabouring his desk 'like a woodcutter'. In 1752 came the Bouffons; and the war blazed up with renewed violence. In 1764 Rameau died; in 1773 Gluck was invited from Vienna to Paris.

There is no need to repeat the well-known story [1] of Gluck's diplomacies and conflicts, of the vicissitudes of his campaign and the signal victory by which it was crowned. But it is worth while to quote from his own writings a statement of the cause for which he contended, since without this we are in danger of under-estimating the debt that we owe to him, and the curious resemblance between his position and that of music-drama in our own time. He is often judged as though his main object was that set forth in the famous preface to *Alceste*—continuity of dramatic texture and a firm resistance to the unreasonable tyranny of the singers. But in his Parisian manifestoes he goes far beyond this. The first letter to the *Mercure de France* gives the place of honour to his librettist Calzabigi, and continues with a sentence which reads like a direct challenge to Rameau:

'Quelque talent qu'ait le Compositeur, il ne fera jamais que de la musique médiocre si le Poète n'excite pas en lui cet enthousiasme sans lequel les productions de tous les Arts sont foibles et languissantes; l'imitation de la nature est le but reconnu qu'ils doivent tous se proposer; c'est celui auquel je tâche d'atteindre; toujours simple et naturelle, autant qu'il m'est possible, ma musique ne tend qu'à la plus grande expression et au renforcement de la déclamation de la Poésie.'

Still more striking is his answer to La Harpe's criticism of *Armide*. La Harpe had complained that the opera represented passions which were beyond the reach of music, which were in themselves so violent and unlovely that they could admit of no possible beauty in the expression. The heroine was 'not an enchantress but a sorceress'; her part was 'one monotonous cry'; there were no airs, and therefore no melodies, only a distressing cacophony forced upon a declamation which would have done better without it. Gluck replies:

'J'avois eu la simplicité de croire jusqu'à présent qu'il en étoit de la Musique comme des autres Arts; que toutes les passions étoient

[1] It has been fully told by Mr. Ernest Newman in his volume on *Gluck and the Opera*.

de son ressort, et qu'elle ne devoit pas moins plaire en exprimant l'emportement d'un furieux et le cri de la douleur, qu'en peignant les soupirs de l'amour.

Il n'est point de serpent ni de monstre odieux
Qui par l'art imité ne puisse plaire aux yeux.

Je croyois ce précepte vrai en Musique comme en Poésie. Je m'étois persuadé que le chant, rempli partout de la teinte des sentimens qu'il avoit à exprimer, devoit se modifier comme eux, et prendre autant d'accens différens qu'ils avoient de différentes nuances; enfin que la voix, les instruments, tous les sons, les silences mêmes, devoient tendre à un seul but qui étoit l'expression, et que l'union devoit être si étroite entre les paroles et le chant, que le Poème ne semblât pas moins fait sur la Musique que la Musique sur le Poème.'

Is it of Gluck we are reading or of Richard Strauss; of *Armide* or of *Elektra*? And if we so look back on the controversies of our predecessors, how, we may ask, will posterity look back upon ours? For, strangest of all, though the same war still continues, the old fortress has been abandoned by both combatants. To us, whichever side we take, the operas of Gluck are now classics; time has so softened their outlines and so mellowed their colouring that they stand to us as examples of pure beauty. We look for the dissonances that assailed the ears of La Harpe; we find harmonies which to us are as transparent as a mountain stream. We look for those outbursts of passion which made the eighteenth century weep and tremble; and we find passion indeed, but so exquisitely melodious that our emotion is too deep for tears.

So far we have considered music in its relation to Tragedy. Comedy is of wider range. It may glow with the imagination of Shakespeare or glitter with the wit of Congreve; it may be the incarnation of common sense like Molière or mere 'excellent fooling' like much of Labiche; it may cut its way by satire like Gogol's *Inspector*, or, like Goldoni's *Locandiera*, delight us by charm and daintiness. In the realm of Tragedy convention wearies and incongruity offends; Comedy has many outlying dependencies where incongruity is part of the fun, and convention passes unnoticed. Across their frontiers music can enter wherever it likes; they set no sentry to challenge it, and at their feast of laughter it is one of the most welcome guests.

Hence the rapid development, at this time, of Italian musical comedy. The Italian composers of the eighteenth century were not reformers; they worked, for the most part, under exceedingly difficult conditions; and they accepted to the full that dangerous maxim that 'an art which lives by pleasing must please at once'. But while, in Tragic Opera, they abandoned all intellectual appeal and all seriousness of purpose, they found in *Opera Buffa* and *Intermezzo* forms exactly suited to their genius. These little pieces, light, dainty, playful, with just enough plot to hold them together and just enough characterization to give point to the dialogue, represented without effort or fatigue their quick sensibility, their native charm, and their inexhaustible gift of tunefulness. It was these *Intermezzi* which the Bouffons brought to Paris, and in so doing created an entire school of French light opera. It was *Opera Buffa* which made the reputation of Gluck's unfortunate rival Piccinni. Only in the nineteenth century did this form also degenerate, and become, in the hands of its most brilliant exponent, a mere 'handful of artificial flowers'.

It was their influence, together with that of Gluck, which trained the operatic style of Mozart. During his early days he was much in Italy; throughout his life he wrote many of his works to Italian *libretti*. In 1778 he visited Paris and arrived there in the middle of the Gluckist and Piccinnist controversy. The first-fruits of this visit may be found in *Idomeneo*, where the effects of Gluck's doctrine and example are beyond question. And, apart from *La Clemenza di Tito*, which was written to order, all his operas after *Idomeneo* are comedies.

To discuss these even in outline would carry us far

beyond the limits of the present theme. It is enough to say that they represent artificial opera—opera as distinct from music-drama—at its best and highest. The set forms which would impede tragedy are here not hindrances but bowers of delight; the characterization, though it never looks beyond the immediate scene, is wonderfully deft and skilful; the declamations flow like a stream; the melodies rise and hover and sparkle like a fountain. *Die Zauberflöte* may be a satire or an allegory or a harlequinade; in any case it is a miracle of musical genius.

One more strand is waiting to be interwoven, in due time, with the general fabric. Folk-drama began from humble origins, from village festival and rustic merry-making; and some centuries elapsed before it found any settled place in a polite and civilized art. Indeed, one of the earliest attempts to put folk-music on the operatic stage was *The Beggar's Opera*, an intentional burlesque; and it was probably the remarkable success of this work which brought the form into vogue. Through the eighteenth century it gradually advanced in skill and favour, growing more and more oblivious of its ancestry, more and more concerned with local stories and the humours of country life, its simple lyric melodies derived or imitated from the songs of the people. So arose Hiller in Leipzig, Dittersdorf in Vienna, Shield and Attwood in London; so at a later stage of development came Weber and glorified the national music of Germany with *Der Freischütz*.

Had Weber possessed more of the dramatist's instinct he might have anticipated by nearly half a century the reforms of Richard Wagner. But his allegiance, like that of Beethoven, was on the side of music. *Fidelio* is really an impossible compromise, a monument of symphonic style, which, except for one superb scene, never strikes the spectator as dramatic. And the same, with due modification, may be said about the work which Weber intended for his masterpiece. *Euryanthe* is ruined not only by a bad *libretto*, but by the conflict of two incompatible ideals. As Wagner sums it up:

Music and Drama

'Never, so long as Opera has existed, has there been composed a work in which the inner contradictions of the whole *genre* have been more consistently worked out, more openly exhibited, by a gifted, deeply-feeling and truth-loving composer, for all his high endeavour to attain the best. These contradictions are: absolute, self-sufficing melody, and unflinchingly true dramatic expression. Here one or the other must necessarily be sacrificed—either Melody or Drama. Rossini sacrificed the Drama; the noble Weber wished to reinstate it by force of his more judicious melody. He had to learn that this was an impossibility. Weary and exhausted by the troubles of his *Euryanthe*, he sank back upon the yielding pillow of an oriental fairy-dream; through the wonder-horn of Oberon he breathed away his last life's-breath.' [1]

Where Weber failed it was not for any other Romantic composer to succeed. Berlioz's *Cellini* was hissed off the stage, Schumann's *Genoveva* withdrawn after three performances; Spohr, safe in his fastness at Cassel, tried a few ingenious experiments, but they came to nothing; for a time it looked as though true art would abandon the opera-house and leave it to the rhetoric of Meyerbeer and the tinkle of Donizetti's guitar. Once more the musicians were 'treating as an end what should only be treated as a means',[2] and in so doing were displacing the artistic balance. The only hope of restoring it lay in the advent of a man who should be primarily a dramatist, but to whom music should be a natural means of expression; who should approach the problem from the dramatic side, yet with such mastery of music as should make it subservient to his purpose.

Wagner's autobiography tells us at first hand how this hope was fulfilled. It is not altogether a pleasant book; there are many details of private life which do not concern us, and would have been better omitted; but, as an account of his artistic career, the work is one of absorbing interest. Some of it has been anticipated in his earlier writings,[3]

[1] *Oper und Drama*, pp. 86, 87 : Mr. Ashton Ellis's translation.
[2] See *Oper und Drama*, Introduction.
[3] Notably in *Eine Mittheilung an meine Freunde*.

but in none of them is the story told with such wealth of incident or such candour of self-revelation—the schoolboy who played truant to write a great Shakespearian tragedy, and justified himself on the ground that he had been placed in a class below his merits; the university student with a drawer full of immature compositions and an overwhelming passion for Beethoven; the theatrical experience at Magdeburg and Riga; the struggling, starving days at Paris; the brief period of official dignity at Dresden; then revolution and exile full of stormy treatises and projects of new work; and so the story closes when King Louis of Bavaria sends his equerry with that offer of freedom and competence to which we owe Bayreuth and all that it has brought us. One point of interest emerges from the volumes with special clearness—the extent to which Wagner, when he had once determined the nature of his message, foresaw the successive stages in which it was to be delivered. It is well known that *Die Meistersinger* was sketched, twenty-two years before the completion of the work, at the time that he was making the arrangements for the production of *Tannhäuser*. It is not so well known that the idea of *Parsifal* was conceived at the same time, and that the *scenario* was written during the intervals of *Siegfried*.

This is the more noticeable because Wagner's dramatic work traces back the history of the art almost continuously from the point at which he received it. We have seen the music-drama begin with religion, change to the conflict of motives and the presentation of human tragedy, develop for a short time into folk-legend, and finally lose itself in the sands of dramatic convention. Wagner reversed this order. He began by adopting the current conventions. In *Rienzi*, for example, Adriano's song is not better than Bellini; *Santo Spirito Cavallieri* is not much better than Meyerbeer; the whole substance of the music is like amateur's work, filling with immense enthusiasm and vitality the accepted formulas of its time. Then came the period of folk-legend, with *The Flying Dutchman* for initiative and *Tannhäuser* and *Lohengrin* for completion. Wagner has told us in full detail how he hesitated between *Tannhäuser* and *Manfred*, and for what reason he abandoned the 'historical grand opera in five acts' which he had already sketched, and took in its place 'that very essence of the folk-poem' which had been brought to his notice in a popular ballad. No doubt he treated these national subjects in his own manner, and his own manner was not that of Weber; but none the less he was feeling his way through nationalism to the most intimate and central emotions of mankind. It is not for nothing that, in the oration which celebrated the transference of Weber's body to Dresden, he spoke of the composer of *Der Freischütz* as 'the most German of musicians'.

Then the stage widens for the larger tragedies of mankind; the immortal passion of *Tristan*, the fundamental problems of right and justice in *The Ring*. Then follows *Die Meistersinger*, the greatest of musical comedies, a triumphant vindication of love and art which is as well illustrated by the conflict of Beckmesser and Walther as Aristophanes's patriotism is illustrated by the conflict of Æschlyus and Euripides. So the course winds upwards from 'frivolity'[1] and spectacular display to national legend, from national legend to the great epic mythology in which human life is symbolized, and to the service of art by which it is ennobled, until at last the summit is attained in the Eucharistic feast of *Parsifal*. Throughout the whole of his work the animating force is love. 'I cannot think of music except as love,' he says—love which is born amid the beauty and goodness of earth and soars flight above flight to the mystic contemplation of eternal beauty and eternal goodness.

With such an inspiration it is little wonder that he has

[1] 'My path led first to utter frivolity in my views of art,' says Wagner in *Eine Mittheilung an meine Freunde*, which, it will be remembered, was written to serve as a preface to *The Flying Dutchman*, *Tannhäuser*, and *Lohengrin*, and to explain their place in his general scheme.

moved the hearts of men. We may grant much that has been said against him—occasional roughness of style, occasional poverty of technique, the faults that follow from a hasty education and an imperfect equipment. His verse can no more stand beside Goethe's than his tunes beside those of Schubert; he is 'not great as they are, point by point'; the work of his early manhood sometimes falls into commonplace; that of his maturity is sometimes heavy and slow of movement. Yet even here the *advocatus diaboli* cannot pass unanswered. Where Wagner's technique is strong it is irresistible. No man before his time ever showed such supreme mastery of orchestral colour. No man except Beethoven has ever compressed his thoughts into such clear, incisive musical phrase. If the stanza-tunes are sometimes ill-rhymed, they are more than compensated by that wonderful diffused melody which overflows the stanza and is the more beautiful for its lack of restriction. If the verse is often unmemorable, at any rate we do not forget the characters that speak it or the scenes in which it is uttered. And, further, it may be urged that to try Wagner by these analytic tests is to judge him on a false issue; the limitations may be real, but they are irrelevant. The sole ground on which Wagner's work can be rightly appraised is its effect in the theatre; and on this ground the verdict of posterity is assured. As the great dramas unroll before us, we have no thought of criticism or analysis; we let ourselves be carried away by the swelling and limitless billows, by the 'unfathomable speech which leads us to the edge of the Infinite and lets us for moments gaze into that'.

Before we proceed to discuss the extent of Wagner's influence on the subsequent history of the stage it may be well to consider a form which, at most, fell but indirectly within its range. During the mid-century romantic opera was running an undistinguished course, often deft and picturesque, but of very little importance. To compare Goethe's *Faust* with Gounod's is to understand why music is sometimes treated disrespectfully by men of letters. But a seed of Weber's sowing was wafted to remote lands, and in course of time grew up and bore fruit. The older Russian composers were passionate adherents of Weber; the younger learned from him the lesson of a folk-opera, based on national legend, and saturated with national melody. Such an opera is *Boris Godunov*, by that great and wayward genius, Mussorgsky. In the first act an entire scene is built from a peasants' hymn;[1] and almost every subsequent melody is either gathered from the folk-songs or a close imitation of their manner. Borodin's *Prince Igor*, too, is saturated with national idiom, employed on a weaker theme than Mussorgsky's, but with greater musical ability. In more recent times Bruneau has used folk-songs for his charming opera *Le Rêve* with special appropriateness to a simple story of French country life. But the finest example of all is Georges Bizet, whose *Carmen*, produced in 1875, shows to what splendid purpose a romantic play can be adorned with national colour and national rhythm. It does not rival the Wagnerian dramas, though many critics, Nietzsche included, have declared that it surpasses them; but it holds an honourable place by the side of *Der Freischütz*.

Wagner's influence may be traced back at least as early as Boito's *Mefistofele* (1868), which in its turn profoundly affected the later works of his friend and collaborator, Verdi. As might be expected, the musician preponderates; but in *Aïda* the change of ideal is evident, and in *Otello* and *Falstaff* it is almost complete. There is some interest in observing that among the followers of the 'new music' Italy led the way. 'How Wagner seems to have stricken these Italians!' complains Meredith's Victor Radnor; and he adds, with the sigh of all musical conservatism, 'I held out against Wagner as long as I could.'

But among all who carried on the Wagnerian tradition

1 'Praise to thee, O God, in the heavens'. It is this tune which Beethoven used in the second Rasoumoffsky quartet. Mussorgsky employs it for a chorus of welcome to the Tsar.

by far the most momentous is Richard Strauss. His *Guntram* first revealed the dramatist on whom the mantle of Wagner has fallen; his two light comedies carry it off with something of a rakish air, as though they had studied their pose from Don Juan; in *Salome* and *Elektra* he sets himself to carry to their furthest conclusion those principles of 'unflinching dramatic expression' which *Oper und Drama* had upheld.

In discussing *Salome* we must begin by conceding the assumption that the subject of a drama may be taken, and even rehandled, from Holy Writ, an assumption which is difficult to traverse in face of such names as Racine and Alfieri. If this be granted, the next point to consider is whether the treatment is worthy of the theme; whether it convinces us as we are convinced by *Saul* and *Athalie*. The plot is undeniably dramatic. An Eastern princess is fascinated—half shudder, half desire—by one of her father's captives. She approaches him, is repulsed, turns to hatred, and demands his life as a penalty. Her father, who regards his prisoner with an uneasy superstitious awe, is forced to a reluctant assent, sees her gloating over her victim in horrible triumph, and at breaking-point of revulsion orders his guards to crush her under their shields.

It is a subject for a great tragedy; but to make the tragedy great two things would seem to be requisite. It must be swift of movement, since it passes over places on which it is not good to dwell; it must never mar its tragic intensity by commonness of phrase, still less by risking that fatal step which lies beyond the confines of the sublime. In neither of these respects does Strauss's *Salome* rise to the height of its purpose. It is sometimes trivial; it is almost always slow in action. The love-scene is unduly prolonged by an indefensible attempt to show the same change of feeling three times consecutively. The scene with Herod is unduly prolonged; we grow weary of the catalogue of treasures and the reiterated phrases in which they are successively refused. Worst of all, the closing tirade, which on all grounds alike of good taste, right feeling, and dramatic propriety should have been cut to the quick, is spread out through page after page of hysteric passion enforced by every device of stress and emphasis that the composer has at his command.[1]

The probable explanation is that in Oscar Wilde's play, from which, with a few cuts, the 'book' of Strauss's opera is faithfully translated, the treatment of the theme is artificial. The style is not Wilde's own; it is borrowed from Flaubert and Maeterlinck and the Song of Solomon. The speeches are deliberate exercises in the beautiful or the fantastic or the *macabre*; and in lashing them with this music of violence and passion Strauss has attempted an impossible task. There are some passages of fine stirring declamation, notably in the part assigned to Jochanaan; there are a few moments of languorous beauty, a few touches of psychological subtlety; yet the chief impression which is left on us at the end is one of strain and distaste.

But in *Elektra* Strauss has come to his full strength. The whole drama is in its kind a masterpiece, grim, forcible, vivid, full of vehement contrasts, yet possessing organic unity, holding from first to last the attention of the spectator enthralled. Every phrase is instinct with meaning; every action is swift and inevitable; throughout the whole stormy course we are carried on a torrent which we are powerless to resist. The character of Elektra is a wonderful study of revenge, inspired by loyalty, embittered by suffering and despair, poisoned at the last to sheer madness. Across her path come, one by one, the sombre figures of her life's tragedy—Chrysothemis, weak and selfish, born to fail in the hour of need; Clytemnestra, livid with long nights of sleepless terror, hung with

1 'With his keen sense of the theatre, Wilde would never have contrived the long speech of Salome at the end of a drama intended for the stage' (Mr. Robert Ross in the preface to Wilde's *Salome*). Mr. Ross adds some very pertinent remarks about critics who, having objected to the 'incident of horror' in the drama, witnessed with uncontrolled delight the same incident on the music-hall stage.

amulets that have lost their efficacy, driven to seek aid even from the victim that she has persecuted; Orestes the avenger, welcomed with all the pent-up joy of a love that has had no outlet, a love which after its moment of pure passion grows lurid with the fire of a baleful purpose; last of all, Aegisthus, the maiden-faced, paying in helpless agony the long debt of treachery and murder. Among all these Elektra pursues her undeviating way. Her great lament for Agamemnon contains already a presage of the day of vengeance to come. She is wholly in Clytemnestra's power, yet she meets her with taunts and defiance. News comes that Orestes is dead; when disbelief seems no longer possible, she turns to Chrysothemis—'Sister, then you and I.' Chrysothemis shrinks back—'Alone then.' When Orestes makes himself known, the revulsion of feeling is too great to bear; the chord snaps, and as she waits quivering at the door you know that the madness is upon her. It shows in the fierce cry, 'Strike once again'; it shows in the terrible irony with which she greets Aegisthus; it nerves her for the sacrificial dance, as of some wild priestess dancing before the altar of the avenging gods; and at the height of her triumph she falls dead.

In Strauss's music, as in von Hofmannsthal's play, the tension is never for an instant relaxed; indeed, all the different arts are here so fused together that it may seem idle to consider any one of them in isolation. But a few words may be said about the musical texture, partly because it has been somewhat misjudged by critics of repute, partly because it may serve, for our time, as one answer to the central problem of the music-drama. Strauss has been charged with sacrificing the art to which before all others he owes allegiance, with writing music which is not musically intelligible, which is a mere jargon of disorganized sounds, in itself unmeaning and incoherent. Surely, it is urged, no plea of dramatic expression can justify the entire dislocation of the laws of musical style.

The answer is that there is no dislocation; the laws of style are fully wide enough to include all that Strauss has here accomplished. We are not children to be frightened by dissonances; 'everything depends', as Mr. Newman says, 'on whether they can be resolved into a higher harmony,' whether they fit their context, whether they prove part of an intelligible sentence. And it may be submitted that in this music the sentences are always deeply significant. No doubt there are some puzzling passages; the cry with which Elektra recognizes her brother is in a new idiom; it uses words with which we are unfamiliar. But they serve their own purpose, they convey their own meaning; and, if they are at present 'super grammaticam', the business of grammar is to overtake them. It ought to be stimulated by the discovery of chords which even Macfarren could not have attributed to the dominant thirteenth. Some are neologisms of which we cannot yet see the ancestry or derivation; it depends upon Strauss whether they take their place in the accepted vocabulary of the art. Others—among them one which has been most in dispute—are the lineal descendants of the harmonies of Mozart and Beethoven, and but claim for their own generation the liberty that has been won by their forefathers. In any case discords are unimportant; it is the texture that matters; and this web is of a master's weaving.

We have travelled far enough from *Parsifal*—from the vision of the Grail and the choiring voices of adoration; and to the heights of *Parsifal* Strauss has not yet attained. But his drama is the direct continuation of Wagner, not only in technique—that is obvious enough—but in its main conception of tragedy. In *Elektra*, as in *The Ring*, the central idea is conflict, the clash of wills, the crown of victory. Siegfried overcomes the very gods, and his death is an apotheosis. Elektra, shattered at the moment of her triumph, achieves it nevertheless by her single-hearted overmastering force of purpose; her hatred is the shadow of her love and her death the price of her triumph.

This is the drama of a strong, vigorous, conquering race, a race which sets the highest value on human will and impulse, which is great in attack, great in enterprise, sweeping away all obstacles, bearing down all opposition. Its exact antithesis would be an art which is reserved and reticent, which expresses itself in faint colours and half-tones, which looks upon emphasis as a danger and upon exaggeration as a crime. In such a drama characterization is tempered and action held in check; there is no vehemence, no outcry; its qualities are gentleness of tone and an exquisite perfection of craftsmanship. The Wagnerian drama is like that of Shakespeare, a full-blooded, lusty giant; the other turns aside to the quieter, more restrained methods of Racine. Hence it is fitting that a countryman of Racine should have headed the most definite revolt against Wagner which the music of the theatre has witnessed in our time. As M. Rolland says:

'Pour nous, ce que nous avons le droit d'affirmer, c'est que le drame wagnérien ne répond en rien à l'esprit français—ni à son goût artistique, ni à sa conception du théâtre, ni à son tempérament musical. Il a pu s'imposer par conquête, il a pu—il peut encore—dominer l'esprit français par le droit du génie victorieux; rien ne peut faire qu'il ne soit et ne reste un étranger chez nous' [1].

And again later:

'On ne comprend que trop la révolte de l'esprit français, au nom du naturel et du goût, contre toutes les exagérations et les outrances de la passion—vraie ou fausse. *Pelléas et Mélisande* fut comme le manifeste de la révolte. Il réagit avec intransigeance contre toute emphase, contre tout excès, contre toute expression qui dépasse la pensée. Cette répugnance à l'égard des paroles et des sentiments exagérés va même jusqu'à la peur de livrer ce qu'on sent quand on est le plus ému. Les passions se disent à mi-voix.' [1]

There could be no better indication of the standpoint from which *Pelléas et Mélisande* is written. It is in no sense undramatic, but it is drama seen through a veil, now grey, now faintly iridescent, behind which the characters move almost as unconsciously as the figures of a dream. The plot unfolds in due sequence and proportion; there

[1] *Musiciens d'Aujourd'hui*, pp. 198, 199.

is not a line wasted or a gesture misplaced; but it is all very far away, and its remoteness gives it a subtle and indefinable charm. The music is soft and caressing; the voices rarely move beyond a narrow compass of notes; the orchestra is kept within a scheme of low values and delicate shades. Instead of the *Leitmotiv* we have fugitive points of colour, touching each sentiment as it passes; instead of Wagner's complex polyphony, we have harmonies which are chosen for their hue, not for their texture; instead of a declamation which enforces and emphasizes, there is a whisper which breathes into the poet's lines a more ethereal spirit of poetry.

Such an art cannot be wholly representative of the nation that has given us Berlioz and Hugo, the luxuriance of *Les Trois Mousquetaires* and the warm vivid colouring of *Carmen*. But it represents one side of the French artistic temper—its measure, its clarity, its chastity of honour which feels a strain like a wound. Debussy's music is too fragile for insistence; it is woven of dew and gossamer, the fabric of a vision which would be destroyed by a clumsy grasp. It is not made for heroism, for the stress of conflict and the large air and the epic majesty of outline; it has not the splendour of romance which will risk everything upon a single throw; it calls the drama back to the service of pure beauty, and in that service it finds its justification and its reward.

The problem, like all artistic problems, remains therefore unsolved; indeed, if it could be solved, it would prove itself valueless. All that we can do is to state for our own time the manner in which the great artists have approached it, and to appraise them by the canons which they have themselves supplied. It is clear that no common measure can at present be set to the ideals of Strauss and Debussy, to the music of *Pelléas* and that of *Elektra*; they stand poles asunder; they admit, so far as we can see, no point of union. But each has in its own way shown how the music-drama can enrich its theme; and it is possible that the ways may after all converge. The day may come when men will regard Strauss as we regard Gluck, and see in Debussy the lineal heir of Mozart. The day may come when a greater than either shall arise and show us that these ideals are not incompatible; that the poignancy of the one and the exquisiteness of the other may be resolved into a fuller and nobler art that shall absorb them both. The dream perhaps was realized by Greek Tragedy; it may be realized again.

CHURCH MUSIC[1]

WE may find some difficulty in realizing that a generation, so near to the present day that many of its members are still active, should ever have taken seriously Matthew Arnold's definition of religion as 'morality touched with emotion'. It labours, indeed, under two fatal defects. First that morality can be touched by many different kinds of emotion: by that which accompanies the sentiment of *noblesse oblige*, or of personal affection, or even of Shaftesbury's aesthetic pleasure; and to describe all these as religious is clearly untenable. The morality in short, which the definition implies, must be touched by one specific kind of emotion, and if we ask 'What kind?' the only answer that can be given is 'Religious'. A more fundamental fault is that it makes morality the substance of religion and emotion a qualifying characteristic or attribute. This, it may be contended, is a reversal of all natural order and proportion. Religion is not a kind of morality; it is a higher synthesis in which morality itself is taken up and absorbed; as the Idea of Good in Plato's *Republic* is the source not only of reality in the objective world but of true apprehension in the subjective. Nor, indeed, need we go so far back as Plato for our allegory. Christian at the outset of his Progress turned aside by ill-advice to seek in the town of Morality a relief from his burden, and the imminent disaster which ensued came near bringing his whole pilgrimage to an end.

Arnold's definition is in many ways characteristic of his time. It was a period of rather quiet and tepid reaction from the fervour of the Oxford movement. His own genius inclined to restraint, equanimity, the golden mean, and these, however useful they may be as guides for conduct, are not really relevant as criteria of religion. At the present time there has come, together with much liberty of criticism (partly, perhaps, because of this), a new outpouring of the essential spirit of worship; the fulfil-

[1] Delivered at the Church Congress at Southport on 7th October 1926.

ment of the Divine element in man by a more direct contact with its Divine source. At every period in religious history this has manifested itself to a greater or less degree; sometimes flowing in full measure, sometimes checked or distracted, but never entirely without witness. And as an example and sign of its influence at the present day I would ask your attention to the great and widespread welcome which has been accorded to Dr. Rudolph Otto's book, *The Idea of the Holy*. With only one aspect of that book have I to deal here and that rather by way of a confirming illustration than of the analysis of an essential argument. The sympathy with which the book has everywhere been received is, I think, a clear indication that it not only expresses but focuses a truth of religion which we all recognize as valid.

According to Dr. Otto the central fact of religious experience is our apprehension of what he calls the 'numinous'; that is the inherent Divinity whom we may clothe with all the noblest attributes that human imagination can devise, but to whom the sum total of all these attributes is at best and highest only the garment that we see Him by. Cudworth in a fine metaphor once figured the Divine nature as an infinite circle of which the centre was goodness, 'the rays and expanding plat thereof' wisdom, and the circumference power. Dr. Otto goes farther than this. Even the goodness of God in any sense in which we can understand goodness is but an attribute of an essential nature which is behind and beyond it; the nature which corresponds to the 'Ineffable' of the Greek mysteries, and which we can know, not in its own substance, but only its effect on ourselves.[1] This effect Dr. Otto describes as the 'tremendum mysterium', that sense of overwhelmingness with its correlative self-abasement which he illustrates from Abraham's plea with the Almighty (Genesis xviii. 27) and might equally have illustrated from many passages in Isaiah. If I might

[1] Suso calls it 'The height of the Divine Majesty, transcending substance'. See Otto, *op. cit.*, p. 109.

venture here to criticize him for a moment, I would suggest that he includes in this conception too personal an element of what he calls 'dread': an instinct of fear or distress which is, I think, not part of true religious emotion, but an alloy with which it is sometimes mixed. The difference between religion and superstition has always seemed to me that in the last assay religion is love without fear, and superstition fear without love. And if this be so, then our conception of the numinous is pure in proportion as it has freed itself from all elements of personal or self-centred misgiving. I would instance the climax in Newman's *Dream of Gerontius* as an example of what I mean. For dread, therefore, I would always substitute 'awe', which, indeed, Dr. Otto also emphasizes; that awe which, partly schematized, we feel in the presence of great genius, but which burns with purest flame in the act of Divine Worship: the sense that we are in the presence of something different in kind from our common human experience, but at the same time something the contemplation of which arouses us, not so much to the sense of our own shortcomings as to the love of its supreme power and goodness.

If this be so, it means that the act of worship carries us up through the empirical world, through even the scientific world of laws or the Platonic world of ideas, and brings us as near as human nature can be brought to the very centre and source of all things. And this makes it especially right and fitting that in the act of worship music should bear an essential part; that it should be one of the ways through which the mystical contact of the soul with God is embodied and expressed. I am in no way depreciating or decrying other forms of beauty in our liturgical use; on the contrary, I would have every avenue—sense, emotion and reason—exalted and ennobled by the skill of architect and painter and cunning workman, by all the beauty and majesty of words, by the dignity of befitting pageant and ceremonial, by every means which can attune the mind of the hearer and purify his soul for the Divine message. But apart from any question of comparison, which it is not, perhaps, necessary here to raise, I would plead that music has a positive and essential place in our worship, and that this entails as a necessary correlative great care in its selection and a great sense of responsibility in its use.

We may accept without cavil the view of the anthropologists that music originates from the heightened expression of feeling: at first, perhaps, only interjectional, then growing more systematized as the feeling itself grows more articulate, until it develops little by little into something that may definitely be described as song. Near the beginning of its history it was probably reinforced by that sheer delight in rhythmic movement which belongs to the childhood of the race as it does to the childhood of the individual; not yet so much for the purpose of co-ordinated effort, though this comes not long after, but rather as a natural ebullient expression of life and movement. Hence comes gesture, and, in very early stages of civilization, the dance. Again, if both these elements in music owe their origin to heightened emotion or to overflowing vitality, we should naturally expect that in any primitive religion where emotion is at its highest and vitality at its most intense, music should at once become the natural medium of worship; and this is abundantly corroborated by history. There is good evidence for holding that the dance was religious in origin. It appears in the Choric Hymns of the Greeks, it is even present in the Old Testament, and traces of its use may be found in the annals of the Christian Church. But far more important than this is the use of music as the natural vehicle of liturgical worship, not as some appanage added to the words by afterthought in order to give them further colour or beauty, but as the very soul and inspiration of the religious feeling which the words themselves can but partly and imperfectly embody. An interesting passage on this subject may be found in Sir James Frazer's book on *Adonis, Attis, Osiris* (pp. 46–7), which runs as follows:

Church Music

'In our own day a great religious writer,[1] himself deeply sensitive to the witchery of music, has said that musical notes, with all their power to fire the blood and melt the heart, cannot be mere empty sounds and nothing more; no, they have escaped from some higher sphere, they are outpourings of eternal harmony, the voice of angels, the Magnificat of saints. It is thus that the rude imaginings of primitive man are transfigured and his feeble lispings echoed with a rolling reverberation in the musical prose of Newman. Indeed, the influence of music on the development of religion is a subject which would repay a sympathetic study. For we cannot doubt that this, the most intimate and affecting af all the arts, has done much to create as well as to express the religious emotions, thus modifying more or less deeply the fabric of belief to which at first sight it seems only to minister. The musician has done his part as well as the prophet and the thinker in the making of religion. Every faith has its appropriate music, and the difference between the creeds might also be expressed in musical notation. The interval, for example, which divides the wild revels of Cybele from the stately ritual of the Catholic Church is measured by the gulf which severs the dissonant clash of cymbals and tambourines from the grave harmonies of Palestrina and Handel. A different spirit breathes in the difference of the music.'

It will be observed that Sir James Frazer, who holds no brief for religious music, assigns to it a naturally creative influence in the progress of religious worship; a far more important place than that of a mere accessory or accompaniment to an act of worship which could as well have proceeded without it. And I believe that music can accomplish this because, more intimately than any articulate speech, it can represent and express the numinous in human utterance. This claim may possibly be met at first with some challenge, even with some incredulity. That is because many of our people have still so little musical training that the art speaks to them in tones as remote and unintelligible as those of an unknown language. A man is still liable to be accused of paradox if he maintains that

[1] J. H. Newman, *Sermons preached before the University of Oxford*, No. xv, pp. 346 sq.

music is inherently significant, that its meaning is not less but more intense than that of articulate speech, that it penetrates still farther into essential truth, that it rises still higher towards essential goodness, that the beauty which, in some measure, all will agree to assign to it is not, as many people seem to think, a matter of sensuous gratification in which the higher elements of human nature have no place, but the very crown and climax of human nature, the nearest that it ever attains to the expression of the Divine.

And yet this is the place that has been accorded to it by almost all philosophic writers who have treated it with understanding. We know what importance Plato assigned in the *Republic* to the right ordering of musical speech; in the *Laws* he is still more detailed and still more emphatic. Aristotle's testimony, though perhaps fragmentary and imperfect, speaks with almost equal conviction. The place of music in medieval education was largely determined by its acknowledged importance in the services of the Church. Most clear of all is the witness of Schopenhauer, who, in the third book of *The World as Will and Idea*, assigns to music the highest place among all forms of human expression. The argument has been often quoted—it is familiar to most readers—and it may here be summarized for purposes of reference. The lowest form of human apprehension, says Schopenhauer, is that which regards only individual things and those only in relation to our own will, i.e. the use that we can make of them. We may imagine this kind of apprehension to be shared by the rest of the animal creation; it appears in man through the ordinary experience of everyday life where the phenomena by which we are surrounded are but so many instruments and tools for effecting our immediate purpose. Next above this comes the scientific apprehension in Bacon's sense of this term, i.e. the inductive power which correlates phenomena and sees them as instances of natural law. Higher still is the imagination of the poet culminating in tragic drama, which Schopenhauer regards as the supreme form of poetry, and dealing not with individual phenomena at all, not with photographic reproductions of particular people or particular scenes, but with the εἴδη of which individual phenomena are the transitory and imperfect embodiments. Hence, the test of great poetry, and even of great painting, is its universality. In proportion as it is a copy of anything in the phenomenal world; in such proportion it sinks below the level of true art and falls under the censure which, in the tenth book of the *Republic*, Plato unjustly passes upon poets at large. Last and highest comes music, which expresses not phenomena or scientific laws, or even Platonic ideas, but the direct emanation of that Divine Will of which the ideas themselves are objectifications. All the so-called representative arts, in short, draw their reality from the ideal world, music from a world which is beyond even the ideal. If this be true it shows the close connexion between music and the numinous element in religion. For this, although, like music, our apprehension of it may roughly be classed as emotional, is nevertheless such that, in Schleiermacher's words, it 'cannot occur except combined and penetrated with rational elements'. True religious emotion, indeed, like true music, is not sub-rational but super-rational. We do not abrogate our reason in its presence or resign ourselves to some languid or pleasurable stream of feeling: the whole nature is vividly and tensely alert in an ecstasy of which reason itself is the assistant and the handmaid. And herein we may find one ready and valuable criterion for distinguishing true music from false. If in our apprehension of it the reason plays no part, if we are not conscious of any fineness of style or of organic completeness of structure, but are merely tasting a series of unrelated and independent sounds, then that music for us has no meaning and no right to its title. To this point we shall return presently, as it is a subject bearing on music in religious worship. At present it is enough to say that enjoyment of music which is purely physical, however pure its pleasure, cannot afford a basis for any discussion of the place which the art should occupy in a service offered by us as an act of worship.

The Christian Church entered from the beginning on an inheritance of religious and liturgical music.[1] In the first instance this was naturally derived from Jewish origins, a fact of great importance in the development of Christian worship, since there can be no reasonable doubt that among all nations of antiquity the Jews were by far the greatest musicians. The Old Testament is full of evidence; not only as to common frequency of practice, but as to a very high level of attainment. In its earlier books we have such examples as the song of Miriam and the hymn of Deborah, examples of religious lyrics to which there are at the time no parallels elsewhere. From the later historical books onwards the testimony still further accumulates. We have the great Singing School established by David at Jerusalem (1 Chron. xxiii. 5, see also 1 Chron. xv and xvi) and its revival after the captivity by Nehemiah (Neh. xii. 27–9, 45–7); we have the Dedication Festival of Solomon's Temple (2 Chron. v. 12), which seems to have been on a more magnificent scale than any musical festival of our own time; the prophets are full of

[1] Among the most accessible authorities for the history of ecclesiastic and liturgical music the following may be mentioned:

(1) For the whole subject, Dr. Guido Adler's encyclopaedic *Handbuch der Musikgeschichte*; especially serviceable for the earlier periods, since these are comparatively little known.

(2) For Jewish music, the article by Rabbi F. L. Cohen on Music, and the article by Rabbi E. G. Hirsch on Psalms—both in the *Jewish Encyclopaedia*; the article on Music by J. G. Prince in the *Encyclopaedia Biblica*, and on Psalms by W. T. Davison in Hastings's *Dictionary of the Bible*.

(3) For the music of the Roman Catholic Church, G. Gietmann's article on Ecclesiastical Music, and the articles by Adrian Fortescue and J. Pohle on the Mass; all these in the *Catholic Encyclopaedia*.

(4) For the general development of Church Music in the West of Europe, Dickinson's *History of Music in the Western Church*.

(5) For points of special interest to English readers, Walker's *History of Music in England*, supplemented by the appropriate articles, biographical and otherwise, in Grove's *Dictionary*. The *Oxford History of Music* may also be consulted when required.

allusions to music—harvest songs, vintage songs, and the like—some of the melodies of which were apparently incorporated for liturgical use; above all, we have in the superscriptions of the Psalms a volume of musical information which, though not yet entirely and finally deciphered, is, even in our limited understanding of it, conclusive. Some of these superscriptions relate to the kind of accompaniment; a single string instrument in one case, in others a small band of strings or pipes, in others (this is probably the interpretation of 'maschil') a rich and elaborate accompaniment for a full orchestra. Other superscriptions deal with methods of performance, e.g. 'in the manner of Jeduthun'[1] (Ps. 77). But most significant of all are those which specify the melody sometimes of a folk-song, to which the psalm is to be sung; e.g. 'To Lilies', or 'To the Lily of Testimony', 'A Silent Dove afar off', 'Destroy not' (which is said to be a vintage song), and 'The Hind of the Morning'. It is clear that where directions are so precise and so varied there must have been a care both for composition and for performance, which implies deep reverence for liturgical music. The orchestras were of string instruments (lyres and harps), wind instruments (trumpets and various kinds of pipe), and percussion instruments, including cymbals, one of which seems to have been used by the conductor for keeping time. As a rule, the number seems to have been about 18 or 20—about the number which constituted Prince Esterhazy's 'Kapelle' when Haydn was his music-master. On special occasions they were very largely increased; we are told that at the dedication of the Temple there were no less than 120 trumpeters. It may be taken as certain that the Hebrews had no knowledge of harmony, that the wind doubled the singers in unison, and that the strings

[1] The exact meaning is under dispute. Jeduthun was the eponymous founder of one of the three gilds of Temple singers (see 1 Chron. xvi. 41, 42; xxv. 1, 6; 2 Chron. v. 12; Nehemiah xi. 17) and it may refer to some method taught by him. Or it may mean some favourite instrument or melody (see Hastings's *Dictionary*, s.v.).

were used for marking rhythmic figures. As to the nature of their music we have very little information, but the fact that they could regard melody as detachable from the words for which it was originally written is very significant, and the early example quoted by Rabbi Cohen in the pamphlet which he contributed to the Anglo-Jewish Exhibition is of totally different character from anything else in ancient music, the earliest-known stanza which we at the present day could recognize as melodic. Into this inheritance Christianity entered. On the night of Gethsemane our Lord Himself sang a hymn with His disciples, said by tradition to have been the Great Hallel, which consisted of Psalms 113–18; St. Paul expressly enjoins the use of 'Psalms and Hymns and spiritual songs' (Eph. v. 19, Col. iii. 16), and very probably quotes early examples of Christian Hymnody, e.g. the passage beginning 'Awake, thou that sleepest' (Eph. v. 14), and possibly the passages recorded in 1 Tim. iii. 16 and 1 Tim. vi. 15–16. It is hardly necessary to add the many references to singing which occur in the Apocalypse and which evidently refer to it as an established practice. Pliny (Epp. 96 and 97) reports to Trajan that the Christians of the early second century were singers of hymns. At some later time, which cannot be precisely determined, there flowed into this stream an important tributary from Greece. About Greek music as a matter of practice we know very little; the theorists who survive are too much concerned with grammatical niceties to be of much use, the philosophers deal mainly with its ethical and educational influence; but it is at any rate certain that the Christian Church took over from Greek usage the different Cithaeoedic modes, with, perhaps, the names of their constituent notes and tetrachords, and very likely some of that practice of subtle and exact declamation in which the essence of Greek music seems to have consisted. At any rate, whether from Greece or from Palestine, the tide of Christian music flowed from the east. The first hymn-writer of whom we have any clear knowledge was Ephraem the

Syrian, who greatly influenced the music of Eastern Europe. Two Church Councils, those of Laodicea and Chalcedon, both gave attention to Church music; indeed, the Council of Laodicea issued a most salutary prohibition against the employment of compositions by unqualified amateurs. The earliest liturgies were of eastern origin; St. Ambrose, the most eminent of the early western hymn-writers, established at Milan the practice of antiphonal singing 'secundum morem orientalium partium'. But if the east were leaders in this matter they were soon overtaken and even surpassed by the hymn-writers of the west and by the progressive regulation of the service under Popes Damasus, Gelasius and, perhaps, Gregory I. The place of the last among these has been somewhat obscured by the extravagant and untenable claims put forth on his behalf, but even if we cannot assign to him any specific addition or invention, there can be no doubt that it was by his authority and influence that the Roman use gradually superseded those of other contemporary churches. We in England have special reason to be grateful to him since the first seeds of our Church music were sown at his instigation by Augustine and Paulinus, who were followed in this matter by Wilfrid and Theodore of Tarsus, the first great musical educators of this country, and so through Aldhelm and Dunstan to the assured harvest of the early Middle Ages. So far as we can tell the practice of polyphonic singing, which entirely revolutionized music, had its origin in the Church service of our country; it may go back as far as Dunstan; it was certainly known in the twelfth century and prevalent in the thirteenth; and although it brought abuses and especially that obscuring of the sacred text which led Erasmus to censure it as a violation of St. Paul's rule against speaking in an unknown tongue, yet the splendour and beauty of sound which it received in such hands as that of the Netherlander Roland De Lattre, the Italian Palestrina, and the Englishmen Byrd and Tallis, have apparelled it in such celestial light as musical art had never known before. We are very near the presence of the numinous when we hear the 'Missa Papae Marcelli' or the Penitential Psalms of De Lattre, or Byrd's 'Justorum Animae' and 'Civitas Sancti Tui'.

It is no part of our purpose to follow the course of ecclesiastical music through all the centuries; the ground which it covered is very wide and details have been abundantly discussed elsewhere. It is a matter of common knowledge that in the seventeenth century there followed on the great period of pure polyphony a tendency towards secularization and dramatic expression affected almost equally by the forms of opera and oratorio, which first blossomed during its earlier years. The tide of lightness and frivolity in music was stemmed during the earlier years of the eighteenth century by Bach and Handel, during the later by Haydn, Mozart, and Beethoven; yet even the Masses of Haydn and Mozart have been brought under ecclesiastical censure. During the nineteenth and twentieth centuries we have been witnessing a curious development of idiom in music, very rapidly changing during its later years, and leaving our composers of to-day with a language almost as different from that of their predecessors as a Romance tongue from Latin. Mention, however, should specially be made of an unduly neglected chapter in ecclesiastic music; that provided by the composers of Spain and especially the writing of what was called the Valencian School. These are works of astonishing purity and dignity, almost entirely untouched by the course of secular events and maintaining even in the nineteenth century a sort of serene austerity so well proportioned that it could dispense with ornament, so solidly built that it offered no crevice for decay; a monument which we seem to have disregarded for no better reason than that it stands beyond the Pyrenees.

But it may be worth while briefly to trace the course of the history in our own country, since Church music was our chief means of expression when, as musicians, we stood in the forefront of Europe. Even when we forgot our traditions and forfeited our inheritance, there was always a little thread of anthem or canticle to prevent the record from being entirely broken. Ousted successively from every other form of composition, English music at its darkest period could take sanctuary in the Church.

In the fifteenth century John Dunstable was by all acknowledgement the first composer in Europe. He seems to have lived much abroad, and among his immediate pupils and successors the greatest were the founders of the Flemish School—Dufay, Binchois, and others. At the same time we have, perhaps, a little too easily accepted the sardonic criticism of Johannes Tinctor, the Fleming, that the English followers of Dunstable were mere imitators and that the Flemings alone carried on his work with original vitality and intelligence. The rediscovery of the Old Hall MS. containing the compositions of King Henry VI and his contemporaries has gone some way to modify this judgement; indeed, Henry VI has some claim for the highest place among royal composers. It is noticeable, by the way, through what a long period English music was aided by royal protection: Henry V sent for his choir to Rouen; Henry VI composed motets for the service at Windsor; Richard III, whose true character Sir Clements Markham has apparently revealed to us, reorganized and endowed the Chapel Royal; Henry VIII was a celebrated musician, and so were at least two of his children. It was not until the time of James I that the royal favour was partially withdrawn, and even so it came back in full measure after the Restoration. Nor should we forget that it was George I who brought Handel to England, and that George III held him in very high honour and esteem.

At any rate, if Tinctor's reproach was ever justified, the occasion of it passed at the beginning of the sixteenth century. With Taverner and Shepherd, Tye and White, Tallis and Byrd and Orlando Gibbons, England produced a century of ecclesiastical music which is still one of the chief glories of our annals. At the death of Gibbons in 1625 began a period of decadence, stayed for a time by the genius of Purcell, but Purcell died when he was 37, and from his time to the middle of the nineteenth century England produced no composer to whom the word genius could rightly be applied. Before his influence could establish a school, Handel came over and at his approach our native music made way. Some historians claim Handel as our own, and no doubt this country made him welcome and he lived among us for over forty years, but we can no more claim Handel than the French can claim Lully. We were the land of his choice and adoption, ours was not the pit from which he was digged. However, during this dark period we still kept a slender light burning before the altar. Greene, Handel's contemporary, had genuine talent, and at least one of his anthems rises to a high level of stateliness and dignity; Battishill wrote a few fine things and would have written more had he not been broken-hearted by a bereavement; the elder Wesley, to whom chiefly we owe the study of Bach in England, produced in his fitful and eccentric life at least two masterpieces; Attwood carried on the tradition of Mozart, and Walmisley that of Attwood; Sebastian Wesley, unhappily influenced at times by the fashion for Spohr, had a really original gift and a limpid stream of pure and expressive melody. With his death in 1876, it may be said that the old order passed away and the renaissance of British music began with the almost simultaneous arrival of Parry and Stanford. Since then the line has been continued by Elgar and Vaughan Williams and Holst, who are now exchanging the ranks of the Hastati for those of the Principes. Among the younger men the attractions of Church music are for the moment less potent than those of some other forms, but there are some whom we still expect to come to us with gifts in their hands.

It will be observed that in this brief historical sketch mention has occasionally been made of errors or frivolities by which the natural course of Church music has been either misled or demoralized. It may, perhaps, be asked how this is compatible with the statement that music represents the numinous in human speech and that it is, therefore, correlative with the numinous in worship. The answer to this may be found in the Preface on the Service of the Church which stands at the beginning of our Book of Common Prayer: 'There was never anything by the wit of man so well devised or so sure established which in continuance of time hath not been corrupted.' Music is no more immune from corruption than any other form of expression, even religion itself, which has to pass through the channels of an imperfect humanity. Indeed, we may say that music is in the greater danger because of the extraordinary apathy and carelessness with which most people regard it. I believe that when their attention is engaged all persons prefer good music to bad, noble to ignoble, but there is, I think, no corner in the field of human civilization in which weeds have been allowed to grow with so little supervision. The result is that some error creeps in almost unperceived, it gains ground because no one cares to eradicate it, and by the time its intrusion is noticed it has taken such a flourishing root that, like a mandrake, it cannot be pulled up without tears. One instance of this is the abuse of medieval polyphony which we have already noticed: parts interwoven until the phrase was no longer intelligible, syllables protracted until the word was no longer articulate, secular melodies used as the staple of liturgical song. Another was the tendency to theatricalism which manifested itself among the lesser composers in the late seventeenth and early eighteenth centuries, and which sprang from a desire to make the details of music expressive without a compensating grasp of its general structure. Another specially prevalent some half-century ago was the tendency to softness and sentimentalism, which meant really the use of cheap and shallow formulae which, even if they had done some little service in better hands, were quite inadequate for the purpose for which they were intended. Others, again, sprang from mere ignorance and want of skill; the admission into the Church service of work which, even if sincere in its intention, was too clumsy and illiterate to deserve a place, and which, I am afraid, was very often a mere outburst of that small personal vanity which so very frequently goes with incompetence. The prohibition of the Council of Laodicea ought to be repeated and extended in each generation.

There is here no need for apportioning any blame or censure. It is natural that men in the first flush of a new technique or a new medium should so misinterpret their functions as to make ingenuity an end in itself. It is not less natural that new forms or idioms of expression should, at the moment when they appear, attract an undue amount of attention by their very novelty; it requires a certain period of sifting before their places can be determined. Even the weaklings and the sentimentalists may in their shallow measure be endeavouring to say something which they have genuinely at heart. As a rule, Church music, even at its least worthy, has been free from that commercialism which is the chief enemy of art and literature. But when all this has been granted to the full we should still be left with an unflinching resolve not to admit to our Church services any kind or example of music which falls short of the highest standard that it can attain.

And this for two plain reasons. First, that when we call our act of worship a service we are dedicating it as an offering to God, and before His Altar we have no right to present anything that is blemished. And secondly, our act of worship brings into the Divine Presence the soul of the worshipper, which must, therefore, be purified and uplifted to the utmost of its spiritual capacity in order that it may gain the strengthening and refreshing which no unworthy recipient has a right to ask. And if it be argued that the recipient must in all cases be unworthy and that, therefore, any such attempt is foredoomed to failure, the answer is that this is a counsel of despair which would equally justify the abrogation of all standards in every other part of the act of worship. But, indeed, as a matter of principle we can hardly doubt that there is here a general agreement. It is needless to labour the point that when we attend the Supper of the Great King we must wear our wedding garment.

This conclusion translated into practice means the application of a critical standard and the rigorous exclusion of all that falls below it. There follows the inevitable question how and by whom this standard is to be applied, and at what point our line is to be drawn. On this point I would venture to speak with entire frankness. The standard should be applied by a council of those best fitted to speak in the name of Church music, whether from the side of the ministry or from the side of musical art or from those, of whom we have not a few in England, who can hold an authoritative balance between them; and the one general instruction under which such a council should act should be, 'When in doubt exclude.' Nothing, in short, should be admitted to the canon of Church music which is not accepted as deserving of its place by a consensus of the liberal and trained judgement of those best fitted to pronounce. A corpus of such music could easily be prepared; some of the work has already been done in various parts of the field; it could, of course, be left open so that further additions might be made from time to time as opportunity arose. It would represent a monument of beauty and dignity and reverence as great in its way as the windows of York or the fabric of Westminster.

Here some objections should be considered. First, that the exclusion of some of the works that have won their way into popular favour would give offence and would be met by resentment and alienation. I do not believe that this objection is of great moment. Almost all the Church music to which it applies was written in one generation by insufficiently qualified composers; it is holding its place merely by use and wont; it could be gradually and imperceptibly dropped out of use with little or no danger of offending the consciences of the congregation. I do not believe that people prefer bad music to good; I do believe, and am indeed convinced by some half-century of experience, that a vast number of people adopt no criteria of excellence at all, that on the whole they prefer any music which is rapid in movement and brief in duration, and that apart from this they do not really distinguish between one idiom and another.

It may be, therefore, that too much attention has been paid to the possible discontent of those who have not really shown any very accurate powers of discrimination. The bad music of a hundred years ago, when, for instance, a parody of 'Rule, Britannia' was sung as a hymn, is now merely a matter of historic or antiquarian interest; practically it has become obsolete. The rapid advance in the understanding of music which has spread through this country in the last few years is far outstripping the bad music of my own childhood; there is an increasing number of people who are offended by what is trivial or false or irreverent. It may, indeed, be urged that of this fact more account might justly be taken. We have frequently heard the plea that music of a quality acknowledged to be inferior should retain its place because 'people like it'; because it strikes some responsive chord of pleasure or association in some section of the worshippers. But we do not hear so much of the steadily increasing number to whom these trivialities give real pain, who are distracted by them from the true objects of worship, who are set in an atmosphere in which their souls cannot breathe freely and naturally, who—to use a more obvious metaphor—are jangled out of tune with the key of worship. It implies, surely, some ill-adjustment of the balance if we are to regard those who are careless or indifferent and to leave on one side those to whom the subject is of vital importance. Part of the reason for this has already been indicated: the fact that many people have never come to the realization that music can be significant and that its significance may cover the whole range from empty and trivial folly to the highest expression of the spirit of man. Those who approach the question from this standpoint are naturally incredulous or impatient when they hear that bad music can be regarded as a cause of offence. People are very apt to regard as insincere any expression of feeling which they do not share themselves, or if not insincere at any rate a hyper-sensitiveness which could be cured by charity and forbearance. With this view I venture entirely to disagree. Bad worship, of whatever kind, has no more place in the House of the Lord than the money-changers had in the Temple; to leave it in possession is not charity but *incuria*.

One has only to consider how such a plea would be received on any other similar question. One cannot imagine an unauthorized amateur being given a free hand to decorate the Church walls; one cannot imagine the liturgy or the lessons replaced at random by some modern and unworthy substitute. Apparently it is only in the music that the priesthood is to be set aside and the preaching of Korah, Dathan, and Abiram accepted as authoritative.

In the best Church music can be found a response for every mood which may legitimately be admitted into worship at all: moods of praise and prayer, of penitence and exaltation, of the joy of God's House and the sacramental communion of His Presence. Its appeal is, in its place, universal, for there is no noble aspect of human nature which it does not touch and no ignoble aspect which it needs to consider. To suppose that it is necessarily intricate, or elaborate—or cold and austere—or beset with difficulties—or in any way unapproachable to the plain man—all this rests on a misunderstanding of its nature and its function. It is the purest expression of that state of the soul which shows itself in the act of worship, and as such it belongs to all to whom that act is a reality.

No doubt the application of this standard would discontinue a vast proportion of the music which has actually been written for use in Church services. That is in itself desirable; it is, indeed, one of the principal ends which reformers should have in view. In every generation false prophets have made their voices heard and the populace has accepted their message with little demur. At present we have a treasure-house into which, by historic accident, a great deal of dross has been allowed to accumulate, but which, nevertheless, contains a full abundance of pure gold. It is good that we should make a gradual clearance, discarding all that is not of the highest value and bringing back all that is into use and currency. That there is abundance lying ready to our hand is plain matter of fact; there is not the least need that any second-rate work should ever be given, for there is enough first-rate to fill our service books by the year together. And as it can respond to every mood of worship so it can present in performance every degree of difficulty from the simplest onwards. Nothing can be farther from the truth than the belief that all good music needs costly resources and elaborately trained proficiency. The hymns in the village Church, which every member of the congregation can sing, may represent within their range as high a standard of composition as the anthems and canticles which are more suited to Abbey and Cathedral. It is not a distinction between the kinds of music with which we are here concerned, but an insistence that all should be in the highest degree good of its kind. Again, I have heard men object that the imposition of a standard would introduce some element of coercion and restraint by which the freedom of worship would be impaired and that this would be done in accordance with some arbitrary criteria which are set on no more stable foundation than individual taste. With the latter half of this objection I would venture once more to express my total disagreement. The matter is not one of fluctuating taste, but of the application of principles which, for acceptance, need only to be stated. Whether they are applicable in a given instance is a matter not for dogmatic assertion but for discussion and debate. In this form of discussion I have been engaged for many years and I have never yet found a case in which we could not reach agreement so soon as the principles were explained and their applicability indicated. It is not, let me repeat, a question of opposing camps or of differences of standpoint; the distinction is between those who have thought about the matter and those who have taken it for granted. And if this be so the first half of the objection falls to the ground; there can be no talk of coercion where all may be convinced. Whether or not it is advisable that there should be a single use for the whole English Church is a matter of discipline and organization on which I have no right to express an opinion, though here, again, I might commend to my hearers the Preface on Services at the beginning of the English Prayer Book. But whether the uses be one or many, whether they be determined by central authority or gradually converge from a number of different practices, there is no reason why they should not consist exclusively of the best and noblest work. In either case the voice of praise and prayer may speak with pure accents and inspired lips, and may to the utmost of its capacity 'render unto God the things that are God's'.

One final word. Dr. Otto, in the work to which I have so often alluded, devotes one appendix to the question of silent worship and one most interesting passage (page 72) to the limitations of music. I am not here concerned to deny that there are moments of silent communion, that these are, perhaps, the most intimate of all, where no articulate expression of any kind is possible, where there is hardly even consciousness, but something like the Nirvana which one of its votaries has described as 'bliss unspeakable'. At such a time any form of utterance may break the spell and distract the attention. Dr. Otto instances the Sanctus of Bach's B minor Mass, which is a magnificent conception of its theme as regarded from outside. As we hear it we look upwards from the earth and see the circling of an infinite heavenly host, where the morning stars sing together and the sons of God shout for joy; but it is a conception of the Sanctus suitable rather for the concert-room than for the Church. It would have been well had Dr. Otto contrasted the corresponding movement of Beethoven's great *Missa Solennis* and especially its opening, where the sound, perfectly simple and almost at lowest degree of audibility, is informed with a spiritual meaning which we seem to feel at the very centre of our soul.

To discuss this matter farther would carry me beyond the limit of my theme. All I am here concerned to maintain is that so far as utterance and expression of any kind are possible so they are at their noblest when they are heightened and transfigured by musical art. Too long have we regarded it as something external to the development of the human spirit, as some appanage or adornment or luxury which can be adopted without ennoblement or discarded without essential loss. It is something far more intimate than this. It is at the very centre and essence of our being: through it we can express thoughts that lie too deep not only for tears but for utterance; through it we can be caught up into the Divine Presence and hear those things that, because they are unspeakable, are higher and more holy than the range of any speech.

THE PLACE OF BEAUTY IN WORSHIP[1]

HEINE tells us a story of the monks of Basle who walked one evening in their monastery garden and heard a nightingale sing with such ravishing sweetness that they exorcised it. I am not concerned to inquire into the historical accuracy of this story: in either case it contains a deep spiritual truth. I can remember in my younger days men and women of the highest possible integrity to whom religion was not only a reality but a supreme reality, the touchstone by which all else in life was tested, but who would also have exorcised the nightingale. There was in those days a real fear, not perhaps prevalent, but existent, that beauty was dangerous to religion; that it was a disturbing, disquieting influence against which the active devotion of the soul would do well to protect itself. I am speaking here to-day because I believe this view to be entirely opposed to the truth: not its contradictory, as the logicians say, but its diametric contrary. In other words, I hold not only that beauty rightly appreciated brings no harm and no danger to religion: I believe that it brings positive benefit, and especially, perhaps, to the act of worship.

The field of inquiry is obscured by two errors, both really irrelevant and both in need of removal. The first is that beauty in worship has to do with some religious party or school, that it carries special doctrinal significance and that it should, therefore, be resisted by those to whom the particular doctrine is not acceptable. A striking instance occurred in the seventeenth century. It is untrue to say that the Puritans were opposed to music—Cromwell and Milton are sufficient instances to the contrary—but they were not unnaturally averse to the old elaborate Church music which they regarded as Roman, as they were to certain forms of Church decoration which they regarded as idolatrous. But this was only to look at the matter in a false perspective. Music is so universal a language that

[1] Delivered at the Manchester Diocesan Conference, November 1927.

we cannot tie it down to any narrow doctrinal significance, and, indeed, it would be specially difficult to particularize its ecclesiastical colour in England, where the stream has been fed by the Roman hymn, the Lutheran choral, and the Genevan psalm. One almost grotesque instance of this partisanship is the belief that some doctrinal significance attaches to the organ as such. I think that I have traced this to an order issued in Scotland about the middle of the sixteenth century which, for fear of Roman influence, prohibited what it called 'curious singing with organs', and thereby cut down to the roots a very promising growth of Scottish Church music. At any rate, this belief survived in the northern part of this country up till quite recent times, and has, indeed, not yet altogether passed away. I remember hearing of an old Scots woman brought up in the strictest traditions of the Faith, who was induced once to visit a church where there was a full choral service with organ accompaniment. When she was asked afterwards what had been her impression, she answered that 'it was mair like Heeven than airth; but, eh, Sirs, what an awfu' way of spending the Sabbath'.

As this error is largely historical, so the other is largely philological. Early in the eighteenth century—somewhere among the seventeen-thirties—a German philosopher named Baumgarten wrote a treatise on the study of beauty and called it by the extremely unfortunate name of 'Aesthetica', as though the whole thing were a matter of sense perception. The subject was new, the treatise attracted a good deal of attention, with the deplorable result that the study of one of the most valuable things in human life is known by a name which degrades it to the lower levels of human nature. Imagine Plato, with his gradual ascent from physical beauty to beauty of soul, and thence up to the beauty of holiness itself, Plato with his supreme Divine Triad of truth, beauty and goodness, confronted with the statement that beauty was entirely a matter of sense perception. Imagine Aristotle confronted with the same proposition: Aristotle, who held that the vital nerve of art was truth and who meant by the aesthetic life that sensuous existence which, as he says, we share with horse and dog and every animal. You may remember a passage in the *Ethics* where he points out that the pleasure which the lion derives from the voice of the ox is not musical, but anticipatory. But, indeed, we have no need of examples, ancient or modern. It is the unfortunate use of the term 'aesthetic' which has really poisoned the wells of judgement. It has encouraged an entirely false impression of the nature of beauty and of the faculties by which beauty is appreciated. It is responsible amongst other things for the remarkable term 'aesthete', which was prevalent in the Oxford of my young days, and which designated a group of young gentlemen in revolt who held that the enjoyment of art should be accepted as a substitute for moral restraint.

Now I am convinced that all artistic delight, and that of music perhaps more than any other, is not of the senses except so far as they are transmitting agents, but of the soul itself: that it takes us behind and above our ordinary world of work-a-day experience and carries us into a region where we can breathe a purer air and devote ourselves to a nobler contemplation.

The Bible is saturated with the love of beauty. The Israelites were no doubt debarred, as they thought, by the second commandment from representations of the human form; they appear to have had a comparatively slight and rudimentary sense of architecture, but they had the keenest delight in beauty of colour. You see it from the hangings of the Tabernacle to the foundations of the new Jerusalem. They were greatly sensitive to the splendour of gold and silver and precious stones, those delights of the eye which are so often used as measures of value. It is inconceivable that their prophetic literature did not make a great deal of its appeal through the sonorous eloquence of its poetry; and for climax we may remember that the Jews were beyond comparison the most musical among all the races of antiquity. You in Manchester have a Musical College of which you are justly proud and the achievements of which are known throughout the country. It would fill but a small place in David's Musical School with its four thousand singing students, and its orchestra for festival days of one hundred and twenty. The Psalms are all full of music: many of them introduced by directions which indicate sometimes the style in which the Psalm is to be sung, sometimes the special character of the accompaniment, sometimes, and this is the most interesting of all, the tune to which the words of the Psalm are to be set. In a word, those who believe that beauty has a real place in worship will find in the Bible abundant and continuous corroboration. 'He hath made everything delightful in its order,' says the writer of Ecclesiastes [1]; and then, speaking of God's gift of beauty to man, he closes his sentence with the wonderful words, 'He hath set eternity in their hearts'. I want no better commendation of beauty than this: that it sets eternity in our hearts.

No doubt there are bad forms of music and bad forms of decoration and these may very well be either distracting or demoralizing, but no more argument is to be found in this than that every human institution or pursuit is liable to corruption, and that the highest and noblest are perhaps more liable than others. The obvious answer is that we should discard corruptions, that we should throw them on one side and concentrate our minds on the abundant store of what is best.

But it is not against hostility that I am specially pleading to-day. That feeling is, I think, diminishing through natural causes as our people come more and more to take a sane and balanced view of life and its resources. A far more insidious enemy and one far more prevalent among us, is *incuria*, that indifference which says it is 'only the music' or 'only the decoration'. Experience is coming to show us more and more that the music and the decoration are very important factors in determining both the

[1] Eccles. iii. 11 (R.V.). I take the marginal reading.

atmosphere of the service and the attitude of the worshipper. I was talking the other day to a clergyman who has the privilege of serving a very beautiful Cathedral. He is himself highly appreciative of beauty both pictorial and musical, and he told me of some special services which he is arranging for people who are not very keen churchgoers, in which he begins with a few moments' silence so that the congregation can drink in the architectural loveliness of the place; that two or three times during the service this interval of silence is repeated; and that every part of the service is as worthy as first-rate tunes and noble and reverent utterance can make it. Why cannot this be done everywhere in due measure and proportion? One does not require a superb building or an elaborate choir; the highest beauty is often the beauty of simplicity: what we want is not to add on expensive devices or decorations, but more often to clear away those which are bad. How many of our great churches and cathedrals, for example, which are monuments of architectural strength and sublimity, are spoilt, at any rate in part, by bad stained glass? How often is a service at which the words come to us charged with the full majesty of our Bible and our Prayer Book often wholly ruined by the interpolation of dull or tawdry or sentimental melodies? It is not so much that we wish to tax the resources of the Church for new discoveries or new inventions, but rather to make a reverent selection from among those that we have. Why is it a commonplace jest that people dislike church-going? Why is it the obvious desire of almost every congregation to come as late as possible and to fly as if the place was on fire the moment after the Benediction? Why, in one word, are the clergy still obliged to advocate church-going as a duty when they ought to be holding it out as a privilege? If the services were such as to attune the soul to worship the difficulty would be not to induce people to come to church but to keep them away. Think especially of the opening of our Church services: the perfunctory voluntary played with one eye on the vestry door, stopping in the middle of a phrase when the Vicar reaches the reading-desk, and in many places scarred across and across with the jangling discord of the late-comers' bell. It would only take three or four minutes to play a choral prelude by Bach or Brahms or Parry which would set the whole congregation in a right frame of mind; and if the need of hurry is so urgent that we cannot afford three or four minutes, then let us at least have silence. Remember that this is not a matter of expensive choirs and elaborate ritual. Some of the most beautiful services I have ever attended have been in village churches where there were nothing but chants and hymns sung by the village choir. No doubt the voices were rough and untrained, but everything that they sang was good of its kind, and that outweighs all elaboration of purpose. It does not cost any more to sing 'Now thank we all our God' than to sing the most sentimental hymn-tune that ever strayed into Church by mistake; and it makes a great deal of difference to the congregation which of these you select.

I would urge particular care in the selection of the hymns. In Churches where the choir is adequate and the opportunities for training are sufficient, I would certainly allow a periodic display of an anthem or the like; but it is in the hymns that the music of the Church is most fully and corporately expressed. The congregation are no longer listeners (though to listen to beautiful music is in itself an inspiration) but actual participators, and they are, I believe, very closely influenced by what they sing.

May I remind you that the Council of Laodicea, among many other wise enactments, ordered that no hymns were to be permitted in church which were not made by fully authorized writers and composers? There was to be no place then, as there is far too much now, for the work of the untrained, irresponsible amateur. Indeed, the Council designated such efforts by a special term of dispraise, calling them 'psalmoi idiotikoi', a phrase of which I will not venture on a translation.

Finally, I would add a word of answer to those who hold

that all questions of a standard of beauty and of its applicability to religious worship are mere matters of personal taste and that one taste is as worthy of consideration as another. *De gustibus non disputandum*, they say, forgetting that the world has continuously been disputing on matters of taste for some two thousand five hundred years. But in spite of the conflict there have gradually emerged certain principles which seem to be founded partly in human nature and partly in the qualities of the medium employed, and which stand firm amid all the ebb and flow of schools and fashions. As I have said before, it is not conflict, but indifference that we have most to fear: that easy-going slackness which allows bad work in our fabrics and in our services, not because it prefers it or because it could defend it if pressed, but because it pays so little regard that it will not take the trouble to form a judgement. I feel certain that this is a very common diagnosis and I believe that it is symptomatic of a very dangerous disease.

During the last fifty years the people of England have been steadily educating themselves to the understanding of beauty and to the higher and purer enjoyment which comes with understanding. Clergy who say that the congregation does not really distinguish are, I believe, making a mistake, the range of which is steadily widening. Those who say that tawdry ornament and trivial tune are attractive and so bring worshippers into the fold may be seriously asked to contemplate how many they are keeping away. And, what is more important than any of these, our Churches are built to the glory of God, and our services are held in His honour. It is God who has made beauty for us and who, in making it, has put eternity into our hearts. Can we doubt that it is our duty in this, as in all other matters, to give Him what is His own?

A COMPARISON OF POETRY AND MUSIC[1]

I HAVE chosen this subject for the reason which animated the Cambridge apprentice in Moore's Diary. Anxious to enlarge his mental horizon he set himself, in such time as he could spare, to attend the public lectures of the University, beginning with those of the Professor of Greek. When he was asked why he had made this choice he replied that in other subjects, such as History or Modern Literature, he might be at a disadvantage confronted with men of greater knowledge than his own: 'Here, however,' he added, with a glance round which included the lecturer, 'here, I presume that we are all much on the same level.' That is how I feel this afternoon. I am certain that there are some very interesting things to be said about the comparison of music and poetry; about the resemblances and diversities of their appeal; but I do not know what they are: I am still groping after them. So I am here not to prescribe, but to suggest, not to indicate, but to search, and since it takes two to speak the truth, the greater part of that function will be yours.

'If music and sweet poetry agree,' says Richard Barnfield, and never doubts that they do—

> As they must needs, the sister and the brother—

laying a sure foundation for that comparison between Dowland and Spenser which to many of us at the present day sounds so remote and unfamiliar:

> One god is god of both, as poets feign:

not, you will observe, 'as musicians feign': it is from the side of poetry that the welcome is offered. And a generation later we find John Milton, the poet, writing to his father, John Milton, the madrigalist:

> Nunc tibi quid mirum si me genuisse poetam
> Contigerit, charo si tam prope sanguine juncti,
> Cognatas artes, studiumque adfine sequamur?

[1] The Henry Sidgwick Lecture, Newnham College, Cambridge, 1925. Reprinted by kind permission of the Cambridge University Press.

A Comparison of Poetry and Music

Ipse volens Phoebus se dispertire duobus,
Altera dona mihi dedit, altera dona parenti:
Dividuumque Deum genitorque puerque tenemus.

'Cognatas artes'—'sphere-born harmonious sisters, voice and verse'. Nor should we feel any surprise that Milton writes in this manner. Of all poets up to our present Laureate he is the one whose understanding of music is most complete and accurate: from the days of his boyhood, when he commemorates Adrian Batten's playing at St. Paul's, to the days of his old age when he found in the organ his chief solace and delight, he dwelt in the inner courts of musical art, his gift of clear and exact presentation never fails him even in this most elusive of subjects.[1] For two centuries, indeed, our music and our poetry were on terms of high mutual regard. Dryden, who comes at the end of the period, when the estrangement was already beginning, paid Purcell a royal compliment in the preface to *Amphitryon*, collaborated with him over *King Arthur*, and wrote in praise of music the ode which, with his accustomed candour, he described as 'the best that ever was or will be in the English language'. Yet as we read *Alexander's Feast* our misgivings begin: music is treated only for its emotional effect, its power of rousing or assuaging passion: there is too much about Jove and Bacchus and the Trojan ghosts and the burning of the palace: the poet stands outside his theme, not as Milton does at its very heart and centre. And in the next generation the breach widened. With the exception of Arbuthnot our Annians were either indifferent to music or antagonistic: Pope, who actively disliked it, wrote his *Ode on St. Cecilia's Day* with manifest reluctance; and, though we may admire the smoothness of its phrase and the skill of its versification, we must remember that it was held of little account in its own time, and that it remained for a hundred and fifty years an unlit lantern until it was illuminated at last by the genius of Sir Hubert Parry.

1 See, for instance, his description of a fugue, *Paradise Lost*, xi, 561–3. It is, so far as I know, the best in all literature.

So through the eighteenth and early nineteenth centuries the estrangement continued. Music fades away from the works of our English poets: Wordsworth, Coleridge, Southey, are outside its influence; Shelley 'pants for the music which is divine' but shows no comprehension of it; Byron has little to show except the songs that he wrote for Braham; Keats has virtually nothing. Nor was France any the more sympathetic. No doubt it made a political quarrel out of the 'Guerre des Bouffons', but there were too many competing issues for this to count as evidence: Rousseau had some music in him, but Voltaire had none, nor had Chénier: Victor Hugo's one tribute to Beethoven [1] is not more helpful than Gautier's famous definition of music as 'le plus désagréable de tous les sons'.

But the most salient instance is yet to relate. For nearly sixty years Goethe may almost be said to have represented the mind of Germany. During the period of its greatest intellectual activity he led nearly every advance: poetry, drama, fiction; the criticism of literature, of pictorial art, of architecture; optics, metaphysics, biology, studies of social conditions in his own and other countries; it would seem at first sight as if there were no topic in the whole range of human intelligence to which he did not offer welcome and hospitality. When he was born J. S. Bach was still alive: before he died Schumann had begun the draft of his first symphony. Within his lifetime falls the entire work of Haydn, Mozart, Beethoven, Schubert, Weber. What, we may ask, has the greatest of Germans to say about the greatest of German arts?

We are told that he was once moved by *Zauberflöte* and conceived for a moment the idea of supplying it with a sequel; but the interest, to whatever cause attributable, was no more than a wave on the surface. We are told that in his old age he petted the young Mendelssohn, who

[1] Note to *Les Châtiments*. The 'admirable musique de Beethoven' there quoted is a mutilated version of a poor melody, very doubtfully attributed to Beethoven and quite unworthy of him.

must have been an extremely attractive child, but the two little poems which he exchanged for a dedication are among the weakest and least inspired of all his writings. Beethoven, with whom he was on terms of personal acquaintanceship, begged him to obtain from Karl August a subscription towards the printing of the *Missa Solennis*: Goethe refused. Schubert, the noblest of all his interpreters in music, sent him the manuscript of *Erlkönig*. Goethe returned no answer. And for the rest, though I speak under correction, I can recall no allusions to music in all that vast field of knowledge and research, except a perfunctory paragraph in the *Annalen*, mentioning some concerts in his house, a note in *Ferneres über Kunst* about the founding of a new Conservatorium, and a few sentences of operatic criticism in which he joins together the names of Mozart and Cimarosa.

For the origin and progress of this gradual alienation one historical reason may be suggested, of which both the obverse and the reverse appear equally significant. In the late sixteenth and early seventeenth centuries, the time of our madrigalists and song-writers, the vast preponderance of music was vocal and the poet looked to it as the natural comrade and illustration of his own art. Shakespeare combines with Morley, Lawes with Milton: the sphere-born harmonious sisters are singing, as Helena says, 'both in one key'. But by the middle of the eighteenth century the current vocal form, outside the services of the Church, was the conventional Italian Opera which, during those years, touched its lowest depth of degradation. Written at breakneck speed, on a rigid and invariable plan, intended only for an evening's entertainment before an audience listless or preoccupied, with no chance of being printed, no hope of appealing to a wider public and no prospect even of intelligent criticism, it set up a monument of folly from which literature very naturally turned in disdain. At the beginning of this period Addison complains that 'music renders us incapable of hearing sense': towards its end Miss Austen, who in *Persuasion* devotes a chapter to a concert without mentioning the music, lays it down as unreasonable to look for the meaning of an Italian love-song. At the same time the more serious composers were beginning to discover and administer an autonomous kingdom of their own—the kingdom of suite and partita, of sonata and quartet, of concerto and symphony, into which the collaboration of the poet was not invited. It is intelligible, it is almost inevitable, that the poet should look upon this new art with impatience: with the laws of its structure he was not conversant, the sound of its voice was pleasant but the speech was inarticulate: it seemed to be always hovering on the edge of a thought which as constantly melted away in the utterance. To such a man, 'Sonate, que veux tu?' is a perfectly natural question, and though we may shelter ourselves for a moment behind the famous mathematician who, after seeing a play of Racine, asked, 'Et qu'est-ce que cela prouve?' yet we feel that the poet's question is relevant and that it must be answered. What is the significance of music and how is it related to the significance of poetry?

And first we may note that these two arts have a common ground which places them at once in direct antithesis to painting and sculpture and architectural design. They are essentially temporal arts, depending for their apprehension on a fixed and determinate succession. We may see the composition of a picture as a whole: we can study its detail from right to left or from left to right, upwards or downwards, as we choose. But with a melody or a sentence all this is impossible: the experience is not complete, is not even fully intelligible, until the last word or the last note, and the order of its recurrence is irreversible. Take the most familiar line of Shakespeare, the most familiar tune of Handel, and try to repeat it backwards: you cannot do so, and it would have no meaning if you did. This implies a resemblance between these arts the importance of which cannot be over-estimated—that they are both continually throwing your attention forward, that at each moment in their course they are rousing the anticipation which it is their aim finally to satisfy. It is, therefore, a point of skill to bring before the hearer competing issues, to set him wondering; now to stimulate him with an effect of surprise, now to let him come to the edge of the solution and help him across; now, and this is best of all, to show him that the true issue was implicit all the time, and that the climax is its organic and inevitable conclusion. No doubt this quality may sometimes be turned to trivial account—some mere clench or conceit, some device of 'keeping the easy rhymes till the end': none the less it is present throughout and it rises to its highest in the supreme moments of structural design. The dull speaker, the dull poet, the dull musician either lets his point be anticipated or buries it in anti-climax: the real artist in words or notes keeps his denouement in reserve so that it strikes the more keenly because the blow has been withheld.

Let me give you one or two instances. And though it is poetry which we are here comparing with music I would ask leave to take the first from rhetoric because it gives the clearest illustration that I know of this quality expressed in its simplest terms. It is a sentence from Cicero's *Pro Milone*:

> 'Domi suae nobilissimus vir, senatus propugnator atque illis quidem temporibus paene patronus, avunculus huius nostri iudicis M. Catonis, fortissimi viri, tribunus plebis, M. Drusus occisus est.'

Observe with what forensic skill this sentence is built up. 'Domi suae'—something happened at somebody's house; 'nobilissimus vir'—evidently a person of consequence; 'senatus propugnator atque patronus'—of great consequence; 'avunculus huius nostri iudicis'—that brings it home: let me see, who was Cato's uncle?; 'tribunus plebis'—of course I know now; and just as the hearer's mind leaps forward to the tragedy of the great tribune, Cicero meets him with that clash of sibilants, like a serpent in act to strike—'M. Drusus occisus est'—Marcus Drusus was assassinated.

Take a quieter but equally famous instance from the ninth book of *Paradise Lost*:

> As one who, long in populous city pent,
> Where houses thick and sewers annoy the air,
> Forth issuing on a summer's morn to breathe
> Among the pleasant villages and farms
> Adjoin'd, from each thing met conceives delight,
> The smell of grain, or tedded grass, or kine,
> Or dairy, each rural sight, each rural sound;
> If chance with nymph-like step fair virgin pass,
> What pleasing seem'd, for her now pleases more,
> She most, and in her look sums all delight.[1]

'Annoy', 'summer's morn', 'pleasant', all preparing for the change from the noisome town to the fresh country air: then the delicious landscape unfolds (how perfect a picture in how few words) and at its close the girl crosses the meadow and completes the scene with a touch of human beauty and human sympathy.

One more example in which the effect is produced by contrast:

> When in disgrace with fortune and men's eyes
> I all alone beweep my outcast state,
> And trouble deaf Heaven with my bootless cries,
> And look upon myself and curse my fate,

—and so Shakespeare continues, glooming through dark minor keys till he comes to that worst pitch of misery where a man despises his own unhappiness; and then, in the space of a crotchet, in the turn of a semitone, the sonnet changes from minor to major, like a shaft of sunlight through an unbarred window—

> Haply I think of thee, and then my state
> (Like to the lark at break of day arising
> From sullen earth) sings hymns at Heaven's gate:
> For thy sweet love remembered such wealth brings
> That then I scorn to change my state with kings.

[1] Compare, for a different kind of structure, on the same theme, Keats's sonnet 'As one who hath been long in city pent'.

'Heaven' and 'state' occur both at the beginning and at the end of the sonnet; but in the two places they are differently harmonized. All through good music there runs this quality of projected attention. Take any great choral tune, *Ein feste Burg*, or *Nun Danket*, or *Moab*; any folk-song like *The Bailiff's Daughter*, or *Early one morning*; any typical melody of Beethoven or Schubert—the Romance in *Rosamunde*, the *Ständchen*, the slow-movement tunes of the *Pathétique* or the *Pastoral* or the late E major Sonata—and note how the beauty and interest of this texture is heightened and enhanced as they approach their cadence. The same is true of composition on a larger canvas—the end of *Tristan* and of *Meistersinger*, the hurricane of the *Appassionata*, the closing miracle of the *Jupiter* Symphony. This does not, of course, mean any such absurdity as that all great music or poetry is a profusion of climaxes: that would obviously defeat its own end and ensure its own downfall. Everything depends on the unit of attention which may be a stanza or an ode, an eight-bar melody or a symphonic movement. It may be a necessary part of the suspense that some passages should be kept at a low pitch: it must be a necessary part that the device is never obtrusive or mechanical, but grows in its place as naturally as a flower: in any case the temporal condition is paramount and the great artist has accepted it and has used it not as a restriction, but as a resource.

Another point of likeness may be noted. Tone and rhythm, which are metaphors, though valuable metaphors, in the representative arts, are in music and poetry vital and essential realities. In both of these music would seem to have the advantage. It falls altogether outside the play and interchange of consonants (for all the letters in its alphabet are vowels), and on this side it is debarred from one of the most telling qualities of articulate speech. But this is compensated, and it may be more than compensated, by the greater beauty of musical sound—the beauty which makes it the highest praise of a language that we should call it musical. I do not deny the moving tones of the great orator: I know that men have read Swinburne for the sheer delight of his verse; but it is no paradox to say that these fall below the resonance of the singing voice or the orchestra or the four magic strings. Music, again, is the only art which has the power of

> Untwisting all the chains that tie
> The hidden soul of harmony.

It alone can make 'out of three sounds not a fourth sound but a star': that new creation achieved by the blending and absorbing of intermingled voices. Nor in rhythm is the supremacy of music less apparent. The Classical poets could work wonders by the counter-change of stress and quantity, but even with them the limit of variation is comparatively narrow. The moderns, who have all but lost this distinction, have attempted to replace it in various ways: the French by free play of sound within determinate systems of metre: the English and German by some lightness of additional syllables, as you may break up a crotchet into quavers, yet hampered throughout by the natural pace of the speaking voice. Coleridge, at the beginning of *Christabel*, deliberately introduced a new melody into English versification: Lamb declared that 'a long line was a line which was long in reading', irrespective of the number of syllables that it contained: most notable of all in this field are the experiments which Dr. Bridges has made in breaking up the conventional designs of his metre. Take, for instance, the poem called *London Snow*. The first line—

> When men were all asleep the snow came flying,

sets a metre with which we have all been familiar since the opening of the *Canterbury Tales*. The second line begins a subtle variation:

> In large white flakes falling on the city brown:

the third and fourth cluster with semiquavers:

> Stealthily and perpetually settling and loosely lying,
> Hushing the latest traffic of the drowsy town.

It is not too much to say that these lines mark an epoch in the history of English verse: yet when you compare them with their analogues in music—with any page of the *Fitzwilliam Virginal Book*, or of Bach's *Forty-eight*, or of Beethoven or Wagner or Brahms, you will see not the lesser skill of the poet, for he has gone as far as language can go, but the lesser flexibility of his medium. Or, again, take the device of syncopation, traversing the bar-metre by a stress thrown on a weak beat, most effective when rightly used, deplorably vulgarized at the present day: compare the finest examples in Milton—

> And over them triumphant death his dart
> Shook, but delayed to strike,

with the finest examples in Beethoven, as, for instance, in the first movement of the *Eroica*; the difference is not one of genius, but one of opportunity. Or, again, take the grouping and phrasing of notes 'across the bar' as in A. E.'s couplet:

> The waters lull me, and the scent of many gardens, and I hear
> Familiar voices, and the voice I love is whispering in my ear.

A miracle, you will say, wrought by three commas; transforming a commonplace metre into a new and living melody. In terms of language it cannot be better done. But contrast it with the lyric movement of Brahms' G minor quartet and you see what genius can achieve, in this manner, with a more responsive instrument at command.

On the other side there can be no doubt that poetry is far more precise and direct than music. One of the most notable qualities of the great Epic writers, especially of Dante and Milton, is their power of presenting the object as it is, of placing it before us in concrete shape and substance. This does not mean that they copy phenomena, any more than the landscape-painter copies nature, but that they crystallize round phenomena the ideas that they hold in imagination. It is because they can

See the world in a grain of sand,
And Heaven in a wild flower,

that they can make the wild flower and the grain of sand real and significant; and one measure of their genius is the clearness with which they perceive the Idea and the certainty with which they embody it. Wordsworth saw the whole world 'apparelled in celestial light', and therefore no detail of it escaped his vision. Shakespeare comprehended all the archetypes of human character, and therefore his personages are as real to us as our familiar friends. But the phenomenal world is the vehicle through which the poet expresses his ideas, and because it is the world of our own experience it brings them into specially close and intimate relation with ourselves.

From this kind of reality music is excluded. It can suggest, but it cannot narrate: it can rouse our emotions but it cannot specify them. A few sounds and movements in nature can be more or less imitated by its tones or rhythms; these lie at the far outskirts and are of no serious account. Descriptive music, in the broader sense of the term, is at best only a half-art, needing words or a written programme or dramatic action to prescribe its meaning. Even then it should be 'mehr Ausdruck der Empfindung als Malerei'. Schubert, for instance, makes no attempt in *Erlkönig* to depict an actual storm—he gives us instead a vague general feeling of turbulence and sinister flight: Wagner in the prelude to *Walküre* begins with the same musical theme as Schubert and writes on it a fine stirring piece which falls short of its purpose only so far as it attempts to be realistic. *Heldenleben* has a programme almost as close in detail as that of the *Symphonie Fantastique*: he would be a bold listener who should endeavour to rewrite the story of either from hearing the music. And in proportion as music withdraws from the drama and the written programme, in proportion as it holds its own autonomous and independent course, so far it recedes from any meaning that could be translated into terms of any other experience. We may find plenty of analogues if we will, and they are often helpful and suggestive, but they are analogues, not interpretations.

Yet within its own domain music has a reality not less than that of any other art. The style of Bach is as perfect as that of Milton, the structure of Beethoven as that of Shakespeare: bad music is, as Coleridge said, the exact equivalent of nonsense verses. But the significance of music is not related to anything outside itself; it is inherent in the succession of notes, the interweaving of parts, the design of themes, contrasted or recurrent, throughout a piece of composition. In all other arts, even in poetry, we can make some sort of abstraction between form and content: in the best music we cannot, they are fused and absorbed into one supreme act of creation. When we hear the slow movement of the Choral Symphony we are not conscious of any specific joy or sorrow, still less of any scene or event: the spell of that enchantment is beyond the reach of any words.

We must not press this distinction as if it were exhaustive. In point of meaning music may no doubt penetrate to a metaphysical world which is behind even the Ideal[1]: so far as vehicle is concerned it needs the ear as avenue, and sound adapted to the ear as medium. There is at the present time a dangerous heresy called Expressionism, which is threatening to invade the domains both of pictorial and of musical art. Its chief principle is, as its upholders tell us, 'the denial of the sensible world'. It is 'indifferent to every perception of sense, and turns away from the outward world in order to behold with the eye of the spirit'. This is false mysticism. No doubt Blake is abundantly right in saying:

> We are led to believe a lie
> When we see with, not through, the eye:

still more, perhaps, when we hear with, not through, the ear; but we must see and hear through these organs, they are

[1] See above, pp. 196–7.

the natural correlatives of sound and colour. And I notice with some misgiving that the plea of expressionism is commonly used to explain pictures which are apparently ugly, poetry which is apparently unmeaning, and music which is apparently cacophonous. One cannot help thinking that the claims of sense, not as tribunal but as witness, are being here too little regarded. 'Heard melodies are sweet, but those unheard are sweeter.' I wonder whether that is always the case. What says the clown in *Othello*? 'If you have any music that may not be heard, to't again; but as they say, to hear music the general does not greatly care.'

Another point of resemblance between poetry and music is that they are specially liable to the same diseases. In dealing with this matter I would ask to leave on one side that deliberate cult of ugliness for its own sake, which stands to art as devil-worship to Religion, and of which the present age has been sometimes accused. It is too serious an accusation to be discussed or considered in the course of a brief and general survey; if it is true it means not disease but death, its basis is probably some form of physiological pervasion, and its proper field of investigation is not aesthetics but pathology. Apart from this, however, there are two maladies which attack the temporal arts with particular virulence, usually at the end of some period of conspicuous achievement. The first of these is anarchy: the claim of a personal freedom which means flat defiance of all law and all regulation. It is not experiment or adventure, which indeed are the conditions of all progress, but blind adventure and experiment conducted at random. For the most part it belongs to the recklessness of youth, and therefore deserves our cordial sympathy; but it is no more a form of art than window-breaking is a form of architecture. Some remarkable instances are provided in Trotzky's *Literature and Revolution*: a book which must be absorbingly interesting to those who have followed the recent course of letters in Russia; and which even to those who read it without this knowledge is very significant. It describes Gorki as 'an amiable psalm-singer'; it treats Blok as a Conservative; it is filled dispassionately with accounts of authors, some of whom are genuine pathfinders while others are dancing round and round in the wildest extravagance. One school is avoiding the charge of voluptuousness by writing its poetry in mathematical formulae; another is inventing nonsense-words like 'Dir' and 'Tschil' and maintaining that the patterns into which they can be wrought 'strike a deeper note than anything in Pushkin'. This is really worse than the literary machine which Gulliver saw at Lagado, for that at least employed real words, and their fortuitous concourses were dictated only when 'they were such as might form parts of a sentence'.

There are dozens of parallel instances in music. I possess at home a copy of a pianoforte sonata in which certain passages are to be played with the fist (presumably on some one else's piano), and others, for which the fist is inadequate, with a wooden plank fourteen inches in length. It presents a very decorative picture to the eye; crotchets like bunches of grapes and minims like spikes of corn; but the sound of it is inconceivable and the sense, to me, non-existent. Again, there are several undistinguished compositions which bid for notoriety by the insertion of inappropriate or meaningless discords; 'put in', like the barking hen of Willie Edouin's riddle, 'to make it more difficult'. They are fairly on a level with the 'transferred epithet' by which something which can have no colour, like a perfume, is called 'black', something which can have no perfume, like a triangle, is called 'fragrant', and something which can have no shape, like Wednesday morning, is called 'isosceles'. It is the more vexing because a great deal of first-rate pioneer work is being done at the present day, work of real genius and accomplished skill, enlarging the bounds of our musical vocabulary and creating new and beautiful forms. If some of our young people would give up celebrating the fifth of November and take their place, beside their comrades, in the general advance, they would be aiding instead of disregarding the cause of music.

A worse fault is pedantry—the fault of those who are so overweighted with learning that they lose all sense of proportion in employing it. Of this the classical instance is Lycophron, the erudite librarian of Alexandria, whose one surviving poem, a monologue of Cassandra on the fall of Troy, is a lamentable monument of misplaced labour. He has heaped metaphor on metaphor, obscurity on obscurity, he has searched the dictionary for rare words and the mythology for recondite allusions—and he has produced in the end a work of which he declared, with all a scholar's pride, that 'he would hang himself if any one understood it'. Here is a comparatively easy passage:

> 'I see the winged firebrand rushing to the capture of the dove, the Pephnian hound, whom the water-faring vulture brings to birth, enoystered in the sphere of a shell.'[1]

'Enoystered': one can imagine the chuckle of delight with which he wrote down that remarkable word. But it takes some investigation to realize that what the lines mean is 'I see Paris coming to capture Helen'.

There is a passage in Schönberg's *Pierrot Lunaire* which seems exactly to match this. Piccolo and clarinet are playing in close canon at the distance of a quarter of a bar: violin and 'cello are playing a canon cancrizans on a new theme: the piano is playing a three-part fugue on the theme of the first canon in augmentation; and the voice is narrating that when Pierrot walks in the cool of the evening the moon makes a white spot on his back. If all this display of counterpoint was successful it would overlay the tiny subject on which it is imposed: as a matter of fact it is so involved that the ear cannot follow it, and it makes no compensation in beauty of sound. But, indeed,

[1] *Λεύσσω θέοντα γρυνὸν ἐπτερωμένον*
τρήρωνος εἰς ἅρπαγμα, Πεφναίας κυνός,
ἣν τόργος ὑγρόφοιτος ἐκλοχεύεται,
κελυφάνου στρόβιλον ὠστρακωμένην.

much of our counterpoint is become so elaborate that it no longer harmonizes: 'the dissonances' we are told 'are inherent in the progression of parts and therefore inevitable'. It never seems to occur to the composer that he might conciliate the parts.

Sometimes the learned scholar becomes adventurous: starting with set purpose and firm resolve to follow the lure of the will-o'-the-wisp novelty. I have never seen *Die Glückliche Hand* and have therefore no right to express an opinion on it. But I may perhaps be allowed to summarize an account of its opening scene, written by one of its ablest and most devoted admirers.[1] At the rise of the curtain the stage is in almost complete darkness. Near the front a man is lying face downwards. On his back is 'a large cat-like animal' which 'appears to have just bitten him in the neck'. At the back of the stage is a violet curtain with twelve holes in it: through these appear the 'greenish faces' of six men and six women who fulfil 'the same function as that of the chorus in a Greek Tragedy'. Half-speaking and half-singing, they 'express their sympathy for the man who has desired earthly happiness and has been given supernatural happiness instead'.

This is what comes of 'schools' and 'movements' and 'coteries' and all the other devices for tempting men into affectation. Sir Arthur Quiller-Couch once implored you to remember that no abstract noun ending in -ism had ever done anything or made anything or exercised any influence. If I may say so, I entirely agree with him. But I would go farther. No one whose designation ends in -ist has, by reason of this, ever done anything or made anything or exercised any influence either. When I see their serried ranks advancing, bent as a rule on some plan for the annoyance of the aged, I comfort myself with the legend of St. Anthony: not the romantic medieval form, beloved of painters, but the original story as told by Athanasius. The saint was lying ill on the mat of palm-leaves which served him for a bed, and the enemy of man-

[1] See the volume on Schönberg by Dr. Egon Wellesz, *s.v.*

kind thought this a favourable opportunity for attack. So he sent a number of his followers disguised as animals—wolf and lion and tiger and snake and many others—who entered the cell and proceeded to make menacing noises. The saint said two wise words: first, 'If you were real, one of you would be enough'; and then, after they had become further infuriated, 'If it be the Lord's will that you should bite me, come and do it; if not, depart.'

No reasonable person wishes to check or discourage the advance. Such a wish would be crabbed, for the advance is young, and futile, for it is irresistible. Mrs. Partington had no chance, and ought to have known that she had no chance, against the Atlantic Ocean: 'She was excellent at a slop or a puddle, but should not have meddled with a tempest.' Yet it may be claimed that part of the function of criticism is to distinguish between the puddle and the ocean; between the shallow little fashion which will have dried up to-morrow, and the unplumbed depths of genius which will last for ever. And this function, if it is to be of any service, it must accomplish betimes. It is no use deferring arbitration until the parties have left the court.

It seems to me that there are two general principles of criticism which may help to guide our judgement of all arts and especially, perhaps, of the two with which we have been dealing this afternoon. One is that the continuity of human history and human civilization is not broken, but fulfilled, by the advent of genius. The great artists are supreme not because they are freaks or usurpers, but because they stand in the royal line of succession: 'nature', no doubt, 'made them and then broke the mould'; but to the making of that mould went the work of many generations. There were contrapuntists before Bach, dramatists before Shakespeare, ballad-makers before Homer himself: each leader is the follower of a past tradition and by his own genius turns it to fresh account. The maxim 'non facit saltum' is as true of Art as of Nature: each of them, for all its infinite variety, finds somewhere in the past the roots of the present and the future.

The other principle, on which one cannot too often lay stress, is that every art has its natural medium and every medium its natural qualities and limitations. The exact placing of these must from time to time be matter of controversy: we should not, I suppose, at the present day accept all the conclusions of the *Laocoon*, though some of us might, in challenging them, feel a doubt as to whether Lessing were not right after all. Yet even within the bounds of a single generic art we recognize that the distinctions are real: the architect does not apply the same design to wood and brick and marble, and we all know what Whistler thought of the critic whose praise of a water-colour was that he might have taken it for an oil-painting. And so between the sister arts of music and poetry—

Facies non omnibus una,
Nec diversa tamen, quales decet esse sororum:

the points of resemblance do not exclude but invite the points of difference: one interprets the ideal world through phenomenal nature, the other need borrow nothing from nature but the sound which is at once its subject and its material. Poetry transfigures the world of experience; music stands apart from it: in the form of their presentation they are akin, in the substance of that which is presented they are separate. It is true that at the supreme moments of both they stand close together upon the summit, but they climb to it from different sides, and if either takes the path of the other it will lose its way.

MUSIC AND EDUCATION [1]

I. THE PLACE OF MUSIC IN LIFE

THE part that music can play and ought to play in the general course of our life has by many people been seriously misunderstood. They have regarded it as something external and insignificant; at best a luxury, at worst an idle entertainment capable of giving transitory and superficial pleasure, but not of striking any deep roots in human nature. We are, indeed, told that one of the sterner races of antiquity prohibited its use altogether, on the ground that its whole effect was to relax the fibres of manhood; and, although this error has been contradicted by centuries of civilized experience, the fact that it was ever promulgated is worth our attention.

Berlioz once divided persons of imperfect musical sympathy into the two classes—*ceux qui ne sentent pas* and *ceux qui ne savent pas*. This distinction, which runs back through the ages, is the cause, in one form or another, of almost all the obstacles that have retarded the progress of musical art. As here stated it is, no doubt, unduly trenchant—it deals with the extreme cases and ignores the 'thousand diamond-weights between'; but it does emphasize the dangers which, in any art, beset erudition without poetry and emotionalism without knowledge. The medieval treatises on music, for example, from Martianus Capella, who wrote in the fifth century, to Alstedius, who wrote in the seventeenth, are with rare exceptions arid dissertations on grammar and accidence, filled with technical terminology of note and rhythm and proportion, but singularly reticent on the subject of beauty. Indeed, the last-named of these authors, writing in the full light of Byrd and Palestrina, can find no better definition of music than 'a mathematical science subordinated to

[1] A course of three lectures delivered, under the auspices of the Rice Institute Lectureship in Music, Houston, Texas, 7, 8, and 9 April, 1926.

arithmetic'.[1] Meanwhile the listener, warned off the whole domain by this *chevaux-de-frise* of unfamiliar terms, came to regard the whole of musical science as a priestly hieroglyphic which he was not expected to understand, took refuge in the native wood-notes of upland and forest, in the simple enjoyment of folk-song and folk-dance, and came, in doing so, much nearer to the heart of the matter. And before them the composer trod his own path, handing down a tradition which was almost certainly empirical in origin, enriching and moulding it through successive generations of transmitted skill, glowing with that inexplicable flame which we call genius, and leading the host as the pillar of fire led the Israelites through the desert.

Music is at once the oldest and the youngest of the Arts. It is the oldest because its origin may be traced to the heightened speech with which primitive man announced some moment of danger or triumph, before the first ordering of rhythmic speech or the first elk on the cave-wall. First the emotionalized cry of terror or delight; then its modification for use as warning or stimulus or jubilance; then the fitting of articulate words into the mould, and the songs of the camp-fire or the hunting-field. Again the most primitive savages of whom we know, and from whom we acquire part of our evidence about antiquity, have a keen sense of co-ordinated rhythm, not only for the strengthening and accelerating of effort, but for the sheer joy in the movements of limb and body; and in this way we can account for the prevalence and universality of the dance. Sir Hubert Parry has well summed up the interrelation of these early practices[2]:

The examination of the music of savages shows that they hardly ever succeed in making orderly and well-balanced tunes, but either express themselves in a kind of vague wail or howl which is on the borderland between music and informal expression of feeling,

[1] Scientia Mathematica subalternata Arithmeticae. See *Alstedius Encyclopaedia*, Bk. XX. It is dated 1620, a quarter of a century after Palestrina's death.

[2] Parry, *The Art of Music*, Chapter I, p. 7.

> or else contrive little fragmentary figures of two or three notes which they reiterate incessantly over and over again.

And later:

> Pure unalloyed rhythmic music is found in most parts of the uncivilized globe and the degree of excitement to which it can give rise when the mere beating of a drum or tom-tom is accompanied by dancing is well known to all the world. It is also a familiar fact that dancing originates under almost the same conditions as song or any other kind of voice utterance, and therefore the rhythmic elements and the cantabile element are only different forms in which the same class of feelings and emotions are experienced.

Yet music is also the youngest, in the sense that of all arts it has most recently developed into forms which we can understand and enjoy. The earliest piece of music which is of first-rate value to us is dated 1240, and there is nothing like it for another two hundred years. The great polyphonic school of the sixteenth century is still a monument of wonder and delight; its idiom has some of the remoteness and stateliness of a dead language. The symphonic forms of Beethoven, the orchestra of Berlioz, the music-drama of Wagner, the *nuove musiche* of the present day are all landmarks in the course of an art which is perpetually advancing. It is not a question of genius—there has never been a greater genius than Beethoven—but of the resources at its command. In music every age has added its own treasures to the wealth that it has inherited, and has bequeathed a fuller heritage for the administration of its successor. The idiom of music has changed far more rapidly than that of language, its method than those of painting or sculpture or architecture; and the result is not to make the old masters obsolete, for they are firmer in our affections than ever, but to show how the spirit which animated them can lead their followers into new paths. We must, no doubt, affirm this distinction as relative, not as absolute, but we can draw some measure of its extent if we reflect that Westminster Abbey dates from the same period as the discovery of organum, and that Titian was contemporary with the early madrigalists.

I hope that it will not be thought fantastic if I find a very rough parallel in the history of the sciences. Chemistry, mathematics, biology have made enormous advances during the last three centuries, yet all these can trace their course in an almost continuous line to early Arabian or Greek or even Egyptian investigators. Compare with them the story of electricity. It cannot be said to have begun before Gilbert's conjectures in 1600; there is an honourable succession through Boyle and Kleist and Franklin and Galvani and Volta, but the door of a new world was opened when Faraday published his researches in 1831. Every decade since then has seen new discoveries, new resources, new opportunities of use, and the extension of our knowledge has taught us that we are now only on the threshold of the subject and that the prospects of its future development are illimitable. In like manner I believe, not that music is going to see composers of greater genius than before—that is beyond conjecture and in any case irrelevant—but that we are only just beginning to learn how it can be employed for the furtherance and enhancement of our civilized life. To this point I shall return in my third address, and shall endeavour then to indicate how this new knowledge may be turned to account: at present I am concerned only to state the belief as a profound and sincere conviction.

The manner in which music affects us may be discussed under three main heads: the physical, the emotional, and the spiritual. I am not here prejudging the question how far these can be regarded as actually distinct—I am fully mindful of Aristotle's warning that divisions of the soul may be but aspects of the same entity—but for the present purpose they may be considered separately. It is no paradox to say that when I cut my finger the pain which I feel is physical rather than emotional or spiritual, and no further committal than this is required by the argument before us.

Physiologists have said that, so far as their evidence attests, two functions would seem to be attributable to the nervous system of the ear. One is the purely specialized auditory function which passes on to the brain those impacts from air-waves which are there translated into sound. The other, proceeding along the afferent nerves to the semicircular canals, is apparently concerned with our power of co-ordinating bodily movements and especially of preserving equilibrium.[1] Experiments have shown that lesions in the canals are attended by a loss of co-ordinating power, and there seems to be enough evidence to establish a causal connexion. Be this as it may—and it is too technical a subject to be argued by a layman—we may safely hold that there is a close connexion between the ear and the well-being of the nervous system in general. The first sign of Schumann's insanity was the persistence in his brain of a single musical note, and Smetana had exactly the same experience. Auditory hallucinations are, I believe, more common than visual: bodily weariness after a certain degree is accompanied by the mis-hearing of tones and can be cured by music which both restores the specific sense and brings about a general condition of repose. There are famous historical instances: King Saul healing his shattered nerves at the sound of David's harp; Charles IX of France sending for Orlando di Lasso to cure him of his insomnia; Philip V of Spain, whose sickness required for its daily medicine four songs from the great Farinelli. Sometimes the story has another edge, as when we read of 'Ethodius the 25th King of Scotland' who could not sleep without the pipes at his bedside, and who was first lulled and then murdered by a treacherous virtuoso. Like the hero of Prior's epigram:

> Cured yesterday of my disease,
> I died last night of my physician.

But the questions with which we are now concerned are physiological rather than ethical.

It is not, therefore, surprising that throughout all the

[1] See for instance Lavignac's *Music and Musicians*, English translation, pp. 39–43.

ages there have been sporadic and empirical attempts to utilize music as a curative agency. Many examples are collected and annotated in an exceedingly rare book by a German doctor named Georg Frankh, who practised in the early part of the eighteenth century.[1] Within its limits the work is as full of queer miscellaneous erudition as Burton's *Anatomy*: it quotes instances of musical cures from Pythagoras and the Asclepiads, notes that Pythagoras used to play the harp every night before going to bed and every morning on getting up,[2] besides doing so at intervals during the day when he wanted his mind to be specially active; and so carries the evidence through Galen and Martianus Capella to Isaac Vossius and George Baglivus, the famous professor of medicine at Rome, who discusses in detail the physical effects of air-vibrations induced by music, and the possibility of discovering 'laws of nature' by which they can be usefully applied. 'Sheer medieval superstition,' some one will say, 'as out of place in our enlightened and scientific age as the Elixir of Life or the Philosopher's Stone or the Talking Head of Roger Bacon.' Let me, therefore, supplement it by a first-hand experience of the last few years. Shortly after the war I was invited to attend the concert of a male-voice choir at Chelsea Hospital. It was a simple programme—a dozen part-songs prepared with the keenest verve and enjoyment by some twenty or thirty men. Every one of them was a patient in the hospital: every one had come there so broken with aphasia that he could neither speak nor understand a word. Their cure had been effected by music: their first sign of consciousness was the recognition of a marching tune, their first utterance the completion of such a tune deliberately broken off, and so by degrees they had been

[1] *Satyrae Medicae*, Leipzig, 1723. It contains twenty essays on purely medical subjects, six dissertations, of which that on Music is No. II, and a posthumous oration on the disadvantages of study (De Studiorum Noxa) edited by his son.

[2] Hawkins, *Life of Ken*, quoted by Boswell, says that Bishop Ken used to sing a hymn to the lute 'every morning before putting on his clothes'.

brought back to the use of speech and the restoration of health. It is true that many of Dr. Frankh's claims are extravagant and ridiculous; this does not prevent us from holding that music can exercise a beneficent effect in certain cases of nervous disorder, and that we do not yet know within what limits its power may be circumscribed.

Closely connected with this is the sheer physical pleasure which the ear receives from certain qualities and combinations of sound: the *timbre* of voice or violin or clarinet,[1] chords as rich as the eye of a peacock's tail, harmonic passages like sunset clouds, the flow of melodies which, apart from their meaning, are as limpid as a brook among the moorlands. Think of the love-scene in *Tristan*, of the end of the first strophe in the *Schicksalslied*, of the clarinet tune in Schubert's Octet, of the famous episode in the slow movement of the first *Rasoumoffsky*: I am speaking for the moment not about the emotional or intellectual force of these passages, but of their pure sensuous delight. It is true that there are some persons who stand outside this influence—some ears to which music is 'un bruit désagréable qu'on fait exprès'; but to the vast majority of normally constituted people this special joy of hearing is not only real but intense.

There is an ambiguity in the English word 'pleasure' from which more precise languages, like the Greek, are entirely free. Sometimes we use it of the subjective feeling ('I shall have much pleasure in . . .'), sometimes of the object which stimulates the feeling ('It will be a great pleasure to . . .'), and the question so dear to moralists as to a qualitative distinction between pleasures is largely obscured by this confusion. For there is obviously no pleasant object the content of which is exhausted by the sensation. It is, in addition, either wholesome or unwholesome, either ennobling or degrading, either self-centred

[1] Madame de Deffand, in one of her letters to Horace Walpole, says that the clavecin, however well played, 'cannot rival the beauty of the harp'. This is clearly a question of timbre alone.

or beneficent, and by reference to these distinctions we may gauge at any rate a part of its psychological value.

Among all sources of physical pleasure music is, perhaps, the purest. It admits, as we shall see later, of varying grades, especially in its emotional appeal; but in its immediate influence on the auditory nerve it would rank, by general acknowledgment, at least on a level with visual beauty, and by most people who are keenly susceptible of both it would have the pre-eminence. And if this be challenged, or set aside as incapable of argument, we may at any rate hold, as psychologists have held since Aristotle, that these two avenues of sense belong to a higher part of our nature than those of touch and smell and taste, which we share more closely with the rest of the animal world. From which it would follow that, on grounds of sense alone, the musician has a special responsibility. It is not reform but anarchy to extend the bounds of the art so as to include sounds which are intrinsically degraded or cacophonous—sounds 'jangled out of tune and harsh' which stab the ear with meaningless discord or isolated and unintelligible noise. Grant that as experience progresses we can adapt ourselves to new combinations of sound, we can do this only if they form part of a coherent design and so bring into play other kinds of receptivity. That has nothing to do with the cult of ugliness for its own sake which is threatening to invade more than one domain of art, and which is the most obvious because the easiest of all ways by which mediocrity and imposture can attract attention. If there were nothing else to urge against the jazz band—and there is everything—it would put itself outside the pale of music by the coarseness and vulgarity of its utterance.

Sense and emotion are so closely interconnected that a great American psychologist has ranged them together as cause and effect.[1] Experiment has abundantly shown that

[1] The passage is well known, but may nevertheless be worth repeating. 'Common sense says, we lose our fortune, are sorry and weep; we meet a bear, are frightened and run; we are insulted by a rival, are angry and

there are certain rhythms and cadences, certain combinations and successions of tone, which are generally stimulative of emotion and which, with some aid, it may be from association and circumstance, the hearer can more or less specify for himself. This is notably the case in song and dance where the music, as it were, crystallizes round the words or the enacted scene, where its rhythm re-enforces gesture, where its tone illustrates the pathos or humour of the poetic phrase: the sorrow of Handel's 'He was despised', the love sickness of Schubert's 'Gretchen am Spinnrade', the jollity of Papageno's introductory song, the farcical burlesque of Beckmesser's Serenade—instances are too frequent to need exemplification. But it is also true that within limits the same conclusion holds of some instrumental music where we have no such adventitious or external means of suggestion. No one can doubt that the slow movement of Beethoven's First Quartet is tragic, or that the scherzo of his Fifth Symphony is eerie, or that the finale of his Eighth is amusing: we may even proceed to analyse, if we think it worth while, some of the points of phrase or colour by which our respective feelings are excited. Many writers, indeed, who can see thus far and no farther, have maintained that the whole essential influence of music is emotional, and have sharply contrasted it with poetry, 'which' as they say 'appeals to the intellect'. This antithesis I believe to be fundamentally untrue; the significance of music is less concrete but not less real than that of poetry: if there be any pre-eminence it is on the side of that 'inarticulate unfathomable speech', as Carlyle called it, 'which takes us to the edge of the infinite and lets us for moments gaze upon that'. But this belongs more

strike. The hypothesis here to be defended is that this order of sequence is incorrect, that the one mental state is not immediately induced by the other, that the bodily manifestations must first be interposed between; and that the more rational statement is that we feel sorry because we cry, angry because we strike, afraid because we tremble, and not that we cry, strike, or tremble because we are sorry, angry, or fearful as the case may be.' (William James, *Principles of Psychology*, ii, pp. 449–50.)

appropriately to our third address, which deals with the place of music in education. It is enough to say here that the whole range of our emotional nature lies open to musical influence, that this influence can be exerted nobly or ignobly, temperately or extravagantly, and that its artistic value and import will depend largely on the choice which it determines. 'Sir,' said Dr. Johnson, irritated by some artificial ecstasies from Boswell, 'I should never listen to music if it made me feel such a fool.' But it is no mark of folly to be deeply moved by the Austrian Hymn, or the Marseillaise, or the Lacrymosa of Mozart's Requiem, or the slow movement of Brahms's Horn Trio; and though we cannot closely particularize the emotion we are none the less conscious of its existence.

To our intellectual nature music appeals through its purity and opulence of style, and its ordered coherence of architectural structure. It no more follows that a piece of music is fine because it contains certain emotional phrases or poignant harmonies than that a play is Shakespearian by virtue of the line

> And so good morrow t'ye, good master Lieutenant,[1]

or that flat verse can be raised to poetry by being winged with such words as 'glory' or 'empyrean'. The value of a musical composition, like that of every other work of art, must be gauged less by its individual details than by its coherence and vitality as a whole. In all ages there have been artistic bunglers like the painter in Horace who set together a man's face, a horse's neck, and a fish's tail; nor is it any excuse to plead that tail, neck and face could please when regarded separately. Almost every one who takes the trouble to write or compose has his moments of invention—stronger or weaker according to the degree of his talent—the great artist is he who knows what to do with them: how to hold them in check and counterpoise,

[1] See *Martinus Scriblerus on the art of Sinking*, written by Pope and Arbuthnot. It is an admirable satire on certain literary follies, and might with advantage be extended to those of musical composition.

how to place each point where its significance will be most vital, and above all how to see, and to make us see, that the structure on which he is concentrating our attention is an organic whole. In a perfect melody no note can be omitted or altered without loss: each presupposes or leads into its context as inevitably as the words of a well-constructed sentence. A bad melody is sometimes monotonous, sometimes incoherent; sometimes, though this is almost incredible, it succeeds in being both at once: in any case, one measure of its badness is that it does not construe —that, as people say, it 'doesn't make sense'—or that, if it does, the sense is so poor and feeble that it fails to engage our interest. And exactly the same holds good of the larger canvas. As the notes or figures in a melody, so the melodies in a fugue or a symphony movement are held together by a living and organic law—a law which is always outstripping the text-book and leaving the pedant to 'toil after it in vain', but the expression of which is a part of the dignity and responsibility of true genius. The plot of a great musical composition is, of its kind and within its idiom, as perfect as that of epic or drama: it may lead to a climax as quiet as that of *Paradise Regained* or of the *Coriolan* overture as tempestuous as that of Hamlet or of the *Appassionata*, in either case, and along the whole line between them, it achieves its end by mastery and domination of its materials. The supreme temples of music are like the Parthenon as Pericles built it—lovely in hue and pillar and colonnade, lovely in architrave and cornice and sculptured frieze, loveliest of all in its complete and majestic perfection.

Yet all these—sense, emotion, intellectual grasp—are but the successive courts which lead to the central mystery. In music more, I think, than in any other art there is an inherent quality which is beyond all analysis or description; which is correlative with the inmost aspiration of the spirit of man. We are dimly and imperfectly conscious of something in ourselves which we call Divine; which is on the farther side of reason as emotion is on the hither side;

which ennobles, absorbs, transfigures our whole being so long as we are under its influence. It finds, I believe, its fullest embodiment in our religious experiences, in those moments of intimate communion with God which, and not petition, are of the central essence of prayer. These moments the purest and most spiritual music can recall as can nothing else in the world; we are not stirred by picture or poem or temple as we are by the *Missa Papae Marcelli*, or the last chorus in the *St. Matthew Passion* or the Sanctus of Beethoven's great Mass, or the slow movement of his Choral Symphony: by these and such as these we are lifted altogether out of the world of experience—we 'are caught up into Paradise and hear unspeakable words'. It is for this reason that such music is a most valuable instrument of religious worship, lifting and purifying our souls that they may be a fit habitation for the Divine presence. And it is for this reason that the heavier responsibility lies on those who would intrude into the Sanctuary with kinds of music which are trivial or vulgar or sentimental; which mince and posture before the altar itself, and turn the act of worship into a serenade.

Music, in one form or another, can touch every aspect of human life. It can be a fitting vehicle for religious observance, it can greatly enhance the splendour of pageant and display, it can excite or soothe, comfort or stimulate; it can rouse our minds to the keenest pitch of interest and expectation, it can not only sweeten our lives with pure and noble pleasure but feed our spirits with the contemplation of Divine beauty. Like every other language it is equally susceptible of use and of misuse: there is no form so austere that it cannot be made dull or vulgar in the handling, there is none so light that genius cannot touch it with magic. People sometimes speak as if all good music were grave and complex—or at any rate as if they believed their opponents to think so: it would be not less absurd to say that all good literature is tragic, to banish from its domain all that company of jest and mirth and honest laughter to which Milton in *L'Allegro* offers a poet's welcome. In music there is abundant room for every mood and we need be at no pains to set one against another. But in music, as in literature, every mood may be nobly or ignobly cultivated—tangled with weeds of illiteracy and impurity or abundant with blossoms of exquisite and entrancing loveliness. It is of high importance to us, both in the conduct of our lives and in the cultivation of our characters, that we should study to discriminate between the various forms of this most potent influence. 'True education', says Aristotle, quoting from Plato, 'is that we shall learn to form a right judgement about our pleasures and pains'; and of all our pleasures those which are wrought by music are among the most keen and the most penetrating.

NOTE A

The most purely sensuous effects in Music are probably those produced by the *timbres* of different voices and instruments and by the 'colour' of harmonies and their combinations. On the first of these there is no need to dwell at any length: it is beyond question that many people are affected by the actual sound of a great singer's voice or of a great violinist's fiddle, apart from any intellectual or even emotional perception of theme or subject. This may, no doubt, be enhanced by some accessory of skill or reputation: one famous and much advertised singer of the eighteenth century was, we are told, applauded 'for five minutes' after singing the first note of his first song at Covent Garden: there is a story that Rubini, after his powers even of vocalization had left him, once held a Parisian audience spell-bound with his 'high B♭'; and the records of our own time could provide a number of other instances. But the centre of pleasure in all such cases is the sheer sensation elicited by the quality of the sound. It seems to be closely analogous to that which we derive from the taste of a peach or the perfume of a flower.

Rather more subtle, but in its way equally sensuous, is the delight which comes from certain effects of harmony, whether as single facts of experience or as parts of a modulating context. I would illustrate these by the most elementary examples, because modern harmony is comparatively unfamiliar to many hearers and its combinations of sound tend to an excess of stimulus which needs a little experience to be wholly pleasurable. This has happened in every age: the ear has to attune itself to the new idiom, and every generation has made and will continue to make its own adjustments. There are a good many harmonic experiments at the present day which recall the recipes of the Roman *gourmand* Apicius: there can be no doubt about their luxury, but they contain too many spices to be immediately palatable. Let us, therefore, begin with simpler fare and with flavours more easily distinguished.

Consider for a moment the following cadences:

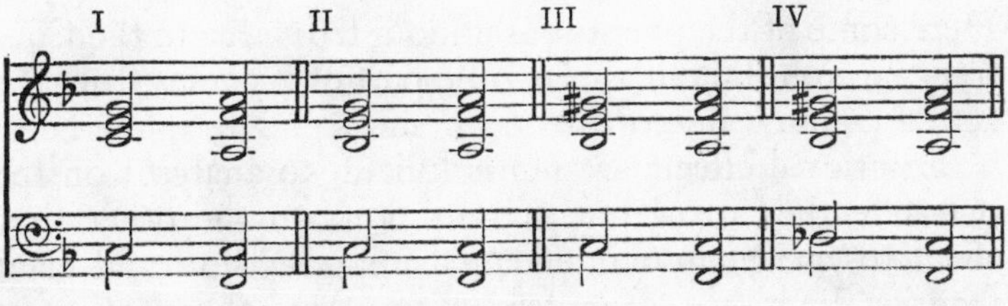

You will readily perceive that each of these has a slightly enhanced colour-value as compared with its predecessor. The dominant seventh in II stirs a nerve which is not touched by the pure authentic cadence of I: there is a further vibration in the augmented interval of III, and another in IV where the bass note almost, for an instant, gives the impression of another tonal centre. Now take the following enharmonic modulation, much beloved by the 'Neo-Russian Innovators' of the 'sixties:

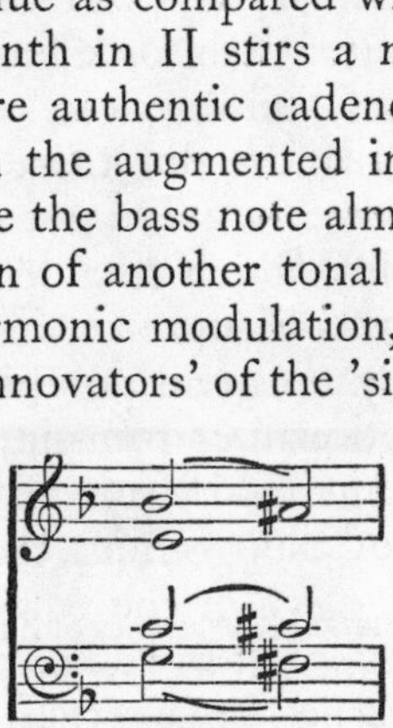

It has much the same effect on the ear as a piece of shot silk on the eye—a shimmer of remote hues which somehow seem to melt out of one another. Again for effects of juxtaposition take the chromatic number from Brahms's Handel Variations, which is like a piece of purple velvet, or many passages in Schumann's *Noveletten* (e.g. the purple second theme of No. 6) or Horatio Parker's well-known harmonization of the chromatic scale:

Here some of the pleasure is undoubtedly due to the Contrary motion, but an appreciable part of it comes from the actual colour-value of the harmonies.[1]

Emotional effects are more difficult to analyse: on the one side they grow out of sensation, on the other they seem to merge into intellectual apprehension and their frontier lines are even less exact than those of most psychological faculties. Many melodies and melodic phrases drive to the very heart of emotion—particularly if their arrow is winged with some feather of association or memory—a song of childhood in old age, or of home heard in a foreign land. But there are many forms of emotional appeal which are due not to association but to some intrinsic quality which rises through sensation into feeling. Wagner was a supreme enchanter in this field of magic—probably no great composer has ever shown such power of emotionalizing music: of making it 'play upon our heart-strings' apart from any question of style or structure. Think of the opening bars of *Tristan*, or the

[1] One of the most remarkable examples of delight in pure colour, apart from its emotional effect, is César Franck. See for example the Prélude in E major, and the whole of the Pianoforte Quintet.

reiterated phrases of the death song in the same opera, or the slow descending theme in the third act of *Walküre*, or the poignant passion motif of *Parsifal*: they are all ready illustrations and there are hundreds like them. Or take, in a very different field, the 'Quis est homo' of Dvořák's *Stabat Mater*:

Notice the emotional appeal of the appoggiaturas at A and B. The whole effect would be gone if Dvořák had written:

But then, being Dvořák, he would never have done so.

On the intellectual side it is impossible even to touch within the limits of this address. To describe it would be to indicate the whole scheme of musical style and musical construction, and to pass beyond these into that sphere of the 'numinous', which Dr. Otto has placed at the climax of all religious and artistic experience,[1] and of which in music Bach and Beethoven are the most sublime examples. Something more will be said about it in the third lecture, but it is far too large a subject to form part of a course,

[1] Otto, *The Idea of the Holy*, Chapters II and III.

and its further elucidation must be left to that educational scheme which it is here my principal aim to encourage.

NOTE B

Since writing the above address I have read Mr. Edward Dickinson's very interesting work on the Spirit of Music. There is a passage in the Introduction which is so apposite to the purpose which I have in hand that I cannot refrain from the pleasure of quoting it:

'The art which the American people have seized upon with the greatest avidity is music. It has entered every phase of social and individual life. It is a means of enjoyment in moments of leisure, of personal expression, of popular education. From the rude folk ballad of the mountaineer to the superfined exhibition of learning and skill in city concert-hall, it meets every shade and degree of taste. It allies itself with poetry, the drama, and the cinema, with religious ceremony, with every occasion in which enthusiasm is to be aroused in the cause of social enterprise. This art, beloved of all men in all ages and climes beyond any other medium for expression in beauty, has had a growth in our country in esteem and practice which none of the other arts have equalled. The rapidity and extent of this growth is a matter of common observation: it is only those directly concerned who are fully aware of the place that music has gained in the large movement of public and private education.'

II. THE PLACE OF HUMANE LETTERS IN EDUCATION

THEORIES as to the ultimate nature and aim of education have usually grouped themselves round one of two focal points. According to the first, the aim of education is the perfection of the individual soul, the cultivation of its faculties for their own sake and in due gradation of absolute value, using the external world, in so far as it does use this at all, chiefly as a means and opportunity of arriving nearer to the ultimate perfection or of rendering clearer our vision of the ultimate truth. One of the clearest expressions of this view is that given by Plato in the *Republic*. His scheme, as presented in the first three books and more especially in the latter part of the seventh, is that for the first seventeen years education should be chiefly occupied with music and poetry and especially with these as strengthening and ennobling the moral nature; that from seventeen to twenty should follow a period mainly devoted to physical training and roughly corresponding with the period of military service which has been common in many continental countries; from twenty to thirty come ten years' devotion to mathematical and abstract sciences—arithmetic, pure and solid geometry, astronomy treated not empirically but in its mathematical relations and regarded as of value wholly in so far as it is a mental discipline. And so these lead on to the five closing years of the university course, in which from thirty to thirty-five the student is devoted to what Plato calls 'dialectic'—the pure metaphysical or theological study of ultimate reality and goodness. From thirty-five to fifty follows a period of public administration, 'the rule', as Plato calls it, 'of the philosopher king', which is not regarded as an end in itself or even as intrinsically desirable, for the soul would be better and purer without it, but rather as a repayment to the State for its cost and charges through the previous years of preparation. At fifty comes the formal discharge from public duty and for the rest of his life the 'philosopher king' is allowed to occupy himself with meditation, returning only at intervals and with bitter reluctance to take his turn at the uncongenial tasks of civic life. Indeed, Plato, with one of those demure touches of humour which make him the most delightful of all philosophic writers, points out in this context that to drag the philosopher from the quiet of his study to the dust and heat of the market-place is possible only by one inducement—the fear that if he refuses he will have to submit to the government of his inferiors.

There are many points of interest in the Platonic scheme. We should not press the criticism commonly and rather unthinkingly urged that the literary and the gymnastic education are relegated to separate periods of life and that in isolation they would not produce their full effect. Plato cannot have meant that there should have been no gymnastic training in the first seventeen years and no literary training in the next three. It is clear that he must have intended a balance of proportion by the complete action of which the body and its emotions should, by the age of twenty, have been brought to their highest state of discipline and control. But two points are specially to be noted. First that the education is expressly designed not for the communication of knowledge, but for the training of faculties. Plato, indeed, states this in terms so plain as to be unmistakable. The Sophists, he says, believe that they can instil knowledge into the mind just as though a man should propose to put sight into blind eyes. True education consists of such a conversion of the whole personality that the eye which has already the potentiality of seeing may be confronted with the light. Hence it will be observed that from this scheme are excluded not only all crafts and industries and applications of science—which, indeed, so far as they existed, were held by the Greeks in some disdain—but all study of human history, of human nature, of all the numberless interests which spring up around us in the community of man and man. It is the more remarkable because one of the greatest glories of Greek literature is that provided by its historical writers and the three greatest of these had completed their work by the time that the *Republic* was written. The other point is that his education is confined to a special class, an aristocracy of intellect and character. In his parable of the three natures he supposes that all men have in their clay a speck of gold or silver or iron and according to this distinction their future careers shall be determined. For those who belong to the iron class no education is contemplated, except, perhaps, such training of skill and resource as is necessary for them to carry out the work by which they earn their livelihood. Those who belong to the silver class are to carry their training as far as the literary and the gymnastic stages: the higher education of science and dialectic is for the golden natures alone.

A doctrine in some respects analogous, but expressed in very different terms, may be found in some of the educational systems of the medieval church. Its apex was theology, as that of Plato was dialectic; it was largely centred on a selected class which corresponded in more respects than one to Plato's Guardians, though its actual range of knowledge was very widely extended by the researches of the Jesuit order among others. The discipline of its teaching was focused on the perfection and salvation of the individual soul. The great sentence of Cardinal Newman, 'Rest in the thought of two and two only absolute and self-evident beings, myself and my Creator', may be taken as the motto and epitome of this view of religious education. Of all things in the world the individual soul is the most important; of all objects which it can pursue none is comparable with its direct relation to God. An interesting medieval example of this ideal may be found in the Statutes drawn up by Dean Colet when he founded St. Paul's School in the early sixteenth century.[1] An image of the Lord Jesus stood over the head master's chair and was saluted with a hymn at the daily opening and closing of the school. The teaching was specially designed to inculcate religion and moral virtue, great stress was laid on the elements of theology and on the Latin language, which was then the common speech of all ecclesiastical organizations. Even in this respect it is noticeable that the authors chosen for study were not the great classics, of whom, indeed, Colet speaks with fierce disdain, but the Christian hymn-writers such as Lactantius and Sedulius, the works of the Spanish priest Juvencus who turned the four Gospels into Virgilian hexameters, and the like: its furthest concession to

1 Colet's general view may be estimated by a sentence of his quoted in Froude's *Erasmus* (page 100) to the effect that education is spoilt when lessons learnt are turned to worldly account.

worldly frivolity is to be found in the innocent eclogues of Baptista Mantuanus immortalized by the old schoolmaster in *Love's Labour's Lost*. Colet includes in his course little mathematics and no science; his boys are to be kept as completely from contact with the external world as if they were in Plato's ideal city; the whole method of education is to be through 'wisdom and chaste eloquence' and its whole object to fit the soul so far as possible for the presence of its Maker.

A remarkable commentary on this general view has been recently afforded in the treatise on *Self* by Mr. Archibald Weir. His position is based on the metaphysical doctrine that in this world none of us can be sure of any reality except his own self, that he has no certain knowledge of any self other than his own, that the development of this self is therefore the one aim and object of his existence, and that though the fact of our life involves us in social conditions which we are compelled to treat as though they were real, yet our attitude towards them must be that they are but the whetstones on which the blade of our own spirit is sharpened. Life, according to Mr. Weir, is one long process of self-discipline, and this discipline involves, as he says, 'a precedence of self over the claims of society'. Three of his quotations throw a very interesting light on the implications of this doctrine. One is the passage from Newman which has been cited above and which he places upon his title-page; the second is the story of Similis, the Roman official who, 'after a most honourable and active career, was retired by the Emperor Hadrian on the score of age'. He lived on in private life until he was able to claim the epitaph 'Here lies Similis, an old man who has lived seven years'. The third is a passage of Plotinus in which he meets those who would maintain the loneliness of the spirit of man in such a world. 'There is no possibility of concealing', he replies, 'that the self's goal is, in the language of Plotinus, in a life without love of the world a flight of the Alone to the Alone'.

It is not, I suppose, necessary to point out that this doctrine is very far removed from what is commonly called selfishness. That, indeed, is the antithesis and opposite of Mr. Weir's ideal, for it essentially implies a constant relation to an outside world of material *desiderata*, that lowest form of apprehension which we share with the animals. From this it is as far removed as in Aristotle's doctrine the lower form of *philautia*, which aims at wealth or power, from the higher kind which aims at filling the true self of man with its appropriate nurture of noble deeds and pure contemplation.[1] Indeed, this doctrine, in some form or another, has been held by a large number of saints and mystics; it cannot be lightly dismissed or set aside; it takes a high view of man's place and his destiny, and therefore of the nature of that education through which his place can be maintained and his destiny fulfilled.

But it is only fair to set against this in direct contrariety the theory of education which emphasizes its practical and administrative aim. According to this second view we are sent into this world not to cultivate our own souls, not to find at once our duty and reward in mystic contemplation, but to help as best we can towards solving its problems, healing its miseries and strengthening its efforts. So far from our depreciating the reality of other selves, it says, in spite of metaphysics, that they are of greater importance even than our own. It is not affrighted by the phrase about gaining the whole world and losing one's own soul, for its motive is not gain, but service. The ideal which it sets before itself is to do what comes to its hand for the amelioration of those lots among which it is cast; and whether its circle of operation be the family, or the city, or the nation at large, it finds the fulfilment of its being not in the striving towards perfection but in the active and operative exercises of its powers on objects outside itself. No one has ever put this more succinctly than the King of Brobdingnag in Swift's allegory who held

[1] See Aristotle's *Ethics*, IX, viii, and compare Bishop Butler's Sermon (No. xi) on Self-love and the love of our neighbour.

that all accumulation of knowledge for its own sake is of far less account than its exercise for the benefit of others, and that the greatest benefactor of mankind was the man who made two ears of corn grow where but one grew before. After all, we have Shakespearian warrant for saying that

> If our virtues
> Did not go forth of us, 'twere all alike
> As if we had them not.

We may find some traces of this doctrine as far back as Aristotle, for although Aristotle was too much of a Greek to lose sight of personal perfection and of the infinite value of the individual soul, he was also too good a citizen to undervalue or to disallow the work which every man should do for the society which he helps to constitute. All through the *Ethics* we are reminded that human happiness consists, not in the possession of high qualities, but in their active and prolonged exercise; and one fundamental difference between his contemplative life and the beatific vision of Plato's Guardians is that Aristotle's philosopher willingly remains in the world and performs his civic duties without constraint and without reluctance.[1]

I have dwelt on the distinction between these two ideals —the ideal of self-perfection and that of active service— because they must affect in some measure the content of any educational system. Yet here we should be careful not to state as absolute what is really a matter of relative proportion. In every true career both elements must be present: without the spiritual culture man would faint and fail in his efforts at public service, or, what is worse, might be warped or poisoned by sordid and unworthy aims; without the wholesome and bracing contact of practical life the mystic has sometimes tended to 'lose himself in an *o altitudo*', or even, as we find in the stories of some ascetics, to impair the natural balance and equipoise of his faculties. It is significant that both schools of thought can

[1] See Aristotle's *Ethics*, X, viii, 6: one of the most important passages in Greek moral philosophy.

claim the example of our Lord by taking a partial and imperfect view of His work. To the one He was the standing challenge of the self against the world, the typical example of the soul which is entirely occupied in communion with God: to the other, and it has equal ground for its belief, His mission was, in St. Peter's phrase, 'to go about doing good,' and an essential part of His work is consummated in the functions of teacher and of healer.

Now it is clear that in proportion as we emphasize the former of these two ideals, in such proportion shall we magnify the place which should be occupied in education by the culture of humane letters. For the function of these is above all things to bring the soul into direct contact with the best and the noblest thought of all ages and in such a way to afford it that training and that discipline by which its highest attributes would be best developed. This is not to deny or depreciate the value as discipline and training of the mathematical and physical sciences; they exercise an invaluable influence in making our thought secure and exact; but it is no paradox to say that a large part of their domain is occupied with the imparting of actual knowledge which can be turned to practical account. The engineer, the electrician, the metallurgist in one sphere, in another the physician, the surgeon, the bacteriologist are all acquiring and using knowledge which is of immediate practical value; and it is obvious that their education must be in some degree determined by the requisition that they should meet the needs which these sciences exist to fulfil. While, therefore, all the sciences have their respective values as forms of mental discipline, all those which we roughly classify as natural—and to which we sometimes rather arrogantly appropriate the name of science—have both in their purpose and in their preparation a direct reference to that external world, a mastery over which is, as Bacon tells us, one of the rewards of education. But for those who are going to follow active pursuits, who are preparing for practical careers, there is still much opportunity for training in the humanities, and the nature and limits of this opportunity we may now proceed to discuss.

I put this forward with the more freedom because of the two educational ideals I profess myself to be on the whole an adherent of the second. Charles Kingsley once said in his blunt way that religion was not 'a set of soul-saving dodges', and in like manner we may hold that we are not fulfilling the real purpose for which we exist by bringing each his own soul to the highest possible pitch of cultivation, but by augmenting the happiness and advancing the progress of the generation to which we belong. Such a view easily lends itself to burlesque. Every one, for example, who has any ambition to help others should constantly keep in mind Dickens's caricature of the hard-faced, tough-hided philanthropist without sympathy, without gentleness, without real kindness of heart, who goes about her business as mechanically as a Prussian drill-sergeant, sowing disturbance and reaping cordial dislike.[1] Another example, less well-known than it deserves, runs through a story by Mr. W. J. Locke. The hero, a man of wealth, ability, and position, is told by his doctor that he has an incurable disease and that there are only six months of life left to him. He takes the blow with philosophic courage, devotes the six months to the service of his friends, helping their fortunes and their love affairs with most disinterested sympathy, and with the result that when, at the end of the six months, an operation following on a new surgical discovery restores him to health and strength, he has mismanaged every life which he has touched and stands alone amid the wreckage without a friend left in the world. But these are parodies which do not really touch the essential truth. The life of public service is not necessarily officious or sentimental; it may have no more ambitious an ideal than that of doing the next job that comes to hand and of so equipping ourselves for this purpose that we can see the object in its true relations and estimate with reasonable probability the effect of

[1] See *Bleak House*, Chapter VIII.

our action upon it. Indeed, the wrong kind of service, miscalled by that lamentable name philanthropy, may often be no better than a particularly unsuccessful species of self-cultivation. Some years ago, when it was a momentary fashion that leaders of London society should pay hasty and sporadic visits to the East-end that they might there indulge in that cheapest of all forms of beneficence which consists in giving, one of them was rebuked by a tenement dweller in words which every philanthropic institution would do well to take to heart: 'Why', she said indignantly, 'must you come here to wipe your souls clean on us?'

The ideal of service, in short, is to be approached only as we depart from self-consciousness and ostentation. Even the sense of power, which is, perhaps, the most intimate of all our feelings, has no place here. The sole admissible desire is that the right thing should be done without any regard as to who does it and still less who gets the credit for it. And because some natural impulses of selfishness and vanity are inherent in human nature, together with our other undesirable tendencies, it is above all things advisable that our education should be such as to eliminate these and to leave us with that clear and dispassionate vision which, as the painters say, 'has its eye on the object'. While, therefore, I do not decry, but omit for the moment as irrelevant, that side of our educational system which aims at the accumulation of knowledge, I should like to emphasize as briefly as I can the very important part which, even in the world of affairs, can be taken by the study of pure letters.

If a man sets before himself the ideal of service with the hope, I do not say of success, but of reasonable efficiency, it is a prime necessity that he should begin by taking his bearings. Much depends upon his maintaining a right proportion between self and circumstance, between claims and duties, between his own capacities and the occasions of their exercise. Sometimes a man fails through diffidence, or hangs back in undue self-depreciation: like

Aristotle's 'man of little soul', who cramps and impedes his actions from a motive which is really timidity masquerading as humbleness. Far more common is the opposite error, that of the man who 'has too much ego in his cosmos', who sees his own powers and his own possessions apparelled in a celestial light which does not shine with equal lustre upon his neighbourhood. Everything which directly relates to himself—family, wealth, virtue, achievement—is set by him in a false perspective; they stand so near to him that they block out the view beyond. Such a man must always be at the height of the fashion, at the front of the movement: he is not content that good should be done unless he has a visible hand in doing it and a visible share in the renown which it brings. To both these men, and especially to the latter, the study of great history and of great literature is an invaluable corrective. The chief problems of human life, though they may differ widely in the manner of their presentation, are throughout the ages fundamentally the same: we shall best preserve our sanity and our sense of proportion in dealing with them if we learn how they have been met and solved by the men who have preceded us. Every one of us is tempted to think that his own experience is unique—that the like of it has never happened before, or that at least it has gained a special significance by happening to him. He will have acquired one of the most profound of all truths when he has realized that he is one private soldier in an innumerable army and that it is of far more importance that he should hold the post assigned to him than that he should dream dreams about a Field-Marshal's bâton in his knapsack.

But the value of great literature is not only that it teaches us to know our place and to maintain this without either belittling or magnifying: it is of still greater consequence in that it strengthens and clarifies our judgement. That we should look at life dispassionately is not enough, though this is the first condition of our looking at it steadily; truth is not so easy of attainment that it comes for the mere wishing; on the contrary, it is the reward of careful search and of faculties alert and well equipped. To such an end the classical writers of all countries make priceless contribution. They set before us our own difficulties, almost as we might state them ourselves, and they treat them with a large and luminous wisdom which, by the very attraction of sympathy, lifts and ennobles our minds; they leave us not with some external and superimposed decision which dominates our personality but with our power stimulated and our understanding enriched so that by their aid we can see with keener vision and decide with a wider and more humane intelligence.

'Consider', says Emerson, 'what you have in the smallest well-chosen library. A company of the wisest and wittiest men that could be picked out of all countries in a thousand years have set in best order the results of their learning and wisdom. The men themselves were hid and inaccessible, solitary, impatient of interruption, fenced by etiquette; but the thought that they did not uncover to their bosom friend is here written out in transparent words to us, the strangers of another age.' And again, for particular example, 'Go with mean people and you think life is mean. Then read Plutarch and the world is a proud place, peopled with men of positive quality, with heroes and demigods standing round us who will not let us sleep.'[1] Indeed, the testimony is all but universal. Hobbes in his paradoxical fashion may tell us that 'if he had read as many books as other men he would be as ignorant as they', but the support of Hobbes is like that of Pharaoh 'upon which if a man lean it will go into his hand and pierce him'. Goethe was the wisest man of his generation, and the most widely read; so was Johnson, so in a very different sphere was Aquinas, and the philosopher whose judgement, on almost every practical question in life, has stood four-square for over a couple of thousand years, is celebrated among us, in Dante's phrase, as 'the master of those who know'.

[1] Emerson, essay on Books in *Society and Solitude*.

Thirdly, the study of fine literature, and especially of the great poets, affords permanent food and sustenance to our sense of beauty. The melody and cadence of noble verse, the poignant phrase which drives to the very centre of the thought and fixes it in our minds as a possession for ever, the close communion through which the poet's imagination touches our own and kindles it as with a coal from the altar—all these are sacramental means of initiation into the deeper mysteries. The world would be a colder and bleaker place for us if we could not be moved to the heart by the serenity of Sophocles, the tenderness of Virgil, the white fervour of Dante, the perfection of Racine; by Shakespeare's orchestra and Milton's organ-voice and the intimate string-music of Wordsworth. The spirit to which they appeal is an essential element of our nature, and the satisfaction of its need is requisite not only as a means of self-cultivation but as an enhancement of our natural activities. For this reason I would urge that the learning of great poetry should be an essential part of all education: particularly in childhood, when the memory is most fresh and plastic, but continued in due measure through later years. It not only trains and tempers the character, it supplies us with an enduring treasury of beauty and delight.[1]

Before leaving this subject I should like to offer one more point for consideration. And although what I have to say is a counsel of perfection, an ideal which none of us can hope to attain, I am none the less serious in proposing it as a goal to which we should approach so far as our conditions allow. It is, no doubt, true that the literature with which we are most concerned is that of our own people. For one reason, this literature most closely reflects the nature of our own thought and the progress of our own civilization. For another it is expressed in a language with the refinements and resources of which we are specially familiar: which we know from inside, as only a chosen few

[1] For all this see the essay on 'Poetry and Imagination' in Emerson's *Letters and Social Aims*.

can know the speech of any other age or nation. Boileau, in an amusing satire, imagines a dispute between Horace and the Parisian *littérateurs* who were forming their language in the reign of Louis XIV. At every step the Roman poet falls into some blunder, using French words and phrases which could be justified according to the dictionary, but which in current usage were solecisms. At every step they correct him—one does not say 'la rive' but 'le bord' of a river-bank, one does not say 'la cité' when one means 'la ville de Paris' and so forth. Horace accepts their criticism, for indeed he cannot do otherwise, and ends the discussion with an ironic hope that they will desist from an equally hopeless attempt to write verses in Latin. All this is legitimate satire; it only emphasizes the deeper truth that if we wish to reap the full harvest of a foreign literature we should read it in the language in which it was written. There are very few translations—the Authorized Version of the Bible is the most notable—which do not lose something of the quality and fragrance of the original: they give us the substance of the thought but not the special beauty and appropriateness of its form. 'A very pretty poem, Mr. Pope, but you must not call it Homer,' was the judgement of Bentley, and his decision may be taken to cover even such marvels as Coleridge's 'Wallenstein', Conington's 'Persius', and Murray's 'Euripides'. In saying this, I do not depreciate the extraordinary skill which these writers have exhibited: I plead only that to reproduce the full tone and cadence of the original version is a task as impossible as to transcribe without loss of balance a sonata of Beethoven for the orchestra or a song of Schubert for the pianoforte.

Indeed, the reason may be given in terms of music. No two languages employ precisely the same instrument, and no two instruments have precisely the same harmonics. What is the English for 'Ich grolle nicht' or 'Si tu veux, faisons un rêve', or 'e il naufragar è dolce in questo mare', or a thousand other magical lines and phrases? How far is 'a young man void of understanding' represented by 'un jeune homme dépourvu de bon sens', or 'Absent thee from felicity awhile' by 'Verbanne doch dich von der Seligkeit'? And when to this is added that all nations look at poetry from their own angles, and that no two angles are coincident, it follows that the difficulty of transference from one to another is almost insuperable. Racine is one of the greatest of all dramatic poets. How often do we see him on the stage of any English-speaking people?

It will be seen, therefore, that I advocate the study of languages not so much for their colloquial use—though there is a great deal to be said on that score—as because they admit us to the inner sanctuaries of literature which otherwise we can contemplate only from the outer courts. And because, in the words of a wise physician, 'art is long and life is short'; because not all of us have the gift of tongues or the leisure for their acquisition, it follows that we must make some choice, contented with the second best in some directions if we can attain the best in others. What then shall be our choice for the period of formal education? French and German stand near to us and have great literary histories, but if we dig our foundations deeper we may acquire at least a reader's knowledge of them in after-life. Italian and Spanish have wonderful gifts of melody, and some of the first names in modern literature: their doors are open to all who have special predilection or special opportunity. Latin, the measure of a pure and exact style, is the tongue of Lucretius and Virgil and Ovid, of Catullus, Propertius, Horace, of Cicero and Livy and Tacitus: if we may have two languages we cannot do without Latin. But if we are to select one which is supreme as a vehicle of human thought, which is almost infinitely rich, flexible and sonorous, and which in the few hundred years of its prosperity embodied a literature which is by all acknowledgement incomparable, I would suggest, even in these days of apostasy, to plead that its ancient honour should be restored to Greek. It has an inherent splendour which even the bungling mispronunciation of later times has not been able to tarnish or overlay. As the inflected speech of a sensitive and artistic people it is filled with problems of rhythm and order and construction, and thus calls into play those gifts of observation and analysis which we continuously associate with the domain of science. And it has this high educational advantage that its masterpieces of literature are not confined to its more difficult and remote fields of study, but meet us with an open welcome from the very beginning of our course. Four of the most entrancing stories in the world are written in a simple and lucid Greek, the structure of which is transparent and the idiom easily acquired: from them, as travellers at a first landing, we can proceed through an enchanted region in which every step brings us new opportunities of noble adventure and delight. It is not too much to say that the study of Greek is in itself a liberal education; that it unlocks a treasure-house of poetry and practical wisdom and philosophic insight, of humour and pathos, of tragedy and romance, of religious fervour and scientific exactitude, to which even our own great literature cannot afford a parallel. America has, during recent years, borne a noble part in educational reform: the revival of Greek learning would add an imperishable laurel to her renown.

It must not be forgotten that I am here speaking about one aspect alone of education; that I am not entering upon that vast domain of discovery and research which is set on the conquest of nature and for which our schools and colleges must in part be the training grounds. To that I pay all honour and would give all opportunity. I am speaking of that kind of education which enables us to take a large and sympathetic view of human nature, to understand its conditions and its problems, and, so far as we have capacity, to help in solving or ameliorating them. It is the education of 'one who loves his fellow men' that I have chiefly in view; its aim is to equip him with wisdom and humour and a sense of perspective that he may play his part among his fellows without misgiving, without ostentation, and without thought of personal reward. For this

I am convinced that the best foundation is the study of great literature, our own first, others in order as we can reach them: we are not sufficient for ourselves, we need the comradeship and encouragement of the great minds that are openly at our disposal. And let no one meet me with a rejoinder about scanty time, and the overcrowded curriculum, and the overburdened life. There is not a school or college upon this earth which cannot, if it will, develop a taste for good literature; there is not a free man or woman who cannot devote an hour a day to reading, and these hours wisely spent will aggregate into a total of inestimable value. The real hindrance to our progress is not insufficient time but time misspent: wasted over mean books and ephemeral topics and transitory interests. We need be satisfied with nothing short of the very best: it lies at our hand in ready abundance, and the touchstone by which we may try it is to be found in the noble words with which Ruskin sums up the aim and purpose of education:

> 'God appoints to every one of His creatures a separate mission, and if they discharge it honourably, if they quit themselves like men, and faithfully follow the light which is in them, withdrawing from it all cold and quenching influence, there will assuredly come of it such burning as, in its appointed mode and measure, shall shine before men, and be of service constant and holy. Degrees infinite of lustre there must always be, but the weakest among us has a gift, however seemingly trivial, which is peculiar to him, and which, worthily used, will be a gift also to his race for ever'.

NOTE

Plato's theory of education as intended primarily for the culture and development of a privileged class has received in modern times a convergent support from an ally whom its author would probably have regarded with some misgiving. The whole doctrine of Nietzsche's *Lectures on the Future of Educational Institutions* is to the effect that education is degraded by being turned to active public service, and that its whole aim should be the perfecting of those chosen minds which he calls sometimes 'the lonely ones' and sometimes 'the few select ones'. This view, like the rest of Nietzsche's philosophy, can most readily be understood if we remember that he first made his reputation with an essay on Theognis of Megara, the most uncompromising Tory aristocrat in literature, and that his entire view of life is taken from this standpoint. His chief objection to Christianity, for example, was that it was based on compassion for the weak and the suffering.

With this may be contrasted a far nobler statement of education as primarily cultural in Newman's lectures on *The Ideal of a University*. Newman delivered these in 1852 when English philosophy was still preponderantly utilitarian, and he therefore emphasizes very strongly the value of knowledge for purposes of mental discipline rather than for purposes of practical equipment, but throughout he endeavours to hold a balance between knowledge for its own sake and knowledge as qualifying its possessor to be a useful member of society. He gives in Discourse 8 an admirable picture of the type of character which he wishes to foster and encourage; and in a famous passage of the introduction he tells us that 'when the Church founds a University she is not cherishing talent, genius, or knowledge for their own sakes, but for the sake of her children, with a view to their spiritual welfare and their religious influence and usefulness—with the object of training them to fill their respective posts in life better and of making them more intelligent, capable, active members of society'. This is a conclusion on which it would seem that all conflicting schools can meet and join hands.

Music and Education

III. THE PLACE OF MUSIC IN HUMANE LETTERS

IT is possible that the close of my last address left you with the impression that I am after all an academic recluse who has no eye for realities, or at best regards them through a study window begrimed by the dust of ages. If there are any here who incline to this view I would reassure them by declaring once more my conviction that the best-educated man is he who is best fitted to occupy his station in life and to fulfil the duties which it entails; that such an education covers the whole personality with all its faculties and attributes; and that I am emphasizing one aspect only because this has sometimes been allowed to fall into comparative disregard. Against such a reaction I make no complaint: it is a phenomenon of frequent occurrence; but I would plead that in matters of educational progress the swing of the pendulum is a dangerous metaphor which may be misused to cover the false belief that human nature is a mere mechanism and that its equilibrium tends toward immobility.

We have seen how large a part can be played in the training of intellect and character by a careful, selective study of language and of the great literatures of which it is the expression. Among such languages I claim a high place for the language of music: among such literatures for musical composition. It follows, therefore, that I should indicate the grounds on which this claim can be made good, and the practical method by which its requirements can be satisfied. The case is one of such inherent truth and justice that if I fail to carry conviction it will be the fault of the advocate.

The issue has been seriously obscured by our inveterate habit of excluding music from our general survey of history and of civilization. Macaulay, for example, devotes twenty-four long, eloquent and copious chapters to the History of England from the Restoration to the death of

William III. He does not restrict himself to political events and issues, though with these he is no doubt chiefly concerned: he aims at covering the whole area, at dealing with every side and aspect of English life during this period. One chapter, indeed, is occupied with the social, intellectual, and aesthetic progress of the country, with poetry and drama, with scientific achievement, with architecture and sculpture and pictorial art: one subject alone, and that of the first importance, is left without any mention. He has plenty to say about Dryden and Shadwell, about Wren and Lely and Kneller, about the growth of the Royal Society and the discoveries of Newton, Wallis, and Halley. But the reader will search in vain for any account of the way in which England was affected by one of the most remarkable periods in all musical history—the period which gave us opera and oratorio, which established the diatonic scale in place of the modes, which reorganized the strings, which inaugurated the orchestra, which filled Church, theatre and chamber with a new melodic idiom, and in which one of the chief creative forces was an English musician. The names which Macaulay has thought worthy of commemoration must extend to many hundreds: they do not include that of Henry Purcell.

More excusable, though hardly less unfortunate, is the common omission of books about music from our great histories of literature. It is, no doubt, true that many musical treatises are arid, and to the general reader unprofitable; that they are concerned with details of grammar and technique rather than with the collection of aesthetic principles; and that they are deficient both in style and in sense of proportion. But when these have been set aside there remains an adequate list of books which are at least deserving of consideration. To this the English contribution has been comparatively slight—it is of English neglect that we are speaking—but in the range from Elizabeth to Victoria it is not without witness. At the end of the sixteenth century came Morley's *Plain and Easy*

Introduction to Practical Music; it was followed in the seventeenth by Playford's *Introduction to the Skill of Music*, and by the admirable *Music's Monument* of Thomas Mace; in the eighteenth appeared the elaborate *Histories* of Hawkins and Burney, after them a series of smaller biographical or critical works—Kelly, Gardiner, George Hogarth, Lord Mount Edgcumbe, John Hullah—all heralding that renaissance of English music which was marked, nearly half a century ago, not only by the compositions of Parry and Stanford, but by Gurney's *Power of Sound* and the first volume of Grove's *Dictionary*. The only two of these who are mentioned in the *Cambridge History of English Literature* (*quam honoris causâ nomino*) are Hawkins and Burney—one as a member of Dr. Johnson's circle, the other as the father of Madame D'Arblay. No account is given of their musical writings.

It must not be forgotten that a notable change has taken place during recent years in the scope and purpose of history teaching. In my young days the history that we learned was mostly made up of battle, murder and sudden death: 'a register', as Gibbon sardonically says, 'of the crimes, follies and misfortunes of mankind.' When I was fifteen I could have given every relevant date in the Wars of the Roses, but knew nothing about the mariner's compass, or the invention of printing, or the building of St. Paul's Cathedral. And it was at a more advanced age that I came across a so-called 'School History of England', from which Shakespeare's name was omitted. But these and similar errors have now been remedied: we are still doing music the injustice of secluding it from the record of our common civilization, on no better ground, apparently, than the belief that it is a special and technical study in which only its practitioners can expect to be interested. And this is the more deplorable because the great events in musical history are closely connected with successive aspects of our civilization and are often illuminating as examples or commentaries. One of the most important facts in the history of the medieval church was the discovery of polyphonic singing: from the Bull of John XXII to the Council of Trent its fluctuations are of religious significance, and beside the famous Theologians and Reformers a high place should be assigned to Palestrina. The social conditions of the eighteenth century may be typically illustrated by the career of Handel: the French Revolution exercised as potent an influence on the Viennese composers as ever it did on the English poets: the psychological effect of Wagner's work has endured and broadened until the present day. We cannot afford to undervalue or disregard these streams of tendency: they are not backwaters, isolated and stagnant, but tributaries which find in the main channel of events their natural outlet: they are as vital to our understanding of human nature as are any other indications of intellectual or social progress.

Here, then, is a field of educational reform, that we should admit musical history to the same place in our annals which we now accord to the history of literature. Our culture is 'like an ill-roasted egg, all on one side', if we are familiar with Spenser and Shakespeare but not with Byrd and Tallis, with Milton but not with Bach, with Goethe but not with Beethoven: if we can interest ourselves in the vogue of the Elizabethan sonnet but not of the Elizabethan madrigal, and trace the growth of drama or novel without a thought to that of sonata and quartet and symphony. All these claim our investigation: all have borne their part in nurturing the spirit of man: indeed, if there be anything to choose between them we may even maintain that the influence of music has been the more subtle and the more penetrating.

But it is not only or chiefly in virtue of its historical record that the place of music is to be vindicated. This is only preliminary or at any rate ancillary to the study of music itself: to that first-hand knowledge of the composer's work without which the most eloquent commentary is useless. And because this reaches to the very heart of my subject I will ask leave to begin from the first elements, tracing as well as I can the course of the musical education which I have in view, and fitting into my scheme, when the moment comes, the stages which most appropriately belong to institutions of university rank.

Here may be noted a very curious and widespread superstition. Music is written in an alphabet of its own: an alphabet of minims and semiquavers, of sharps and flats and naturals, ruled for convenience on a stave of five lines and punctuated for convenience with a succession of upright bars. Like every other alphabet this is conventional: like every other it has its own system of fixed and determinate symbols, each with a special significance. It differs from the ordinary scripts of spoken language somewhat more widely than they differ from each other: we may even allow that it contains one or two anomalies which have grown up by custom and which men have not thought it worth while to eradicate. But it is legible in exactly the same sense in which we apply this term to the English alphabet, or the German, or the Greek, or the Russian, or any other which is used as a vehicle of human speech. Like them it has to be learned: when learned it can be read. Yet a vast majority of educated people maintain that the silent reading of music is an impossibility: what they call reading means playing or singing at sight or, in the farthest extreme, following a performance with the score: that a man should profess to read Beethoven 'with his feet on the hob' is an audacity which they are prevented only by natural politeness from denouncing as imposture.

To all this we may find analogies from outside. The cross housekeeper in *Lorna Doone* declares that no one can read print; that those who appear to do so have learned the passage by heart, and are only affecting to decipher it in order to impress their auditors. Some people of backward education do all their reading aloud: 'Si je lis haut', says M. Colladan in Labiche's comedy, 'c'est pas pour vous, c'est pour moi. Toute fois que je ne lis pas tout haut je ne comprends pas ce que je lis'; and I have observed people at a higher educational level who, when they add up columns of figures accompany the process with moving lips and a running murmur. But no one attaches any weight to this evidence: no one holds that it is impossible to do what many people do all day: the marks on the printed page are the symbols of audible speech, yet we convey them direct from eye to brain without any conscious mediation.

It is much the same with music. To read it silently is usually harder than to read prose or verse because one usually has to co-ordinate a number of different lines, but it is certainly not impossible or unprofitable, for an increasing number of people are doing it with genuine pleasure. In more complex cases it may, perhaps, be analogous to map-reading, where a trained eye can follow the shape of the country from the contour-lines; only in the most elaborate modern scores has one to read too slowly for enjoyment. And I believe that the younger generation, to whom the idiom of these works is familiar, does not even here find any real difficulty. This, at any rate, I can affirm from personal experience, that the silent reading of the great classics is not only a delight in itself, but vastly enhances the fuller and rounder pleasures of the audible performance. You may hear a given Beethoven quartet perhaps twice in a year: learn to read it and you have it always at hand. What would be our knowledge of Shakespeare if we could not read him silently?

Our ideal education in music should, therefore, begin through the natural avenues of reading and writing. The practice of musical dictation, now customary in many English schools, is the method to be employed: after acquiring the first alphabetical rudiments the child writes down a melody which it has just heard, or conversely, sings or plays a melody which it has just seen on the blackboard. In both cases the tune, whether apprehended through the eye or the ear, has to be swiftly memorized and it is remarkable in how short a time the exercise can be done with sureness and accuracy. At first only short and simple phrases are used (it would be the same with any other dictation); these can be extended as time goes on and experience matures: it is of further assistance to let the pupil learn pieces by heart and read them silently while they are still familiar; and in this way proceeding step by step from known to unknown it is possible to bring the faculties of sight and hearing into a very efficient co-ordination.

From the outset children should be accustomed to hear well-selected examples of the best music, and of the best alone. The ideal way of presenting these is that a competent teacher should play them with a running commentary pointing out not some fantastic conjecture as to their poetic meaning, but their felicities of phrase and melody and harmonic texture, of colour and surprise and climax, of coherent stanza and organic structural form.[1] At this stage the pieces should be short, for young attention easily wanders and a thread once broken is almost beyond mending; they should be clear, telling and rhythmic, so that they can most readily arouse and maintain the interest of the audience. Lyric numbers of Handel, of Mozart, of Beethoven are admirably suited to the purpose, so are the marches and polonaises of Schubert, the *Kinderscenen* of Schumann, Chopin's Mazurkas, the best of Mendelssohn's *Songs without Words*, the Hungarian dances of Brahms: there is abundance of first-rate quality and it grows more welcome as it grows more familiar. But above all things it is necessary that we should rigorously exclude every composition which is mean or enervating or vulgar. The two most famous of all educators have laid it down as a principle that children should be protected from every degrading sight or sound: discrimination comes with growth of years and maturity of judgement, and is far more likely to be rightly exercised if it is founded on a solid tradition of excellence. Much of the so-called

[1] If an adequate pianist is not available his place may be taken by a gramophone with carefully selected records. In any case there should be some descriptive analysis of the pieces performed.

music which is written for schools is wholly unworthy of its place: without purity, without talent, without significance, securing its place apparently by accident and keeping it by mere carelessness and apathy. For there is nothing in the world to which we apply a less effective standard than to music. I do not believe that people prefer the worse: they are ready enough to discard it when their attention is engaged: for the most part they listen in contented indifference which it requires a dynamic shock to disturb. Let me give two instances, both from my own experience. I once presided at a musical festival organized by a group of Sunday Schools. A special list of hymns had been provided ranging from a quality comparable with Shakespeare to a quality comparable with Martin Tupper. Next year I was asked again and pleaded, in accepting, that the bad hymns should be replaced. Back came a most courteous and kindly answer: the Committee understood that there were some tunes to which I took exception, they had no idea which these could be, but if I would indicate them my wishes should be respected. Still more notable was an Educational Conference which devoted one of its days to an exhibition of school orchestras. The competitors played with spirit and enthusiasm, they had been carefully drilled and their performance was very creditable. But the programme was a nightmare. Out of some twenty-four pieces there was only one which had any claim to be regarded as music: the others were dull and trivial futilities which, for the most part, did not even make sense. I was invited to criticize, and after commenting with genuine admiration on the attack and accuracy of the performance, added that in those competitions with which I was familiar the organizers paid special attention to the character of the music and allowed nothing of inferior value to be admitted. 'Quite right,' said the superintendent with fervour: 'so do we.'

It may be said that these illustrations prove too much; that if the distinctions were as wide as I have described them they could not so thoroughly escape the notice of reasonable listeners. But two points may be offered in rejoinder. First, that in music as in other arts—and perhaps more than in other arts—the degrees of merit and demerit, of attainment and failure, tend to shade into each other. It is impossible to divide all music bluntly into good and bad as you distinguish the squares of a chess-board into black and white: there are infinite gradations on the way—and hence, although the extremes are as far removed as the *St. Matthew Passion* from Barnby's *Rebekah*, it requires some effort of attention to follow and interpret the scale. Secondly, this attention is one which the ordinary public has not yet learned to bestow. We have been so long browbeaten into the belief that music is a hieroglyphic mystery into which we have no right to penetrate; we have come to regard ourselves as the ignorant laity beyond the gates, we accept without question everything that is offered us; and we are constantly liable to mistake for the true initiate any temple-slave in masquerade. One of the urgent reasons for a better musical education is that it will encourage us to rely more on our own judgement; and the surest way of strengthening our judgement is that we should feed it, during its most receptive and plastic years, on the purest, noblest, and most life-giving fruits of truth and beauty.

At some stage in musical education, and probably at this period of school life, there should be some systematic drill in the elements of theory. It is of great assistance afterwards to know such technical terms as designate ordinary matters of fact, and though in music these are mostly dull and uninspiring, they are not many in number and are not difficult to learn. At worst they are no harder than the 'terms of art' used in architecture or painting or literature, they are far easier than those which are coined every day by the terminology of science. I have read a book on psychology in which one of its most eminent professors is described as a 'hormic interactionist', and even this pales beside 'strophanthinized', 'phenyldiethylammonium iodide', and 'the morphology of the Telencephalon of Spinax'.[1] 'Thou didst talk', says Sir Andrew Aguecheek, 'of Pigrogromitus, of the Vapians passing the equinoctial of Queubus: 'twas very good, i' faith.' Much advantage, too, would be gained by studying at this point the elements of harmonic texture: not from the text-book, still less from the figured bass (which together with the canto fermo in semibreves should be banished from every class-room) but from the living model, the mastery of Bach, the transparence of Mozart, the 'curiosa felicitas' of Chopin: beginning with simple relations of treble and bass alone and showing in gradual accession of parts how skilfully the web is woven, how evenly the dialogue is maintained. Most important of all, because vital to the understanding of the larger classics, is a study of the chief architectural forms in music: mass and madrigal, opera and oratorio, suite, partita, and overture, the fugue and all that it implies, the complex organism of sonata and quartet and symphony. These form the very plot and ground plan of all musical composition: if we do not understand their principles we are like a theatre-audience to whom the whole construction of the play should be unintelligible; and though we may in such a case get some momentary entertainment from particular actions or episodes, it is no paradox to hold that we are less favourably placed than our neighbour who knows the language.

It is an arguable question how far the students whom we have chiefly in view—those who are taking music as part of a liberal education—should be encouraged to play on instruments or to compose. Of the two I incline to lay stress on the latter. Many more people have an aptitude for it than is commonly supposed; and even if the results are of no great value the attempt to produce them is abundantly rewarded by a quickened sensibility and a more intelligent appreciation:

[1] I omit, because I am unable to pronounce, such names as Dicyanohydroxymethylcyclohexylethanedicarboxylicanalyde, and Hydroxyketomethyldihydropyridenecarboxylonitrile. They must make the exchange of chemical repartee very difficult.

As a wise workman recognizes tools
In a master's workshop, loving what they make.

Solo playing I should discourage except in cases of real aptitude, but all who can should take part in the practices of the school orchestra and the pieces should be adapted so as to admit of as many recruits as possible. Above all, choral singing should be universal. The cultivation of the solo voice is best deferred until after the period of adolescence: a period at the beginning of every day should be set aside for class-singing, not only because it is a delight in itself, but because it is the best of preparations for the work that is to come after. And if any one complains of encroachment, and talks of the overweighted syllabus or the overcrowded curriculum, I answer that the quarter-of-an-hour so expended will be more than repaid by the enhanced alertness of mind and the readier acceptance of discipline. A great prima donna once said to me, 'You cannot be in a bad temper while you are singing'; and to have attained that is itself an achievement.

For this purpose two books are required: a collection of hymns and a collection of secular songs. Both should be specially edited by the best panel of judges available—it would be an easy matter to choose such a panel in this country—and kept on the highest level of words and music without favour or compromise. The books need not be long, a hundred each would probably be sufficient, for they must be acquired and loved by each generation: they should certainly not be 'written down' to the supposed capacities and sympathies of children, but should be of a quality which will make them life-long possessions. Both should, of course, be drawn from all available sources: the hymnaries and song-books of many countries may be brought into requisition, and from their varied gardens may be gathered a wreath in which no blossom is flecked or ill-shapen.

We are now in a position to consider the end and aim towards which this address has been directed—the assignment of music to its proper place in the studies of a university or of an institution of university rank. Ideally speaking, we should presuppose that before this stage is reached the ground which we have already surveyed should have been traversed; that the student as he approaches this threshold should bring with him a general school education in music and some knowledge both of the outline of its history and of the elementary principles of its structure. But this, though highly desirable, is not a *sine qua non*. Institutions and colleges of higher education are sometimes obliged to make good certain deficiencies in science or letters which are due to imperfections of earlier training; and though this is a real drawback and hindrance in the educational course, we cannot at present legislate as though it were altogether absent. We can minimize it; we can prepare for a time in which it vanishes before a better co-ordination; to ignore it as an existing problem is to shut our eyes to known facts. We must therefore acknowledge, as a possibility, that students in whom this course of training is not presupposed may yet qualify if they are so minded for the university course. They will require to be provided with special preliminary classes in which they make up for lost time: there is no need to bar the door on them at the outset. I remember the winning of a first class in *Literae Humaniores* by a candidate who, at entrance into Oxford, was unable to read Greek; and although this was a very exceptional achievement of genius it cannot be ruled out of consideration.

In whatever way the elements have been acquired it is on their foundation that the university course should be built. For this the personnel and equipment can be easily stated, and, in a country so generous to education as America, should not be difficult to provide. The music department should be in a separate building, at some distance from the rest of the university, and constructed with walls which are, so far as possible, sound-proof. Providence has not thought fit to supply us with ear-lids and our sense of hearing must, therefore, be allowed some adventitious protection. Readers of Burney will remember the practising room at St. Onofrio[1]:

'On the first flight of stairs was a trumpeter, screaming upon his instrument until he was ready to burst; on the second was a French-horn bellowing in the same manner. In the common practising room there was a *Dutch Concert* consisting of seven or eight harpsichords, more than as many violins, and several voices, all performing different things and in different keys; other boys were writing in the same room; but, it being holiday time, many were absent who usually study and practise there together.'

In our music school there should be abundant class-room accommodation, both for lectures and for seminars, a private study for each member of the staff, and an adequate concert-room, staged for full chorus and orchestra, with every mechanical contrivance for extension or adjustment, and equipped with piano, organ, gramophone, and wireless receiver. Much of this equipment, at any rate the piano and the gramophone, should be duplicated in the various class-rooms, and be used daily for the illustration of lectures on musical analysis and construction. But far the most important of all material resources, the centre from which the whole of the teaching radiates, should be the music-library. The object of this should be principally and in the best sense of the term utilitarian: a tool-chest rather than a treasure-casket. All to the good if it can also contain some specimens of bibliographical rarity and value: Morley or Mace or Dowland's *Ornithoparcus*; a black-letter MS. on vellum, or the holograph score of a famous master: but its main office is not that of the collector but that of the teacher and guide. The first charge, then, on its ample and recurrent revenue must be the scores, whether original or adapted, of all the great compositions which are appointed for study, chosen with the widest and most impartial catholicity from every age and style. Palestrina is not too remote nor Stravinsky too modern;

[1] Burney: *Present State of Music in France and Italy*, p. 336. (31 Oct. 1770.) St. Onofrio was at this time the most famous conservatoire in Europe. Among its principals were Leo, Durante, and Porpora.

Grieg is not too innocent nor Brahms too austere; every coin of true mintage should have its currency and only the dross and pinchbeck refused. After these come the chief accessible histories and works of reference: Grove, for example, and Riemann, and Guido Adler, quarries of information in which all strata alike are comprised; and after these again a careful selection of the books that have been written about music, the works of biographer and critic and commentator, and even as need arises of the prosodist and the grammarian. Here, however, a word of caution is necessary: musical criticism is extraordinarily difficult to write. The famous classical examples—Berlioz, Schumann, Wagner—need not here be brought into evidence: all that those men wrote is of high biographical value and it does not concern us much if we hold that for perfect equipoise Wagner was too polemic, Schumann too fantastic, and Berlioz too prejudiced. But apart from these, the moments of high success have been rare and disputable. There are some interesting and distinguished writers from Hanslick to the present day: the torch is even now being upheld by Bekker and Pfitzner, by Henderson and Ernest Newman, by the younger writers who are bringing to their subject a new breadth of sympathy and a new alertness of intelligence: yet I do not think it possible to claim that even the best musical criticism has attained the serene and unconscious security of judgement which marks the essays of Dryden and Emerson and Sainte-Beuve; it is still feeling its way, trying to express some of the most subtle truths of aesthetic in a language that was framed for other ends. And this acknowledged sense of difficulty has had an ill effect on the practice of the art as a whole. Where no one has fully achieved there has been a lenient eye even for gross and palpable failure; to write bad musical criticism is as easy as to write a bad novel, and, in an age when every one reads and no one thinks, even the feeblest of efforts is allowed to pass muster. All this aimless and ephemeral writing should be rigorously excluded from our bookshelves; all critical treatises that ask admittance should be subjected to the severest scrutiny, and those alone should be accepted which can without impropriety be compared with literary analogues; which at any rate the masters of literary criticism would recognize as apprentices in their workshop.

The question of personnel obviously depends on that of opportunity. If the institution is situated in a large town, where are already many music-teachers, it can in some measure utilize them as visitors or specialists. When it is remote or isolated it must clearly rely upon its own natural resources. In either case it must have a professor and a lecturer of first-rate standing: both learned, both endowed with insight and sympathy, both intent on showing the true significance of music and its relation to other forms of human study. To these must be added a librarian, and such other lecturers or demonstrators as the course of experience may suggest. At least one member of the staff should be a capable executant at the keyboard.

The cardinal object of such a department is to train the listener. Students who show special capacity as executants or composers may be given every facility for instruction and practice: they correspond to students in other departments who have a talent for research; but the curriculum should be so framed and the courses of teaching and examination so devised that they are within the grasp of any one who loves music and who is prepared to give the requisite time and care to its comprehension. A considerable part of the teaching, therefore, would be occupied with what the French call a *lecture expliquée* of the great classics: the principal themes of a movement played on the piano, written on the blackboard, stated, interpreted, discussed, the whole organic construction gradually unfolded and explained, the work set in due relation with the condition of music at its time, its indebtedness to the past as clearly shown as its influence on the future: all, in short, done for Beethoven which the teachers of literature would do for Shakespeare or Goethe. And if a discontented critic complains that music will be strangled by 'the clammy fingers of the educationalist', I would answer with all respect that he is beating the air. Nothing is further from my desire than that the mind of the student should be either stunted by second-hand admiration or desiccated with irrelevant detail: these are not methods of education but its calamities and diseases. But a vast majority of mankind is at present outside any judgement of music because it does not understand the language in which music is written. All that I want, for the sake both of music and of liberal education, is to break down that barrier. We hear too much of the 'unlearned love' which seeks not to know but to enjoy. It is a false antithesis: Browning was far nearer the truth when he told us that admiration grows as knowledge grows. But the hostility of the artist to the educator, of the poet to the philosopher, is mostly half-humorous. Remove the pedant from behind one of them and the mountebank from behind the other—the true men will join hands readily enough. No artist has ever more eloquently satirized the pedagogue than Sir Walter Raleigh, who lectured on English literature for over thirty years. The study of musical texts, with the theoretic and historic background which they imply, should be one of the recognized options of the curriculum and, at any rate in arts and pure science, should have equal citizenship with all other options. Undergraduates who are not offering it as a part of their course may well be encouraged to attend the more general classes: if they have any love of music they will not be sent empty away. Every concert within reach should be heralded by a lecture on its programme: the only reason why an intricate classic bores some people is that they cannot disentangle its melodies; and they will have a very different experience if they come to the concert-room with the clues already unravelled. On the other side, every one who can play an instrument should be invited to join the college orchestra, and every one who is not constitutionally unable to sing should be pressed into the college choral society. In both of these it is possible that the conductor will at first be confronted with some difficulties of balance; these will adjust themselves in the course of experience; and it must be remembered that a great deal of admirable music is written within a narrow range of orchestral resource. Much can be done with a piano or organ and a body of strings: if one or two wind instruments can be added the door is thrown wider open: the tradition once set is certain to be followed and will add much to the pleasantness of university life.

It is worth considering what influence could be exercised by such a department on the music of religious worship. The standard of an entire continent might be set by a choir, selected from all the available resources of the university, adequately trained and rehearsed, and properly directed in the choice of music for performance. A choir so constituted would be hampered by no prepossessions, baffled by no difficulties; it could give the motets of Palestrina, the cantatas of Bach, the hymns and anthems to which almost every civilized nation has contributed; it could build up and display to the world a monument of religious and liturgical music which would endure for ever. In almost all places of worship the present selection is either too narrow or too undiscriminating: either it leaves untouched a heap of valuable treasure which it might have for the asking, or, more frequently, debases its jewel-work by the admixture of paste gems and tinsel setting. Sometimes the bad music has crept in by carelessness and maintained its place by mere use and wont, sometimes it has been admitted on some paltry ground of compromise or personal favour: in either case it should make room for the abundant sufficiency of the very best. In chapel as well as in concert-room our universities may rightly uphold the banner of noble, generous and sympathetic melody.

It may be said that in dealing with this last topic I have wandered from the centre of my theme, and have entered on a larger and more disputable field of investigation. With this criticism I should not agree: the service of music to religion is one of the supreme facts of human nature, and no system of musical education can afford to leave it out of due account. At any rate, no decision on this particular issue will affect my main contention: that music can have and ought to have a place among the humane studies which enter into a liberal education. It is a language of extraordinary beauty and subtlety with laws of organic growth which will repay the work of investigation: it possesses a literature of composition which may be set beside any literature of poetry or prose: its doors are open to every student who is not physically disqualified, and its rewards are among the most precious with which the spirit of man can be enriched. Too long have we stood outside the threshold of this art, hearing dimly and confusedly the harmony of voices within: we have but to enter and we are assured of welcome and companionship.

SOME LANDMARKS IN EDUCATION[1]

IN the old days of motoring there was a famous story about a nervous passenger who, for the first time, was being driven by an enthusiastic and rather reckless amateur. After some jolting and discomfort he succeeded in shaking out the words, 'Would you mind telling me what is this old graveyard that we are passing through?' 'Graveyard?' said the driver. 'Graveyard? Oh, milestones!' I cannot help being reminded of that story when I attempt to comprise within a brief oration an account of the principal landmarks that stand in the course of educational history. I can only hope to select those that seem to me of most importance, and to collect them together so that they will seem to you not so much a succession of gravestones as of monuments.

Educational conditions in classical antiquity were in so many respects different from ours that their schemes may serve more for contrast than for comparison. Education to the Greek writers was the privilege of a leisured class which had virtually no professional work to perform and which cultivated its mind in such times as were set free from the easy task of public administration. In the Persian Schools, as described by Xenophon, there do not seem to have been even any lessons, except some small amount of technical training for the priesthood. The rest of the school day was occupied partly in the cultivation of the body and partly in the practice, under supervision, of debates on moral and legal issues. Herodotus sums it up as comprising three branches of instruction—to ride, to shoot with the bow, and to speak the truth: an admirable education for an open-air, aristocratic life, but not bearing very exhaustively on the problems of the present day.

In like manner the Athenian education was essentially that of free citizens whose daily needs were supplied by the labour of others. The Athenian gentleman served his

[1] Delivered on the celebration of the one hundred and fourth anniversary of the foundation of Birkbeck College (University of London), 1927.

country in the assembly and in the law courts and in the army, and betook himself to Socrates or Plato or Aristotle more for the general improvement of his mind and character than for any acquisition of skill or knowledge. Indeed, the educational systems both of the *Republic* and of the *Politics* concentrated far more on character than on attainments. There was an almost over-sensitive fear lest the teaching should be turned to any practical account, and it is significant that the first teachers in Greece who used their instruction as the practical equipment of a career were held by their contemporaries in great disfavour, and have come down to us under the depreciatory title of the Sophists. Even in the later days of Greek University education, when the term 'Sophist' had risen into high repute and was indeed the equivalent of what we should call 'Professor', the subjects which these men taught and by which they attained fame and fortune were not those which required exact knowledge or investigation, but rather a fluent tongue and a brilliant display of rhetoric.

Something of the same conditions prevailed in Roman education, though this seems to have been more consciously directed towards the aims of civic and administrative life. At Rome also oratory was the most natural avenue to a civic career, and it is characteristic that our most important book on Roman education is a treatise on oratory by Quintilian, one of those amazing Spaniards who came over to Rome in the first century of the Empire and seems to have swept the entire board both of literature and of administrative office. History has shown more than one instance of an invading nation which has won its victories in peace and not in war. Among such instances a notable place should be assigned to Rome in the reign of Augustus and his immediate successor.

We may, perhaps, trace the origins of our modern scheme of education to the conditions which prevailed during the decay of the Roman Empire and especially to the works of Boethius and Martianus Capella, both of whom lived in the fifth century and exercised a vast influence on the civilization of the Middle Ages. The latter of the two is, indeed, something of a literary portent. He was an African rhetorician of considerable repute in his day, who wrote amongst other things a work called *The Marriage of Mercury and Philology*, which continued in some sense to be the basis on which was built the formal education of the Middle Ages. It is in nine books, written in a frigid, artificial style which makes it very hard reading, and, as an example of literature, truly deserving of the oblivion into which it has now descended. But it popularized a scheme of education which lasted, with certain necessary developments, for nearly a thousand years.

The first two books are occupied with an account of the wedding of Mercury and Philology (the very collocation of their names is significant); the other seven are devoted to the seven sciences who attend the ceremony as bridesmaids. Three of these, Grammar, Logic, and Rhetoric, formed what was called the Trivium, or threefold way, with which formal education began. The other four, Music, Arithmetic, Geometry, and Astronomy, formed the Quadrivium, or fourfold way, which represented the further stage in educational method. For the most part the seven books are dull and arid disquisitions on purely technical points of detail. There are a few exceptions. The section on geometry, with which Martianus Capella includes geography, gives a brief and succinct account of such countries as were known to the geographers of the time; the section on music opens with an account of a concert, which, though too vague to be of much service to us, is not without interest. But the reader of to-day may go through the entire work and find very little either of instruction or of entertainment. At the same time the book is of great historical importance. The two schemes of the Trivium and the Quadrivium held their own in the academic world almost to the time of the Renaissance, and we may therefore certainly count Martianus Capella as one of the landmarks in educational history.

Meantime, however, there was coming from another

quarter a stream of learning which did an immense amount to fertilize the rather barren fields of Western Europe. It will be observed that in the Trivium and the Quadrivium there is not very much room for anything which we could describe as natural science, and indeed, all scientific method was very much hampered and checked by the clumsy systems of the Greek and Roman numerals. Towards the ninth century, however, or a little earlier, the Western world began to feel the influence of Arab learning. The Arabs had preserved in translation many of the lost works of Aristotle, and the discovery and translation of these revealed a new world of investigation and research. Beside these they revolutionized all sciences which involved calculation by bringing with them what we significantly call Arabic numbers. It is not possible to tell from what source these originally came; a good case is made out for India, but it was almost certainly the Arabs, and particularly one Mohammed Ben Musa, who brought them over and popularized them. Their far greater ease of manipulation, and especially the system called algorism, that is, the use of the zero to alter the values of numbers by altering their position, gave a new resource to the arithmetician and to the scientists who were dependent on him, and indeed, so strange and bewildering were the results that in some writers of the time *ars metric* is used as a synonym for magical arts. Hardly less important than their contribution to the theory of numbers was the advance that they made in the study of medicine, and secondarily in some degree to chemistry, botany, and the allied sciences. The great medical school of Salerno was started early in the twelfth century and set a classical tradition which was followed by many schools and Universities in Western Europe. Other schools, like that of Paracelsus at Basle, were started in direct and conscious opposition to any traditional learning, and in spite of their petulance, succeeded in making some genuine discoveries; the more remarkable because medical science, like all investigations into nature, had to make its way through a good deal of suspicion and hostility and ignorance which seemed sometimes almost invincible.

Not that the investigators were always free from blame. They were sometimes self-interested, often jealous, and not infrequently light-hearted and imaginative. I have seen a facsimile of an early English herbal illustrated with admirable drawings of the plants described, on one page of which, to fill in an empty corner, the author has invented an impossible plant which he calls a 'pereterion'—compounded of a number of incongruous parts from different flowers—and describes it with the same gravity and thoroughness as if he had it on the table before him. It must be remembered that science was not always at this time conducted in a very scientific spirit.

To these were added two preliminary types which need here be touched upon but briefly, since they are fully described in Mr. Adamson's excellent *History of Education*. One was the distinctively churchman's education, largely Latin, Theology, and Music, which was conducted in the ecclesiastical schools, and had definitely the service of the priesthood as its aim; and the other was the court education, as exemplified in the charming picture of the Squire which Chaucer draws in the Prologue to the *Canterbury Tales*. A boy of good family in the Middle Ages went naturally into court service, first that of some great noble, later, if he were fortunate, that of some reigning king or prince. Up to the age of fourteen he was called a demoiseau or valet, was brought up with the ladies of the court, and was educated chiefly in games and in the acquisition of easy and gracious manners. From fourteen to twenty-one he was a squire and went through the course which is outlined in the *Canterbury Tales*. Thus he learnt to play and sing, to make verses, to be an adept at military exercises, to ride, to shoot, to carve at table, and above all to turn a pleasant compliment and behave himself as a member of civilized society. At twenty-one, therefore, he was not only a gentleman, but a gentleman of very considerable accomplishments. And if it be asked whether all the education was concentrated on the sons of the family and whether the daughters were left out in the cold, the answer is that there is considerable evidence of women's education during all this period. Some of the exercises were, no doubt, set aside as manly, but they learnt their full share of the accomplishments and amenities of life, and in some cases a good deal more. It required a considerable amount of energy and a trained mind to be the successful châtelaine of a medieval castle.

May I give you an example? Towards the end of the thirteenth and the beginning of the fourteenth century the French King Philip IV, who was a man of great missionary enterprise, inaugurated a scheme for converting the Saracens of the Eastern Mediterranean to Christianity. This involved the setting up of what we should call a co-educational college in France, in which the boys were to be taught Oriental languages in order that they might appeal to the Saracens by convincing their reason, and the girls were to be taught the science and art of medicine, in order that they might conciliate the Saracens by healing their diseases. It was expected that the preaching of the boys would be more effective if the girls had already brought the audience into good bodily condition, and it was even hinted that when the time came and the conversions had begun, the whole scheme might be consolidated by intermarriage. I am sorry to say that the college never really matured. I am not certain whether it ever actually opened its gates: at any rate there were few or no graduates.

Then came the Renaissance and a new landmark in the revival of Greek learning. We need not lay too much stress on the statement that the flow of Greek to Western Europe was set free by the Turkish capture of Constantinople. There was certainly some influence before that. But we need have no doubt that in the fifteenth century the flood came full spate, first to Italy and then to France and England. The brilliance of the Greek teachers and the revelation of beauty contained in Greek poetry and Greek art brought about a real awakening of men's minds and constituted another and very important landmark in the history of European education. Erasmus and Colet brought the new Greek learning to Oxford and were met at first with considerable opposition. Oxford has always had at any rate its Conservative Party, and this stood out vehemently against the new learning. Indeed, the University broke into two hostile parties who called themselves the Greeks and the Trojans, the latter maintaining the walls of Ilium against the Greek invasion. And I can still remember a passage in Sir Thomas More which says of it that 'either from hostility to Greek, or from a distorted zeal for other studies, or, as I am more inclined to think, from an inordinate love of sport and frivolity' it entirely refused to lend an ear to the innovators. When I read, as I still sometimes do, of eminent scientists who find all sorts of inadequate reasons for opposing the study of Greek, I like to think of the description of their predecessors handed down to us by Sir Thomas More.

Into the middle of this came the educational system of Rabelais, described in the twenty-third and twenty-fourth chapters of his first book. I find it difficult to speak of Rabelais's educational system with complete patience, partly because it seems to me very bad, and partly because it has been praised as if it was the last word in educational method. I do not deny that it is an excellent compendium or catalogue of different subjects which, reasonably applied, might form an invaluable system of education; that, indeed, it is a quarry from which our schools and colleges might with advantage hew some of their materials. But it is only a quarry, not a building. It sets out to occupy the entire twenty-four hours and comes lamentably near to fulfilling its purpose. The unfortunate pupil gets up at four in the morning, and while he is being massaged somebody reads aloud to him. He then has two hours in which to dress, which would seem an excessive time but that while he is dressing he is required to repeat everything that he learnt the day before. I do not remember any mention of breakfast, but when dressing time is finished there follow three hours of serious lessons, a game of tennis, carefully supervised, and then dinner, which seems to take place about ten or eleven in the morning. All through dinner his tutors lecture to him on the properties and sources of every single thing which is on the table; not only the meat and the vegetables and the fruit, but all the accessories as well. Immediately after dinner the cards are brought, and the sympathetic reader expects with a sigh that there will be a moment of leisure. But no; the cards are employed to teach arithmetic and are followed by a period of advanced mathematics and music, in the latter of which the pupil is required to master no less than seven instruments. After this come three hours more lessons. He is then taken to the riding school and made to ride for an hour; stopped in the garden and taught botany on his way home. When he reaches home he has supper, and at supper there is the same continuous disquisition on all the viands, where they come from, and how much they cost. After supper comes a lesson on astronomy, at the close of which he is required to repeat such as he can remember of the curriculum of the day, and especially to quote from as many classical authors as possible. It is not stated at what hour this unhappy child is allowed to go to bed, but I venture to give the assurance that as he sinks on his pillow and turns to sleep, the last sound that enters his somnolent ear is Q.E.D.

The use of Latin as a common language among educated Europeans suggested another curious and interesting development of education which had a considerable vogue in the sixteenth century, and which was no less than an attempt to conduct the whole intercourse of school life in that language. It was largely promoted by Roger Ascham in England, by John Storm at Strasburg, and by Michael Cordier (Macaulay's 'old friend Corderius') at Geneva. Not only did they require that Latin should be an habitual medium of conversation, at any rate in school hours—a requirement which I believe the statutes of some of our grammar schools have still unrepealed—but they encouraged and facilitated this by writing a number of little plays and dialogues expressing in easy Latin the ordinary events of school life. If we are to have a universal language Latin would certainly be a far better choice than Esperanto or Ido, but perhaps it is just as well that this fashion has passed away. It is an admirable vehicle for what Dr. Rouse calls the Direct Method. If it were in force throughout the school day it might cause embarrassment in more directions than one.

Still education was regarded as a liberal training for specially selected or privileged pupils, and of education so conceived we have, perhaps, the finest description extant in Milton's famous letter to Hartlib. I will ask leave to quote it for the sheer pleasure of saying the words: 'I call a complete and generous education,' he says, 'that which fits a man to perform justly, skilfully and magnanimously all offices public and private, of peace and war.' The more deeply you ponder upon that sentence, the more you will see that it goes to the very heart of the highest and noblest education. The three qualities are carefully selected and contrasted, and it seems to me that they cover the field between them.

Towards the end of the century in which Milton lived there came into the educational field a very interesting Bohemian called Comenius. He was an enthusiastic student of Bacon, especially of the *Novum Organum*, and he tried to found education on the same basis and to carry it out by the same method which Bacon had advised for the study of nature. Bacon, it will be remembered, claimed for his method that it equalized all intellects. Comenius held that the differences of intellectual endowment were so slight as to be inconsiderable, and proposed a sort of inductive method of education in which, as he held, such differences as there were would be wholly obliterated. It has not proved to be a very practicable scheme. There are still wide differences of ability which no method can bridge over, and though it is worth paying a tribute to the splendid optimism which believed that an educational highway could be laid down which all could travel equally and to the same end, yet we may doubt whether, even if this were possible, it would be a desirable ideal. To abolish the distinction between grades of ability, even if it could be done, would be dearly purchased if it involved the obliteration of the different kinds.

Of English education in the eighteenth century the less said the better. There were, no doubt, some bright spots; but the general atmosphere of Oxford and Cambridge was of almost Cimmerian darkness, and the majority of the schools were not very much better. As a matter of fact, life in our English Universities was far too comfortable. A boy with ability or patronage gained a scholarship which took him within the walls and maintained him at little intellectual cost. In due time he succeeded to a Fellowship and became a more or less learned vegetable, doing very little to instruct others and not much to improve himself.

This, no doubt, was in part a natural consequence of a customary method which was imposed on all alike, and which cost but slender trouble to devise and almost none to maintain. A landmark of the first importance was passed in the latter part of the eighteenth century, when Rousseau shifted the centre of gravity in education, and instead of imposing it on the child as a scheme from above, began with the investigation of the child's mind and worked outwards from that. In other words he began at the end not of the teacher's desk but of the pupil's desk. So far as we can assign any discovery to any one he may be said to have discovered what learned people now call the psychological method in education, which begins by endeavouring to find out what the boy or girl is good for, taking it for granted that they are all good for something, which I entirely believe; but that, which I also entirely believe, they are not all equally good for the same things, and that, therefore, different educational methods must be adapted to fit their different requirements. We know how successfully our modern educational scheme has been based on this principle. We do not drive all people nowadays into the same mill. We recognize, for instance, that there is a difference between the humanistic and the scientific types of mind; between the type, for example, which loves mathematics, and the type to which all mathematics are mere bewilderment, but which, as has often happened in England, can rise to very high eminence in other fields of intellectual work. There are indeed as many differences of mind as there are of feature, and education has to take these differences into account, to fit its scheme so as to suit their needs, and to provide them, as far as possible, with the resources and the equipment which they want for their training in school and for their careers afterwards. If, therefore, we are ever tempted to depreciate Rousseau and to call him a sentimentalist and other hard names, let us at any rate remember that we owe very largely to him the freedom and flexibility of our present education.

I have left no time for more than the briefest mention of two other setters-up of educational landmarks: Pestalozzi and Froebel, who carried on Rousseau's work from the beginning to the middle of the nineteenth century. Of these Pestalozzi's is the greater and more original mind; Froebel, indeed, began as one of his assistants and learned from him a great deal of his own method. Both had to encounter considerable difficulties. Pestalozzi was once in his life confronted by financial ruin; Froebel saw his schools closed by the Prussian Government, partly because they were too successful. Both contended vehemently in the face of obstacles, and both have become household words in educational history.

Let me close this hasty and imperfect sketch on the name of one man who has never to be mentioned here, or indeed throughout English education, without the highest regard and reverence—Dr. George Birkbeck. Many of you will remember how his praises were sung in the centenary year which is only recently over. I am therefore speaking after the event when I ask you once more to accord your tribute to the very great work which he did to the education of this country. By establishing the Mechanics' Institutes he opened a door through which countless numbers of his fellow countrymen have passed. He brought education down from its formal strongholds and set it to mingle in the streets with the mass of the people. You will have read of the fierce opposition with which his proposals were at first received, the dangers of revolution which they were expected to herald, the overthrowing of society which they were accused of involving. We can afford now to smile at those idle predictions, and to recall that some of them were even faintly heard when, under great pressure, the British Government first voted money for school building. But the attacks on Dr. George Birkbeck were so extreme that they defeated their own ends. Censure which is tempered and qualified and mixed with praise is very often a difficult opponent to meet; censure which is violent and passionate produces little or no effect, since no one believes that it means what it says. And now that the clouds of battle have rolled away and we can look on Dr. Birkbeck's work as it had been developed and consolidated during a century of continuous advance, we may say without flattery and without partisanship that he occupies one of the highest places in the educational work of this country.

There have been plenty of other landmarks—the great names in the public school and University life of our nineteenth century would afford material for many addresses—but it is sufficient if I have enabled you to see that the process of education has been in spite of ebbs and flows a continuous process ever since people took it seriously in hand, and that being a continuous process it is still far from its end. You, who are growing up now, will see far better educational methods and systems brought into being than belong to the generation of us who are passing away. I am very glad indeed to see that and to welcome it. I am quite certain that the advances which education has made in the past—and they have been very real and very valuable advances—are only an earnest of the further progress that it has before it in the future. I feel assured that there are many of you here present this evening who will see that progress beginning and so help it as to make it of good augury for future generations to come.

IAGO [1]

THE pivot of Verdi's *Otello* is the scena of Iago in the second Act which begins, 'Credo in un Dio crudel' —a deification of that power of evil to whose service he holds himself predestined and devoted. It is an outburst of unrelieved wickedness, casting ferocious scorn upon human suffering, human virtue, human life itself: Satan is God and Iago is his prophet.

It is not too much to say that for some three hundred years and more this was the accepted view of Iago's character. When at the beginning of the nineteenth century Ducis presented *Othello* in Paris, he was obliged, we are told, to re-write portions of it so as not to offend the artistic susceptibilities of the audience by a character of black and unredeemed villainy. Coleridge about the same time was lecturing on 'the motive-hunting of a motiveless malignity'. Later on Swinburne, who was not always sympathetic in criticism, dismissed the matter by describing Iago as 'an artist in tragedy', perhaps the least convincing of all explanations. It was not until Mr. Bradley's great essay that we began to see the character in its true perspective and in due relation to its circumstances. Mr. Bradley is, indeed, so thorough and so comprehensive that it may seem needless temerity to glean after his harvest, yet even he seems to have left one or two points which are worth further investigation. It is not Shakespeare's manner to people his plays with embodied characteristics of good and evil. He draws his characters in the round. And it may therefore still be questioned whether, when Kean played Iago as a human being, he was not more in the right than Hazlitt, who censured him for doing so: whether, in short, the 'villain', as he is bluntly described in the Dramatis Personae, is not meant to be a consistent villain of flesh and blood rather than an impossible combination of malice and hypocrisy.

At the outset of the play he is twenty-eight years of age, which means that he has been about ten years in the

[1] From a lecture delivered at the Sorbonne, December, 1927.

service. He is a good soldier, who has fought well 'at Rhodes, at Cyprus and on other grounds Christian and heathen', who has risen to the office of standard-bearer, and who believes himself to have a claim to that of lieutenant. Again he is evidently popular, a genial companion at the canteen who can take his glass and sing a good song; and, what is more to the purpose, he is the trusted adviser of everybody upon the stage. 'Honest Iago' they call him, and when any one of them is in trouble—Roderigo, Cassio, Othello, Desdemona herself—he is the one person in whom they all confide and to whose counsel they all appeal. It is clear that he has never been found out in any act of treachery or mischief, and, accomplished hypocrite though he be, yet ten years is a long period for a successful masquerade. Again he is wholly and inherently selfish: intent on his own advancement and unscrupulous as to the means of securing it; but there are two qualities which from a certain form of selfishness are almost inseparable. The first is a superficial good nature which likes popularity and is quite ready to purchase it by gift and service so long as they involve no serious cost. Many of the most selfish men in the world are agreeable and even kindly until you cross their interests: then they are adamantine. The second is an instinctive dislike of the sight of pain except where the temper is made cruel by anger or fear or jealousy. It is not pity, it is not compassion; it is a personal feeling of discomfort which is a spurious counterfeit of these. And because the world takes little pains to distinguish counterfeit from sterling, such persons are accredited with a sympathetic disposition when in reality they are only anxious to rid themselves of an annoyance. We have, therefore, but to suppose that, up to the scene which immediately precedes the play, Iago had never found any occasion to sting; that his life had run on a straight course with no rival to remove and no injury to avenge: if this be granted there is no difficulty in explaining his popularity and the confidence which every one reposes in him. He had all the external qualities of 'a good fellow' and nothing had as yet occurred to bring out the latent evil below the surface. Thirdly, his intellectual power, though extraordinarily keen and subtle, had very obvious limitations. He can treat the immediate situation, he can weave the immediate strand of the plot, with a skill and a dexterity that are almost uncanny; and it is evident as the play proceeds that he takes an intense pleasure in the exercise of his sinister ingenuity. But he has almost no foresight. His plot, as will be seen presently, is from hand to mouth, it constantly puts him to new shifts, it hurries him into a catastrophe of the nature of which he had, when he began, no expectation. His intellect in short is comparable to that of a chess-player who can make a brilliant next move, but who cannot see six moves ahead.

Fourthly, and this is in some respects the most important point of all, he is 'a filthy cynic' in his estimate of women. He simply does not believe in woman's purity, nor does he regard his disbelief as a matter of any moment. He takes the view which was commonly held by medieval satire and comedy that all women are 'guinea-hens', that all love is appetite, and that a deceived husband is a target for laughter. He uses the vilest terms when he tells Brabantio of Desdemona's flight, and has evidently no idea that they are offensive.[1] He sets forth his doctrine to Roderigo in an easy familiar tone as though it were a commonplace of reasonable judgement.[2] His way of entertaining Desdemona, on her arrival in Cyprus, is to regale her with epigrams upon the unchastity of her sex.[3] And, for climax of testimony, he comes so near to believing in his wife's infidelity that he actually taxes her with it[4]; and yet it does not seem to make any difference in his treatment of her.

[1] Act I, Sc. I. [2] Act I, Sc. 3. [3] Act II, Sc. I.

[4] In Act I, Sc. 3, he doubts: 'I know not if't be true'. In Act II, Sc. I, his suspicions have ripened: 'I do suspect the lusty Moor Hath leap't into my seat'. By Act IV, Sc. 2, he has certainly accused Emilia, for she speaks of the false informer that 'made you to suspect me with the Moor'. Yet through the intervening time he makes her not only his comrade but his accomplice.

Such is the character,—cold, selfish, unscrupulous, not gratuitously malicious, impure and therefore sceptical of purity, keen witted but almost wholly devoid of imagination—into which there falls like poison a rankling sense of injustice. His friends have applied that he may have the lieutenancy: it has been given to Cassio, whom, rightly or wrongly, he regards as his inferior. It is idle to inquire (though it has often been inquired) whether his description of Cassio is a fair statement: you do not expect an angry man to speak fairly of a successful rival: the key-note of the play is that he is mortally aggrieved and offended by Othello's action. When Roderigo says:

> Thou told'st me thou did'st hold him in thy hate,

Iago answers not with a plain affirmative, but with a flash of rage—

> Despise me if I do not,

and then breaks like a flame into the tirade about favouritism and neglected merit which is one of the most genuine outbursts of emotion in his entire part. There is, I believe, no understanding of the play unless we realize that Iago's first motive is a rankling sense of personal wrong. He hates Cassio because he is jealous of him: he hates Othello for having given him cause of jealousy: he makes up his mind to cry quits upon both of them. But it is not a diabolic attraction to evil for evil's sake: it is a very human passion of revenge smarting under injury.

As yet there is not the smallest indication that he wishes or contemplates the death of either. If he had there were plenty of means at his disposal. He simply wants to hit back: first to wound Othello without losing his favour, then to degrade Cassio and 'have his place'. And here comes in the second of his three motives. His desire for revenge, though keen, is not so keen as to obliterate his ambition. He wishes 'to serve his turn upon the Moor', but he wishes also that the Moor shall appoint him lieutenant. And so from the first he stands committed to a double game.

For his revenge upon Othello Fate seems to bring an immediate and ready opportunity. The Moor has just married by stealth Brabantio's daughter. Why not raise hue and cry upon him and have him arrested? The Signory will annul the marriage, perhaps impose some penalty in addition. Of course Iago must not appear, but the night is dark and he can slip away before the lights come.[1] And what subtle irony to go to Othello, while the blow is still impending, and with a smooth and plausible face offer him condolence. Politic, too: for it will give honest Iago another claim when the lieutenancy falls vacant. So, with his next move fully considered, he sets Roderigo battering at Brabantio's door: everything at the moment falls out as he would have it: and in Act I, Sc. 2, he is at Othello's side, pouring out his fears in sympathetic voice:

> But, I pray, sir,
> Are you fast married? Be assured of this,
> That the magnifico is much beloved,
> And hath in his effect a voice potential
> As double as the duke's; he will divorce you,
> Or put upon you what restraint and grievance
> The law—with all its might to enforce it on—
> Will give him cable.

The trial takes place, and Iago's weapon bursts in his hand. With that want of imagination which is his essential weakness he had never expected that Brabantio would be unselfish enough to leave the decision to his daughter, and that Desdemona would be loyal enough to declare, before the full Signory, in favour of her husband. The marriage is not annulled but confirmed, and Othello,

[1] Act I, Sc. I. 'Farewell, for I must leave you:
It seems not meet nor wholesome to my place
To be produc'd, as, if I stay, I shall,
Against the Moor.'
Said to Roderigo, when Brabantio goes out to fetch lights.

appointed to high command in Cyprus, leaves the Court with his wife, unscathed.

As he is going out Brabantio speaks:

> Look to her, Moor, if thou hast eyes to see:
> She hath deceived her father, and may thee.

And these words set Iago musing. There is a still better revenge in store. Desdemona has shown herself loyal in the court-house, but she is a woman and no woman is chaste. 'Virtue, a fig! 'tis in ourselves that we are thus, or thus.' She may be a precisian in appearance but 'the wine that she drinks is made of grapes'. And here is the young fool Roderigo pining for love of her and threatening to drown himself in despair. One could help him and pay off the Moor at one stroke. After all it is no very great injury. Othello has played false with Emilia, or at any rate there is suspicion of it; fair retaliation allows that he should be requited in kind. Fidelity is as empty a word as virtue. 'It cannot be that Desdemona should long continue her love to the Moor.' 'She must change for youth; when she is sated with his body, she will find the error of her choice.'

There cannot, I think, be reasonable doubt that Iago is speaking his real mind. It seems false criticism to caution us that we 'must disbelieve everything that he says'. When he has anything to gain by falsehood he lies without hesitation and without remorse: when he is forming his plans we must surely assume that he is expressing his own view of the forces which he intends to control. It is a part of this view that to be deceived is the common lot of husbands and that the pain of deception is the sense of being outwitted, of being made a laughing-stock. In Iago's time this was the favourite jest of every barrack-room in Europe: it was his punishment that he took it for earnest.

Roderigo goes away comforted, and Iago, left to solitary meditation, plans an amendment to his scheme. Cassio is 'a proper man': he shall be represented as the lover, whether truly or falsely makes little difference: there is an equal chance for the faithful friend who warns Othello that his honour is imperilled, who denounces the marauding villain, and who as a natural result succeeds to the villain's office. The two strands of the double game twine into a single cord which, as he tests it, appears to him unbreakable. 'I have't,' he cries exultantly, 'it is engendered'; and with these words enters upon a course, of which if he had foreseen the upshot, he would not have advanced another step. What he intended was to clear off a couple of scores and by so doing to become Othello's favourite and deputy. What he effected was the murder of two persons with whom he had no quarrel, the suicide of Othello, and his own death by torture.

The scene shifts to Cyprus. Iago has the honour of escorting Desdemona, and her sweet and gracious welcome of Cassio rouses his foul mind to the hope that his plans are maturing.[1] Indeed, he is so totally incapable of comprehending her purity that he actually debates with himself whether he will not also become her lover.[2] Then his thought turns again to Cassio:

> I'll have our Michael Cassio on the hip;
> Abuse him to the Moor in the rank garb,
> For I fear Cassio with my night-cap too,
> Make the Moor thank me, love me, and reward me
> For making him egregiously an ass
> And practising upon his peace and quiet
> Even to madness.[3]

In this speech, immediately after he has looked on Cassio as a possible rival, Iago shows for the first time that he has some dim comprehension of the meaning of jealousy. And even so the lines quoted above are of a strange irony in the light of what follows:

> Make the Moor thank me, love me, and reward me
> For making him egregiously an ass.

[1] 'That Cassio loves her, I do well believe it;
That she loves him, 'tis apt; and of great credit.' (Act II, Sc. I.)

[2] *Ibid.*

[3] Act II, Sc. I. See the whole scene.

That is Iago's view of the situation as it stands before him at present.

Meantime an opportunity occurs of striking at Cassio more directly. A holiday is proclaimed, with a night of festivity and rejoicing. Iago deliberately makes Cassio drunk, induces Roderigo to provoke him, Montano intervenes, there is a scuffle, a blow, an outcry; Othello is summoned, Cassio censured and degraded: one score is paid off and the path to preferment reopened. This is the only episode which Iago manages exactly as he intends; the only one in which his ingenuity is triumphant. On this field he is master of the circumstances, he plays upon each character in turn, he is dealing with forces which he understands, and he directs them unswervingly to his purpose.[1] It is significant of the whole play that this complete and rounded success is by a higher tribunal of the Fates most emphatically reversed on appeal. Cassio by a treacherous plot is disgraced in the eyes of his General; the Venetian Senate, which has heard nothing of the matter, shortly afterward supersedes the General and appoints Cassio in his room.

As yet, however, none of this can be foreseen, and the next move looks as though the Fates themselves were playing on the side of Iago. Cassio comes to him for advice, is recommended to win over Desdemona as advocate, and by gratefully accepting this counsel, walks, it would appear, straight into the web that is to enmesh him. It only follows to warn Othello: a little counterfeit anxiety, a few insidious hints, and the whole thing is achieved. But as his plot proceeds it grows more dangerous. There must be evidence of some sort, and every piece of evidence is only an additional opportunity of confronting him with the truth. He is evidently uneasy: he braces himself up to the deed in a speech of fierce and savage irony[2]—sure sign of a troubled mind—you can see that there is beginning

[1] Act II, Sc. 3 (first half).

[2] Act II, Sc. 3—beginning
'And what's he then that says I play the villain?'

faintly to form within him the conviction which he afterwards puts into plain words [1] that he himself stands in much peril. In the first of his three scenes with Othello [2] he employs his hateful skill at its wariest. In the second,[3] after he has obtained the handkerchief, he grows bolder and is beginning to instil his venom with a more lavish hand when suddenly his whole sky is rent by a thunderbolt. Othello who was to have 'loved and thanked him' flies at his throat in an outburst of half-articulate fury:

> Be sure of it: give me the ocular proof:
> Or, by the worth of mine eternal soul,
> Thou had'st been better have been born a dog
> Than answer my wak'd wrath.

And again:

> Make me to see't; or, at the least, so prove it,
> That the probation bear no hinge nor loop
> To hang a doubt on; or woe upon thy life!

And again:

> If thou dost slander her and torture me,
> Never pray more.

Here comes to a climax the third and last of Iago's motives. He is afraid. For the first time Shakespeare makes him speak in heightened and emotional language: his tone grows vehement, almost melodramatic, even his iron self-control is for the moment shaken. And because he is essentially of the temper which fear makes cruel, so from henceforward his purpose becomes darker and more terrible. His life is at stake: he must at all hazards win the cast: whatever stands in his way he is now relentless. Yet even here is a tiny gleam of compassion which flickers for a moment before it goes out. Cassio is the person whom he has chiefly to fear: 'The Moor may unfold me to him: there stand I in much peril.' Cassio, therefore, must die swiftly and speedily before any explanation is

[1] Act v, Sc. 1.
[2] Act iii, Sc. 3 (earlier part).
[3] Act iii, Sc. 3 (later part).

possible. But as yet he does not fear Desdemona. In his abominable code it is a commonplace convention that the suspected wife should lie in self-defence, and that the husband should place no credit in her protestations. He has nothing to gain by her death: 'Let her live,' he pleads.[1]

By the next interview[2] even this spark is extinct. Between Act III and Act IV Iago has had time for further reflections. After all, it is possible that Othello may believe Desdemona; if that were to happen there could be no doubt about the issue. Better make all secure even if it cost another life in the making. And so follows that scene of unbearable cruelty—the false confession, the torture strained beyond breaking-point, the horrible exulting triumph, the planning of Desdemona's death-warrant,—which fills to the very brim the measure of human wickedness. But it is not 'motiveless malignity': it is malignity sharpened and accentuated by a keen sense of personal danger.

As if to make this clear, Shakespeare at once adds two scenes in close relation. At the end of Act IV, Sc. I, the Venetian senators come to supersede Othello and appoint Cassio to the generalship. Earlier in the play Iago would have heard this with jealous anger: now he passes it by without even the comment of an aside. It will serve later for an argument to Roderigo: for himself he has matters of more immediate moment to consider. Again in Act IV, Sc. 2, Desdemona sent for him to ask his advice about her husband's estrangement. He comes with conflicting impulses. He has plotted against her life, against her honour, but he cannot see her in sorrow without a feeling of discomfort. His tone softens as he addresses her—first 'Madam', then 'Lady', then 'Fair Lady': he soothes her with mechanical words of consolation, 'Do not weep, do not weep. Alas the day!' There is no possibility of his relenting—he is too deeply engaged. There is no question

[1] It greatly heightens the drama to regard this plea as genuine.

[2] Act IV, Sc. I. Observe that Shakespeare places it in a different Act from the two preceding interviews: i.e. after a short lapse of time.

of true pity—he is now beyond its reach. But for the moment he lets his thwarted ambitions and his personal fear fall into the background until he is set once more upon the alert by a sudden challenge from Emilia:

> I will be hanged, if some eternal villain,
> Some busy and insinuating rogue,
> Some cogging, cozening slave, to get some office,
> Have not devised this slander: I'll be hanged else.

'To get some office.' It is a bow at a venture but it pierces the joints of the harness. At once he fears that he is suspected. 'Fie,' he answers hastily.

> Fie! there is no such man; it is impossible,

and as she proceeds with more urgency he apprehensively bids her 'speak within door'. Desdemona's plea gives him time to collect himself, and his tone again grows gentle: but 'office' and 'Cassio' are running through his head, and he answers her with 'business of the state' and 'messengers of Venice': a reply natural enough in any case, but especially significant here. His mind once more oscillates between personal fear and thwarted ambition, and when he leaves Desdemona's presence, it is to plan forthwith for the assassination of his rival.

But the stars in their courses fight against him. It is the poor dupe Roderigo who is killed: Cassio escapes with a hurt grievous indeed but not mortal. All hope then turns on the death of Desdemona.[1] Cassio cannot possibly speak until the morrow: even then he is disgraced and discredited, he has been caught with Bianca, he has wounded a man in the open street: his testimony may be negligible if Desdemona is no longer living to confirm it. And so Iago, holding this welter of emotions and apprehensions in an iron grip, offers to the scene his words of regret, sympathy, even moralization; and when the stage is clear reveals his innermost heart in the hoarse cry:

[1] Observe the tremendous irony with which this situation reverses that of Act II, Sc. 3.

This is the night
That either makes me or foredoes me quite.

His last thought, before the final downfall, is of the narrow razor-edge on which he stands between safety and ruin.

It is curious that he does not fear Emilia. Once already she has nearly imperilled him, yet he holds her in such light account that he actually sends her with a message to the citadel,[1] where, if the crime for which he hopes has been committed, she must inevitably discover it; and if not she may delay or prevent its commission. It is a stroke of sheer folly: the reaction of a brain overwrought by excess of scheming: it is done instinctively, without forethought, to play out the scene. What more natural than that he should send his wife on such an errand? So might Lady Macbeth have sent Banquo to watch in Duncan's chamber.

When she confronts him by Desdemona's death-bed (for under some irresistible fascination he has followed her to the place) we see that his strength is gone, that nothing is left but the wreckage of his quick and resourceful villainy. He mutters a faltering excuse, 'I told him what I thought': he threatens, 'Get you home: be wise, and get you home': as the peril grows more visible he breaks into a torrent of foul abuse: at last, in panic rage he loses all self-control and confesses his guilt by stabbing her. He is so purposeless that he tries to escape by flying from the room: forgetting that he is in the centre of the citadel and must assuredly be apprehended before he can reach the gates. When he is brought back under arrest he knows that all is over: he speaks one word of bitterness, then relapses into a fixed and stubborn silence, and so he goes to his death.

The play is almost as much Iago's tragedy as Othello's: the tragedy of a nature, selfish indeed at the outset but not malignant, which is driven into unforeseen crime by successive impulses of resentment, jealousy, and fear. There

[1] Act v, Sc. i (end).

are some indications that he sometimes hates himself, and the whole black business: he speaks of it as devil's work: he says of Cassio:

> There is a daily beauty in his life
> Which makes mine ugly:

yet he is caught in the toils of his own sin, and if he struggle is but the more deeply implicated. That he is the wickedest man ever portrayed upon the stage may be admitted without reserve: the contention is that Shakespeare has made him not a mere personification of evil but a possible human being with human qualities. At first he has virtue enough to win the liking and esteem of his fellows: he has bravery, he has geniality, he has even a faint sort of kindliness and good nature. The beginning of his downfall arises from the desire to avenge a wounded self-love and a wronged self-interest. Of the two plans which he proposes, one only, the displacement of his rival, is clearly seen by him: of the other he can neither understand the nature nor foresee the issue. When his plot is once begun every step forces him to go farther, until he reaches a point where, on peril of his life, he dares not recede or hesitate. And at that point the abyss opens.

THE USE OF COMIC EPISODES IN TRAGEDY [1]

THE practice of interweaving tragic and comic strands, characteristic of English Drama in the seventeenth century and of Italian Opera in the eighteenth, has been vigorously attacked and stoutly defended by critics who have not always fully realized that the main office of the critic is neither attack nor defence, but interpretation. To make an arena of literature is to clear the field for combatants who hardly ever join weapons, for they hardly ever strike on the same plane. One censures for lack of passion where the other praises for chastity of form: one maintains that the plot moves slowly, the other that the characters are skilfully developed. So in Dryden's essay Lisideius blames tragicomedy on grounds of artistic impropriety, Neander answers him on grounds of indulgence and relief. 'Tragicomedy', says the one, 'is like an ill-wrought web: many of the scenes have nothing of kin to the main plot . . . the actors keep their distances as if they were Montagues and Capulets, and seldom begin an acquaintance until the last scene of the fifth act.' And again—'There is no theatre in the world has anything so absurd as the English tragicomedy: 'tis a drama of our own invention, and the fashion of it is enough to proclaim it so: here a course of mirth, there another of sadness and passion, a third of honour, and fourth a duel: thus in two hours and a half we run through all the fits of Bedlam.' To which Neander rejoins by shifting his premisses. 'Why', he asks, 'should Lisideius imagine the soul of man more heavy than his senses? Does not the eye pass from an unpleasant object to a pleasant in a much shorter time than is required to this? and does not the unpleasantness of the first commend the beauty of the latter? . . . A continued gravity keeps the spirit too much bent, we must refresh it sometimes as we bait on a journey that we may go on with the greater ease. A scene of mirth mixed with tragedy has the same effect upon us which music has between the acts; and

[1] Address to the English Association, February, 1915.

that we find a relief to us from the best plots and language of the stage if the discourses have been long.' Here, no doubt, the form of the dialogue enables Dryden without inconsistency to argue on both sides; but even when the matter comes to a more personal issue he can change his ground with the same confident and disarming frankness. The plot of his own *Spanish Friar* is commended by him in the dedication for the same division of interest which makes him, in the parallel of Poetry and Painting, dismiss it as 'an unnatural mingle'.[1]

Professor Schelling calls the term tragicomedy a misnomer, and the entire accuracy of his stricture is borne out by the alternative definitions which he is forced to draw from plays to which the name has been applied. 'It may result', he says, 'in two ways, either by deepening the situation of comedy into a serious mood by the infusion of a sentimental or a pathetic interest; or by the resolution of a situation essentially tragic into reconciliation.' If this is so we must simply revise the usage which has given the title of tragedy to the *Eumenides* and of comedy to *Much Ado about Nothing*. Indeed, most of the so-called tragicomedies of the seventeenth century fall readily on one or other side of the line. *Philaster*, for instance, is pure romantic comedy, so are *The Renegado* and *The Maid of*

[1] The defence has, it is true, a tone of special pleading. 'There are evidently two actions in it; but it will be clear to any judicious man that with half the pains I could have raised a play from either of them: for this time I satisfied my own humour, which was to tack two plays together, and to break a rule for the pleasure of variety. The truth is the audience are grown weary of continual melancholy scenes; and I dare venture to prophesy that few tragedies except those in verse shall succeed in this age if they are not lightened with a course of mirth. For the feast is too dull and solemn without the fiddle. But how difficult a task this is will soon be tried; for a several genius is required to either way; and without both of 'em a man, in my opinion, is but half a poet for the stage. Neither is it so trivial an undertaking to make a tragedy end happily; for 'tis more difficult to save than 'tis to kill. The dagger and the cup of poison are always in a readiness; but to bring the action to a last extremity, and then by probable means to recover all, will require the art and judgement of a writer, and cost him many a pang in the performance.'

Honour: *A King and no King* is placed by Dryden in 'that inferior sort of tragedies which end with a prosperous event'. Poetry, as every one knows, lends itself very ill to exact schemes of nomenclature and classification: we do not improve matters if, like over-ambitious gardeners, we confuse our classes by the production of artificial hybrids. It is of some moment to ascertain, if we can, how and for what reason the tragic and comic spirits have so often been allowed to alternate and even to intermingle.

We may begin with the type in which incongruity is at its most obvious—the Opera of the eighteenth century. There, between the acts of *Agamemnon* or *Alexander* or *Mithridates*, it was the custom to give Intermezzi—little simple comedies of which *La Serva Padrona* is the best-known example—occupying pleasantly enough the time needed for scene-shifting, but containing, as Lisideius puts it, 'nothing of kin to the main plot'. That the practice was extended to oratorios will surprise us less if we remember that the opera seria often took its subjects from Bible history, and that oratorios were usually presented in a theatre.[1] But in both alike the explanation is the same. The discrepancy was veiled partly by the music, partly by the very intermittent attention of the audience,[2] but chiefly because the tragic operas were not in any real sense of the term dramatic at all. They sometimes contained passages of fine poetry, especially when Metastasio was the librettist, but they were bound by so uniform a convention of characters and sequence and plot that any experienced playgoer knew the whole course of the story from the beginning. They were cast in dramatic form because this gave special opportunities for costume and stage-carpentry; but they were essentially musical performances in which the audience was no more offended by incongruity of mood than by a scherzo after a slow

[1] Kozeluch's three most famous works were *Judith*, *Deborah*, and *Moses*: two of them operas, the third an oratorio.

[2] The plans for the first opera-house at Vienna were rejected because the boxes did not contain room for the card-tables.

movement or a bourrée after a saraband. Indeed, it must have been a genuine relief to turn from the rather stilted and artificial beauties of the *bel canto* to these tiny unpretentious interludes which were at least human and amusing; and it is possibly due to the absence of such relief that Dryden's heroic plays (which are fully as 'spectacular' as grand opera) were comparatively unsuccessful. They had not the inherent strength of tragedy, and they grew wearisome by 'stealing from themselves'.

The problem, then, becomes more interesting when it deals with plays in which the tragic issue is essential or at least predominant, and comic incidents or characters are introduced as accessory to the design. And here may I pass very rapidly over a piece of what Macaulay would call 'fourth-form learning'? In the earliest meaning of tragedy the root-idea is not that of pain—hardly even of conflict, though this makes its appearance at any early stage—Aristotle's phrase for it is 'the representation of a serious action', μίμησις πράξεως σπουδαίας,[1] and the word which he selects is that used all through the *Ethics* for the 'good' man, and more distinctively in the famous passage which says that 'earnest is better than jest'. With tragedy a so-conceived laughter is out of tune, not so much because it is unsympathetic as because it is irreverent; because it jars with the gravity and dignity of the theme. In the lighter, more jocund, more relaxed moments of the festival it was welcomed; but it had in the truest sense of the term 'no kinship' with the mystic sacramental hymns among which, if the traditional story is true, even the loftiest tragic episodes were at first allowed only a cramped and grudging admission. The

[1] So says Milton:

Sometime let gorgeous Tragedy
With sceptred pall come sweeping by,
Presenting Thebes' or Pelops' line,
Or the tale of Troy divine,
Or what (tho' rare) of later age
Ennobled hath the buskined stage.

earliest proverb coined by Greek Tragedy[1] is a protest that all dramatic action is an encroachment on the priestly prerogative. And this consorts not only with the religious origin of tragedy among a people whose highest ethical ideals were gravity and dignity, but with the intensely religious impression which even we gain from the tragedies of Aeschylus and of Sophocles. The one 'carries his theme on a wave of religious emotion' as strong and fervid as that of Isaiah, the other bathes it in a great peace in which suffering itself is hallowed by submission. But with Euripides the standpoint is changed. The gods are no longer impeccable and unquestioned arbiters; the heroes are made human, and their acts viewed in the light of common day. In the *Hippolytus* the sinner is not Phaedra, but Aphrodite: at the end of the *Ion* Apollo slinks behind the scene lest he should be forced to make open confession of his shame: Telephus and Peleus, poor and in exile, lay aside the high ritual phrase as they lay aside the ceremonial Ionic dress, and speak in the garb and in the manner of ordinary mankind. So the drama comes to appeal more directly to the sympathies of men: the sense of conflict quickens, and with it the pity and fear that belong to everyday life. The old religious light which irradiated everything is beginning to fade away: what is to take its place lest tragedy becomes too poignant to be endured?

One answer which Euripides found was his treatment of the choruses, those lyrical outbursts of pure music which, though they are in the key of the plot, sing their own melody. But for its choruses the tragedy of the *Trojan Women* would be almost unbearable; they give in perfect beauty those moments of rest and recuperation which are needed to relieve the overstrained nerve and the overwrought emotion. And there is another and a more intimate means. Sympathy is with joy as well as with sorrow: the conflict brought to its most acute point of issue may determine on the happier side, and the spectators

[1] Οὐδὲν πρὸς Διόνυσον.

after a suspense, artfully prolonged by moments of relief in the plot, may see the balance incline in the direction of their hopes. Such for instance is the treatment of the *Iphigenia in Tauris*, of the *Ion*, of the *Hypsipele* (so far as we know it), and especially of the *Alcestis*, in which the scenes of pure comedy between Admetus and Pheres and between Heracles and the old butler are a necessary preparation of the final event. And of these plays three at least have every right to be called romantic comedies.

There is on this point a curious piece of evidence to which scholars have not perhaps paid the full attention that it deserves. One of our best authorities for the vocabulary of the Greek classics is the lexicon of Photius compiled at Byzantium in the tenth century. Under the word *κροταλίζειν*, which appears in the *Hypsipele*, he gives a definition, and adds 'as used by Euripides the comic poet'—*ὥς φησιν Εὐριπίδης ὁ κωμικός*.[1] It is surely noticeable that a master of Greek scholarship should ascribe comedy to one whom Aristotle calls *τραγικώτατος*, but who among his fellows most often sets out to compass a happy ending and who deliberately discards the heightened and prophetic style of his predecessors. We may recall another poem which was called a *Divina Commedia* because the 'end was prosperous, pleasant, and desirable, and the style lax and unpretending, being written in the vulgar tongue'.

Roman tragedy consists for us of a few fragments too slight for any induction, and of the academic plays of Seneca which have survived to the odd fate of discrediting their apologists. It had no root, and therefore it withered away. But when Church and Ostrogoth had combined to demolish the debased Roman theatre, a modern drama arose which was again built on a religious foundation. This time there was an essential difference of theme. Leaving aside the important question of nature-worship, which no doubt influenced the Greek drama as well as

[1] This is Porson's reading. There have been attempts to alter it, but they do not seem very successful.

that of modern Europe, it seems clear that the main stream of our Western dramatic literature took at any rate one of its sources from the mystery of the Crucifixion, the conception of God not as victorious and triumphant, still less as blameworthy yet irresistible, but as blameless and yet suffering. From this it spread in natural course to stories like the Sacrifice of Isaac (where the ram caught in the thicket is treated rather as an afterpiece than as part of the drama), and to the legends of Saints and Martyrs, which for the first time in dramatic literature ennobled suffering for its own sake. In the Greek drama the justification of pain is usually retribution: 'to leave a good man in adversity', says Aristotle, 'is not tragic but abominable.' In the Christian drama of the Middle Ages the good man is usually the victim, and the justification of his torment is the martyr's crown. It is clear that, given the unlettered public before whom these plays were performed, such a drama is laying down a special necessity for relief, for the relaxing of tension, for the healing of a sympathy which may be wounded by too keen a stroke. And so the plays were given on the holiday festival, in honour of which they introduced if possible a scene of levity and amusement, and where this was out of keeping you were held but a short time before you could go on to the juggler or the bout at quarter-staves. When the Moralities followed, with their abstract characters and their nakedly didactic purpose, they anticipated even more fully George Herbert's maxim:

> A verse may find him who a sermon flies,
> And turn delight into a sacrifice,

and were ready to bid for the attention of their audience either by spectacular effects, like Anima, 'with little devils running in and out under her skirts', and Belial, 'with gunpowder burning in pipes from his hands and ears', or by episodes of the Vice and the Devil who fought with wooden daggers and pelted each other with genial insults and light-hearted buffoonery. And at this point we are not very far removed from the comic scenes in Marlowe's *Faustus*.

Into this vigorous and rather turbid stream flowed the Classical Renaissance, which among other things brought Seneca to England: Seneca with his sententious maxims and his philosophic disregard of human limitations, Seneca who is so bleak a Stoic that he can represent Medea murdering her children upon the stage. So on the one side came *Gorboduc*, cold, dignified, and moralizing, and on the other the fierce melodramas which culminated in *The Spanish Tragedy*. And because such a conception of tragedy was all the more in need of lightening we have the 'tragical comedy' of *Appius and Virginia*, and *Cambises*, that 'lamentable tragedy mixed full of pleasant mirth',[1] in which one of the characters is flayed alive before the eyes of the audience and the plot is periodically broken by the humours of 'Huf, Ruf, and Snuf, the three ruffians', who do little more than reincarnate the Vice of the old-time moralities.

There are, then, two reasons why the English dramatists treated their form with greater freedom or greater laxity than the French. One is that so far as they accepted the classical tradition they followed worse models. A few years after Jasper Heywood's translation of Seneca, Jodelle was writing tragedies which, weak and immature as they are, nevertheless draw their inspiration direct from Greek originals. In the great days which followed, Racine certainly drank from the same source: indeed among all the masterpieces of classical French tragedy there is only one —Corneille's *Médée*—which derives from Seneca, and that brought to the task a hand trained in a better school. The second reason lies in a difference of national temperament; the finish and perfection of the French writers as against the English luxuriance, and even eccentricity, which Continental criticism regarded sometimes with admiration and sometimes with severe distaste. The liberty which Shakespeare claimed as a birthright would have

[1] Like *Pyramus and Thisbe* 'very tragical mirth'.

seemed to Racine no liberty at all, but mere anarchy and chaos, and it is worth remembering that before Voltaire's death France had become seriously and genuinely shocked at the vagaries of the English theatre.

So when our Elizabethan dramatists entered the field they had little care of paths or signposts. The Moralities were still going on with their licensed alternations of solemnity and laughter; spectacular dramas found their analogy in the pageants and public shows; the University plays brought a certain modish wit into prominence: the chronicle histories threw all the unities to the winds and ranged at will over an entire reign and an entire kingdom. The playwrights had, as a rule, no theories about their art, they were far too fully occupied in being artists; the critics, even when Sidney was of their number, had little influence in an age of almost universal controversy. Our poets adventured into the drama as our sailors adventured into the Spanish Main: at no time in the history of any art was prescription of less account or a man more free to deal with his own subject in his own way.

As a natural result we find among our Elizabethan plays almost every variety of treatment. Sometimes the tragic note is maintained throughout: Marlowe's *Tamburlaine* never lightens with a smile the 'stormy monotony of Titanic truculence which blusters like a Simoom through the noisy course of its ten fierce acts'[1]: Chapman's *Bussy d'Ambois* admits a few touches of humour, but there are none in *The Revenge*, or in *Charles Duke of Biron*: Jonson's two tragedies contain no scene that can be called comic, and in the preface to *Sejanus* he offers a proud apology for condescending from the tragic throne, even if it be no further than to the Forum or the Senate-house:

'Nor is it needful, or almost possible in these our times, and to such auditors as commonly things are presented, to observe the old state and splendour of dramatic poems, with preservation of any

[1] There were, apparently, some comic interludes in the acting version, but they were discarded when the play was published. See Jusserand, iii. 115.

popular delight. But of this I shall take more seasonable cause to speak, in my observations upon Horace his Art of Poetry, which, with the text translated, I intend shortly to publish. In the meantime, if in truth of argument, dignity of persons, gravity and height of elocution, fulness and frequency of sentence, I have discharged the other offices of a tragic writer, let not the absence of these forms be imputed to me, wherein I shall give you occasion hereafter, and without boast, to think I could better prescribe, than omit the due use for want of a convenient knowledge.'

At the other extreme lie all manner of wayward designs, from the farcical episodes in *Faustus* to the incongruous jests in *The Revenger's Tragedy*: Middleton's *Mayor of Quinborough* turns from the convulsions of a kingdom to the humours of a county election: Greene's *James IV* is so much concerned with Oberon that some critics have suspected an interpolating hand. Yet again there are, especially among the later Elizabethans, plenty of instances where the connexion is more close and organic; where the discrepant notes of tragedy and comedy are resolved into a dramatic concord. We could ill spare the three conspirators from *Perkin Warbeck*: in *The Virgin Martyr* the two rascally slaves not only throw the figure of Dorothea into fairer relief but are themselves the instruments of her martyrdom. More subtle, and more intensely dramatic, are the rare cases where the two strains are intermingled, where they are together inherent in the same person or situation. Such for example is *Vittoria Corrombona*: the wit of the heroine is as true a stroke of portraiture as is the flippancy, with which it is so vividly contrasted, of her coarser and more unscrupulous brother.

But the question of greater moment to us is how did Shakespeare use this form?—Shakespeare, whose practice is the rule and measure of criticism. And first, it may be noted that there is not one of his acknowledged tragedies in which the element of comedy does not appear. Even *Macbeth*, the closest-woven of all, has the scene of the porter: even *Hamlet*, which raises the most tremendous of tragic issues, has the players and the gravediggers and

Osric the waterfly.[1] In that house of many mansions there is not one from which laughter is excluded. It may be sardonic, as in *Troilus and Cressida*; or pathetic, as in *Lear*; it may be as gallant as Mercutio or as shrewd as the cobbler-politician in *Julius Caesar*; through one or other of its forms it is always at hand.

Now, setting aside the Clown in *Titus Andronicus*, whose scenes, if Shakespeare wrote them, appear to be legacies from an earlier method, we may say that in the tragedies *proprio nomine* the comic episodes fall roughly under two main divisions. And though here again classification is tiresome and unsatisfactory, the differences seem wide enough to require separate discussion.

One kind is that in which the comic scenes actually take their colour from the main scheme of the play, and are obviously and vitally necessary either to give circumstance to the plot or to prepare for some climax that is coming after them. To take a musical parallel: Beethoven, the most Shakespearian of composers, establishes his marvellous unity of structure partly by throwing out at the beginning of a movement a passage which immediately arrests the attention, and which is justified and explained by the latter development of the music,[2] partly by trans-

[1] A parallel example may be found in *Henry VIII*. The prologue announces a subject which is of the very essence of Aristotle's definition:

> I come no more to make you laugh; things now
> That bear a weighty and a serious brow,
> Sad high and working, full of state and woe,
> Such noble scenes as draw the eye to flow
> We here present.

Yet the play has room for the typically Shakespearian scene of the crowd and the testy gatekeeper.

In the *Pilgrimage to Parnassus* a clown is drawn on the stage by a rope. He protests. Dromo answers: 'Why what an asse art thou. Dost thou not know a play cannot be without a clowne?' Clowns have been thrust into plays by head and shoulders ever since Kempe could make a scurvy face. See Jusserand, iii. 115. Apparently the clown was expected to improvise.

[2] A classical instance is the beginning of the *Eroica* symphony. Indeed wherever Beethoven places at the beginning of a movement a point of harmony or rhythm which seems merely decorative, it is safe to assume that he will afterwards show it to be structural.

cending, while he observes it, the customary alternations of gravity and levity which his favourite form inherited from the suite. The scherzo, for instance, the 'jesting movement', is not necessarily with him a piece of pure merriment: it always brings the relief of swift movement and dancing rhythm, but the dance may be gay or martial or sinister according as the previous course of the music has determined.[1] So it is with these comic scenes of Shakespeare. Menenius, for instance, the 'humorous patrician', is not merely a foil to Coriolanus: he is the character who makes the conflict human and therefore possible. The commoners who are dispersed by Flavius at the beginning of *Julius Caesar* are forerunners of the crowd which at a critical moment of the play gathers to hear Mark Antony. No tragic scene could carry us so well, as do the brawling servants, into the heart of the feud between Montagues and Capulets: no one but Mercutio could so vividly set before us the youth and brilliance and impulse amid which alone this tragedy could have taken place. And the unity is bound still closer when it is attained not by contrast but by similarity of mood. Pandarus and Thersites are fit jesters for the one play in which Shakespeare tried to believe that man was hateful: the grim humour of Apemantus sorts well with the soured and disappointed temper of Timon: the drinking scene in *Othello* is a feast on the crater's edge: one feels through it all the ominous trembling of the earth.[2] Most poignant of all is the Fool in *Lear*, whose brave and pitiful gaiety drives straight to the heart. We

1 Contrast, for example, the scherzos of the third, fourth, fifth, sixth, and seventh symphonies.

If a joke occurred to the greatest dramatist of the period (i.e. before Shakespeare), while writing the main scene of his tragedy or picturing the death of his hero, he would put in the joke without hesitation. Jusserand, iii. 116. [I do not feel sure about this.]

2 Contrast it with the 'Auerbach's Keller' scene in *Faust*: made sinister by the presence of Mephistopheles, but little more than a parenthesis in the main plot.

laugh at the home-thrusts and the absurd stories and the snatches of biting verse, but it is with a laughter on the farther side of tears.

The other kind appears at first sight to be the least organic which any dramatist could devise. There are several instances in which a comic character, usually a servant or a countryman, enters for a single moment, touches the outermost fringe of the story, and then disappears entirely from the stage; for example, the clown in *Othello*, the porter in *Macbeth*, the gravediggers in *Hamlet*, the peasant who brings the asp in *Antony and Cleopatra*. Against these a good deal of critical artillery has been turned: the gravediggers were severely censured by Voltaire: Coleridge, in a famous passage, attacks 'the disgusting scene of the porter, which I dare undertake to demonstrate to be an interpolation of the players'. Now it brings bad luck to disagree with Coleridge, but I cannot see how in this matter he can possibly maintain his challenge. The physical effect of the knocking, which so moved De Quincey, is in itself a masterpiece of stagecraft, and no one but Shakespeare could have spoken of 'the primrose way to the everlasting bonfire'. Even if it were an isolated example it would be beyond impeachment, and as we have seen it is one of a group.

What is the explanation? Surely not mere contrast of colour, mere relief and breathing-space, a 'stopping to bait', as Dryden says, on the tragic journey. Were it so it would be sufficient for a lesser man—the swiftest and most transient contrast may be artistic if it hits the right moment—but from Shakespeare we look for something more. And as we look we notice that all the cases here cited stand on one common ground: that the character momentarily introduced understands no whit of the tragedy which is gathering round him. Othello, says the clown, 'does not greatly care to hear music', therefore if the waits 'have any music that may not be heard let them fall to 't', if not they may pack up their instruments and be gone. He has no idea that at the moment when he speaks Iago is advancing with net and trident to strike Othello down. The porter knows nothing of what has happened in Macbeth's castle; he only grumbles because he has been roused from sleep by an unseasonable knocking. The gravedigger may argue wisely about crowner's-quest law, but death is such a commonplace to him that he can sing at his work. The Egyptian peasant brings his asp because Cleopatra wants a new pet: to be sure it is a strange choice, and he feels bound to warn her that 'the worm is an odd worm' and that she must 'give it nothing for it is not worth the keeping'. When she asks 'Will it eat me?' the barbed irony flies so far over his head that he returns a jesting answer: when he takes his leave with a 'yes forsooth: I wish you joy of the worm', he gets his pay and goes back to his field and has nothing more in his mind than a vague inarticulate wonder at the caprices of royalty. It never occurs to him that he has been witnessing the crisis of a tragedy: still less that he has borne any part in bringing it about. And here, as it seems to me, Shakespeare lifts the veil and shows us for an instant one of the most tremendous truths which even he has revealed.

For the experience of these clowns and rustics is the experience of every one of us. Just as in the biological world light is nothing to the creature without an eye or sound to the creature without an ear: the vibrations are there, but no organ is open to receive them; just as on our higher plane there may be at this moment countless forces and influences which we cannot perceive or can only perceive dimly and at rare moments: so in the world of human life we are constantly touching the fringe of great issues, great events, great tragedies; we catch a glimpse of the conflict, we may even, for good or ill, take an unwitting part in it, and then the scene closes and we go on our way and know no more. It is not that fleeting sense of the infinite which came to Wordsworth in his youth and which gradually left him (if, indeed, it left him at all) as he grew to manhood: that brought its own message and its own interpretation. It is not even that strange impression, strange and yet common, which Professor Murray describes in the introduction to the *Hippolytus*:

'Probably most people have had the momentary experience—it may come to one on Swiss mountains, on Surrey commons, in crowded streets, on the tops of omnibuses, inside London houses—of being as it seems surrounded by an incomprehensible and almost intolerable vastness of beauty and delight and interest—if only one could grasp it or enter into it.'

This which we see in Shakespeare is something more intimate and human: a chance meeting with a stranger, a few words half-uttered or misunderstood, and we leave behind us a tragedy which has failed of its appeal to us because we had not ears to hear! It is true that in Shakespeare the gap is too wide for any real sympathy: to him, as to Dryden, tragedy 'is great and consists of great persons', and his uncomprehending peasants are men of mean estate: that is merely an accident, or a convention of the tragic form as he received it. None the less he rouses in us that curious uncanny feeling, to which our everyday life bears witness, that on either hand of us are things great and momentous, and that we see them as we see the reports of battles in our daily papers, without imagination enough to guess their significance.

Johnson explained Shakespeare's freedom on the ground that he appealed from rule to nature: a wise explanation, for the appeal to nature is in all dramatic art the ultimate rule. The audience is always part of the *dramatis personae*: its psychology is as important to the playwright as that of the characters whom he portrays. There is no *a priori* standard except that which is founded upon the essential attributes of mankind: all attempts to make one have foolishly endeavoured to turn the customs of the past into the regulations of the future'.[1] Not of course that the artist should court his public: he who does so is like the politician who tries to be popular, and whose well-deserved

[1] A remarkable instance is the attempt to judge Tchekov's plays by the reference to the technique which he intended them to supersede. The history of every art is full of these *nuove musiche*.

failure is one of the most just objects of derision. But the great artist is he who absorbs his public, who is large enough to contain all that they think and feel, and who because he sympathizes can also foresee. Mere incongruity, like mere triviality, is condemned not by the critics' rule, but by its own inability to endure: the 'courses of mirth' which Lisideius assailed were already dying when he dealt them their mortal stroke. But when the German purists attacked some farcical passages in *Faust*, 'you cannot touch them,' Heine answered, 'it is the finger of Goethe'; and that is the answer which the world has come to accept. To say that the supreme artist is above criticism is self-contradictory: he is no more above criticism than the Emperor Sigismund was above grammar. But he is above the kind of criticism with which impatient schoolboys relieve their feelings when they first begin Greek: the criticism which is based on no surer foundation than an inability to understand. It is perfectly right that one should set out upon the study of a great classic with obstinate questionings: one can pay it no worse insult than that of 'wondering with a foolish face of praise'. But the more faithfully one studies the more nearly one comprehends. Interrogation passes into assent, assent into admiration, admiration into love. And to love great art is to claim, however humbly and remotely, a kinship with those who have made it.

EPILOGUE

1928

'BECAUSE I have reached Paris,' says R. L. Stevenson, 'I am not ashamed of having passed through Newhaven and Dieppe.' To those of us who have followed for some years the difficult pursuit of music criticism it has become abundantly plain that we shall never reach Paris: that Dieppe is the farthest point of our reasonable hopes, and that we shall be fortunate if we do not stay weather-bound in Newhaven harbour. Whatever we look to achieve we shall not attain finality: we are well advised if we set that ambition behind us and satisfy ourselves with the humbler task of interpreting a transitory period to a transitory generation.

This is not to deny that there are fundamental principles in music and that on their validity its existence ultimately depends. I firmly believe that there are such principles; that they can be discovered and stated; and that they rest partly on the nature and limitations of the material employed, partly on those elements of human nature and their various interrelations, by reference to which our significant forms are determined. But like all laws of equal generality these are eternally true because they are eternally abstract; they cannot serve as guides to judgement or even as constituents of experiences until they are expressed in the idiom and vocabulary of actual practice. And because the idiom and the vocabulary and the practice are those of the creative artists in each generation it follows that all criticism which is concrete enough to be useful must be in great measure inductive; following not leading, explaining not prescribing the artistic method of its own time.

Consider what happens in a great constructive period. The artist—Palestrina or Bach or Beethoven—finds under his hand a mass of traditional material, all of which is derived from the work of his predecessors and to which he gives the special shape and colour and vitality which are proper to his genius. It is a commonplace to say that supreme genius has never invented or replaced a form: it is come not to destroy but to fulfil. At the same time because it is genius, and therefore intensely personal, it sees the traditional material in a new light, fills it with a new content and widens, though without breaking, the bounds which it has hitherto accepted. Hence the listener who is accustomed to stand upon the old ways is often baffled and bewildered by a new work which when it becomes familiar is readily accepted as the outcome of a natural and organic growth. The very qualities which give it distinction are those which tend at first to obscure its value. That is where the critic finds his opportunity. His function is, it has been well said, to 'translate' his impression of beautiful things—to make them intelligible to the untrained reader who is still faltering and stumbling through the elements of their original language. Nothing can be more misleading than are the metaphors which describe him in terms of the judgement-seat or the tribunal or, worse still, the gladiatorial arena. He belongs to none of these: if a picture be needed he is better described as liaison officer between genius and its environment; bearing the messages of the one for the acceptance of the other. No doubt it is necessary that he should, to the full extent of his power, comprehend their purport, though he will never fathom the depth of the transmitter's mind: it is equally necessary that he should know the passwords and be able to distinguish friend from foe and true man from knave; but his main business is the delivery of his burden in clear and unmistakable form. And because genius and environment are constantly changing, because every generation brings up its own conditions, its own methods, and even its own desires and aspirations, it follows that the messages will change also and that even with the same general end in view they will indicate new points of vantage and new methods of attack.

It seems advisable to emphasize this because of the rapid change through which the progress of music has passed during recent years. Our young composers are extending the bounds of the art on every side; our young critics are transvaluating our values with an enthusiasm worthy of Nietzsche; our public is beginning to awaken from its dogmatic slumber and to claim an unwonted freedom of judgement: it is abundantly worth while to explore the new world which they are making and to trace its interrelation with that which is passing away. There can clearly be no question of summarizing under any one category the tendencies and achievements of the new age. If this were ever possible, which I doubt, it is not possible now. This period is above all others eclectic: it has the largest inheritance of resources, and makes the most lavish use of them; it has employed every variety of texture and every kind of structural form, it has revived the modes and adopted the quarter-tone scale, it has taken some of its themes from the folk-song and some from the higher mathematics, it has brought together every conceivable combination of instruments, it has speculated like a Russian philosopher and experimented like a medieval alchemist. We may doubt whether the history of any art can afford an illustration of such wide and ceaseless activity. One result, if indeed it be not cause rather than effect, is a very considerable improvement in the spread of technical skill. Take for instance the field of executance. The great peaks remain unapproachable—we have no one who can play the violin so well as Joachim or the pianoforte so well as Madame Schumann—but the level of the tableland is vastly higher: there is a much larger number of competent virtuosi, and it is no exaggeration to say that a clever boy from the Royal College has now as great a command of his instrument as had many concert soloists a generation ago. A ready analogy occurs from the cricket field. We elders are still of opinion that there has never been any one like W. G. Grace; but there are twenty times as many people who can make their century in a first-class match, and every year the public schools turn out a score of boys who, by the old standard, would be good enough to play for their county. But whereas in sport I can see no drawback to the general improvement—unless it be the number of unfinished matches—in the dustier arena of musical performance there is a real danger from which we are not entirely free. To be overoccupied with technique is to forget that it is ancillary to interpretation: we are sometimes dazzled by our pianists and violinists until we can no longer see what they mean. A considerable number of the great classics are now played too fast, too brilliantly, with a rhetoric too urgent and stimulating: how many people, I wonder, pay any attention to the 'Maestoso' in Chopin's *Polonaises*, or have ever heard the finale of the *Appassionata* as Beethoven intended it?

The same qualities, among many others, are, I think, observable in the present state of composition. To begin with, there can be no doubt about its technical proficiency. It has acquired an astonishing command over its methods and its material, and it is evidently much interested in the problems which they respectively present. The old composers now and then allowed their invention to droop, and relaxed on an Alberti bass, or a Rosalia, or a cadence as commonplace as a stock epithet in Virgil. It is true that they usually compensated for loose workmanship by some special jewel of passion or melody: it might even be maintained, if it were not special pleading, that these moments of careless ease bring them into closer touch with our common humanity. In any case the method of the present day makes no concession to such weakness. Its typical compositions are extraordinarily ingenious; they 'file out to the fraction of a hair'; they polish until the surface looks like Japanese *cloisonné* work, they invent the most recondite patterns and arabesques, they fashion them with an accuracy which never seems to hesitate or falter. Whatever else is to be said about them there is no bungling in their work: it hits with unerring mastery the target at which they aim.

But the placing of the target is a matter of some

importance, and here there is room for some differences of opinion. At present each man is setting up his own, without any respect for the King's Regulations; and the result is that the shooting-range looks ragged and disorganized. The new age is very impatient of prohibitions and restraints: an attitude which is intelligible and even laudable when we remember the text-books of our youth, but which needs some forethought if it is to be of any constructive value. The rules of an art, by which we mean its conventions, are there for general guidance and mutual understanding, but they are not invented *a priori*, they have grown from accepted practice and they are liable to be suspended if the practice alters or if a preponderating advantage is to be obtained.

Let me give an illustration from the pages of the English grammar. The double negative, which is common in Chaucer, has been discountenanced by modern English usage: we frown upon 'I never didn't' and 'I shouldn't wonder if she wasn't in now' because they upset our habits without any countervailing gain. Yet Sir Walter Raleigh, than whom we have no better authority, quotes as a supreme example of emphasis:

'There 's nothing not so difficult, not to drive, when there 's a many on 'em, very, isn't a pig.'

This is surely irresistible. Not only is 'very', as Raleigh says, 'a pinnacle of distress', but the negatives beat like hammers round the argument and clench it into conviction. Yet again what are we to say of Lewis Carroll's verdict when two disputants urged on him the respective claims of clergy and laity to a vacant head-mastership: 'I think that no one who is not a layman ought not to be elected.'

It is precisely the same with the grammatical forms of music. Far too much ado has been made about consecutive fifths and unresolved discords and polytonality and all the rest of it. They are but colours on the palette and the only question that matters is of the picture. Yet even here a word of caution may be not superfluous. All my life long I have welcomed every movement which made for freedom in music, and have never wavered in my conviction that freedom means responsibility; that anarchy in music, as elsewhere, is no more than a passing phase, and that a free people is one that makes its own laws and observes them. And I cannot help wondering whether some of the laws which are now beginning to emerge are not really defiant 'orders of the day', whether in other words the negative side of the revolution is not continuing a little too long. The prisoners in Stevenson's fable were liberated from gyves on the right leg, and wore them on the left instead. It would be a pity if our new leaders were to substitute a convention of revolt for a convention of obedience.

This, however, is of comparatively small importance. The idiom and vocabulary of music will look after themselves in the future as they have done in the past: all we need to ask is that the word should have a meaning, and, if possible, an etymology. But there are two more serious obstacles to be encountered; and, although genius will assuredly surmount them both, it may be as well to discuss them as they make the critic's task of interpretation unduly difficult.

To one of them I have alluded elsewhere—the danger that this over-elaboration may defeat its own end, either by losing the due sense of perspective and proportion or by straining beyond reasonable bounds the possible receptivity of the audience. Du Maurier once drew a threefold picture entitled 'Music of the past, of the present, and of the future'. The first panel was 'A melody by Mozart', and the guests were listening. The second was 'A brilliant fantasia by Herr Rumbeltumtowski', and the guests were conversing. The third was 'Twenty-four interdependent logarithmic studies for pianoforte, violin, and 'cello with an exposition in four modern languages'—and the guests were escaping. No doubt the receptivity of the audience is not a fixed measure, but grows with experience into adaptability; but Du Maurier's fears are not far from realization when we find Mr. Edwin Evans (whom no one will suspect of bigotry) writing as follows about Herr Alban Berg's recent concerto:

'It is constructed on Schönberg's twelve-note scale: everything in it is the result of abstruse calculations, and however fascinating its problems may be to the eye, there is no ear in the world which can take them in during performance. Hence this over-organized composition is in effect like an unorganized arbitrary succession of sounds.'

When some of us advocate the cause of silent reading it is not this which we have in view.

On the other point it is harder to speak because, amid the multiplicity of our materials and ideals, every plea may be traversed by some notable exceptions. To them all honour is due, for they are keeping alight a torch which might otherwise be extinguished. Apart from them, and, I think, as a general tendency, our representative music is lacking in repose and in the gift of happiness: it has forgotten, or disallowed, Schiller's maxim that Art is joyous: it is admirable and astonishing, but it is not equally delightful. A characteristic outcome is the truceless war which our young people are waging against Romance: they regard it with a cynical and disillusioned eye; they call it by derisive nicknames; they pierce it with disdainful epigrams and with mordant shafts of irony. Part of the cause is no doubt the natural reaction which separates every age from its predecessor; part is a reticence intensified by the experience of the Great War; part is due to that preoccupation with the details of craftsmanship which has been already noted and which is almost incompatible with the free play of emotion. But whatever the diagnosis, they are wrong: they ignore a priceless element in human nature: they 'escape the title of fool at the cost of a celestial crown'. It is not a question of maintaining the intellectual basis of true music—no one has ever done that better than Beethoven; their cause is not intellectual but intellectualist, self-conscious, deliberate, academic, the work of a declining rather than a renascent period. We may freely assert that the claims of undisciplined sense and emotion have inflicted the worst outrages upon art that were ever perpetrated; there is no need for us to fly into the opposite extreme, and, because the Capital is iniquitous, go and starve our feelings in the Theban desert.

So my quarrel with the young people, if indeed I have one, is that they are not young enough; that they will not let themselves go, that they sit cold and calculating over their inkstand while passion and adventure beckon to them in vain. They have become their own masters, and are under a self-imposed tyranny. They have won their claim to do anything that they like, and always seem to be asking themselves 'what shall we do next?' They have an amazing amount of knowledge, and a range and felicity of skill which no generation has ever surpassed: what they seem to lack is that divine spontaneity which all skill and all knowledge cannot replace. If this be true they are advancing the cause of music rather by perfecting her instruments than by revealing her secret, and their reward will come not in their own achievements but in those of the creative age for which they prepare. And if it be untrue I shall have added one more to those whose sight is grown too dim for reading the signs of the times.

There is at any rate one point on which we can all agree—the eminence that has now been attained by this country in musical scholarship and criticism. When I was young we were at low-water mark: Gurney's *Power of Sound* came out while I was an undergraduate—an interesting work and unjustly neglected—but it stood alone, and of our journalist criticism the less said the better. We owe an immense debt to our pioneers: to Grove and Parry and Stanford, to Fuller Maitland and Barclay Squire, to 'S. L.' and Herbert Thompson and Ernest Newman, who not only lifted musical criticism from a dusty corner of the practice-room to an honourable place in the library, but who laid for it a foundation of method and philosophy on which our present superstructures are being well and truly built. And we have good reason to be proud of our architects: Terry and

Mrs. Newmarch; Dent and Buck and Fellowes, Colles of the *Dictionary* and Fox Strangways of *Music and Letters*, and so onward to those brilliant leaders of *les jeunes* Dr. Dyson, Mr. Heseltine, Mr. Cecil Gray, who are bringing to their work a store of wide knowledge and keen judgement with a freshness of outlook which is the best of auguries for the future.

In dealing with the later development of criticism in this country, by which I mean not only published writings but the trend of current opinion, I am naturally concerned, in some measure, with its attitude towards the past. And here I would dwell for a moment on the reaction against Beethoven which seems to be characteristic of the present age. It is obviously sincere, it represents a definite and intelligible standpoint, it is maintained with vigour and ability; on all grounds it merits the most serious consideration.

The attack ranges from complete denial to a partial and restricted acceptance. 'The music of Beethoven', says one of our greatest critics, 'is no longer convincing to modern ears'; and those who would modify this verdict confine their plea to the compositions of the third period. The early works, we are told, are but derivations from Mozart and Haydn, and lack the clarity and transparency of their originals; and the works of the middle period are mechanical in structure and are imbued with the sentimentalism of their age: only from the B♭ trio does the real Beethoven emerge with music that is not for an age but for all time. And among these latest compositions are selected as specially pre-eminent the C♯ minor quartet, the Hymn from that in A minor, and the Grosse Fuge for strings.

Now we may take it as common agreement that Beethoven is greatest in his third period and that he there crosses a frontier-line into a new region of art. If this music is 'not convincing to our ears' then no music of the past is convincing; it is at best a toyshop and at worst a lumber-room. Indeed, this view is so extreme that I cannot help thinking it has been imperfectly expressed or understood—that it is a hasty generalization which needs re-shaping. At any rate we may here discuss the more moderate opinion, which is also more prevalent, that the third period has supreme value, but that the other two are obsolete.

One charge against them is that of mechanical structure. In particular we are told that the 'first movement' form (Beethoven's favourite type of design) is dull and monotonous, built on one unvarying plan and so uniform that two-thirds of the way through we have virtually reached the end. 'Our interest', say the objectors, 'is fairly well sustained up to the beginning of the recapitulation: after that we have nothing before us but a flatter reflection of the country that we have already traversed. Every bar, every phrase, every melody can be anticipated before it comes; there is nothing in the further course of the music to stimulate or engage our attention: it is literally as tedious as a twice-told tale.' I will not ask my objectors to finish the sentence, for indeed there is something genuine in this dislike of repetition. We are all a little impatient at the 'da capo' aria (how much even 'ma in Italia' loses on the second occasion), and there are some ritornelli which seem to visit us too often and to linger too ceremoniously on the threshold. But the sonata-form is not in like case, and before we make up our minds about it there is some more evidence to be heard.

An artistic form can be judged only in relation to its conditions and its purpose. It would be absurd, for instance, if we were to rush hot-foot from our breathless modern drama and censure Aeschylus because his action is from time to time suspended by choral hymns, or Shakespeare because at some moments of crisis his characters make longer speeches than they would in real life. To Shakespeare the speeches are an essential part of the presentation; to Aeschylus the choral hymns are the very staple of the drama, and if we do not approach them in their own spirit it is we who are the losers. Now Beethoven's world was permeated with a sense of tonality and of key-relationship: ours is not. The modern methods of polytonality and continued chromatic change are incompatible with this form of expression—they obliterate it, or rather replace it with a structure of their own. I am not arguing whether this new music is in principle better or worse than the old—it has gained something and lost something; I maintain only that it is essentially different and that unless we recognize this difference we cannot hope to appraise the Viennese masters. It is clear that the old sonata-form can no longer serve as the vehicle of composition: that indeed has long been foreseen. But given tonality as a basis, it remains the most complete and organic way of dealing with its problems: it affords to them the best and most satisfying of solutions. Its triad of Duality, Plurality, and Unity is valid only within the limits of a definite key-system: within those limits it is paramount.

'But', it may be said, 'this end would be better attained without any exact restatement. We want new material, or at least new treatment of the material, to prevent our attention from flagging.' My answer is that the restatement is not exact. One of the most astonishing signs of Beethoven's genius is his power of manipulating his plot, inside the recapitulation, so as to prepare for the entry and presentation of the transposed second subject. Here he abbreviates, there he extends his phrase, there again he develops it: in one work a simple modulation is sufficient, in another a whole section is hardly long enough, and so far as I remember he never repeats a device. He is at a less crucial point of the intrigue than when he closes the development section, and his contrivance is therefore, as a rule, more quietly handled, but it is never commonplace and it never fails of its purpose. Look at the first *Rasoumoffsky*, at the *Eroica*, at the Pianoforte Concerto in G: these are but typical gifts of an abundance that is spread on every hand. No doubt the constituent themes are the same, or but slightly altered: that only means that the characters who contended in the first act have come to be reconciled in the last. It is not like the recurrence of the da capo aria, where there is an actual loss of lyric or dramatic significance, that was a mere convention even in the time when it flourished. The structures of the sonata are in relation to their medium real and significant forms, and of their significance Beethoven was the greatest exponent.

A more fundamental objection remains—that the fault of these works of the middle period lies not in their structure but in their sentiment. Here the controversy needs to be stated clearly, for it may be *à outrance*. Surely it does not mean that we are to banish sentiment altogether from music—Byrd's *Justorum Animae*, and Handel's *He was despised*, and the last chorus of the *St. Matthew Passion*, and the Lacrymosa of Mozart's *Requiem*. I would as soon think of mocking at the *Antigone* or the *Vita Nuova* or the death-bed of Lear or Cleopatra; and if any one can read these unmoved his name, I think, is Bartholomew Smallweed. It must mean, therefore, that in these works of the middle period there is some quality of sentiment by which the present generation is irritated or repelled. What is this quality? Is it coarseness or extravagance or unreality, is it unctuous or neurotic or epicene? Of course I admit that there are weak passages in Beethoven, as there are in every artist that is subject to our common humanity, but in his best work, with which alone we are concerned, I can find no affirmative answer. When I first heard the C minor Symphony I went in the strength of that meat forty days: I can remember now, at the interval of half a century, the place, the conditions, and the effect that it produced. So it was when Joachim played the Violin Concerto, or Rubinstein the *Appassionata*, or Piatti the Violoncello Sonata in A. These were not transitory moments of pleasure but enduring delights, as real now, if not as vivid, as at their first experience. Yet all the works which I have enumerated are at the very core and centre of the despised period. Again, I fully acknowledge that with all their greatness they are surpassed by the compositions of his later life. There is no music by which I am so deeply moved as by the Cavatina, the finale of the A minor quartet, and the slow movements of the B♭ trio, the Choral Symphony, and the Opus 106 sonata. But these stand in the line of succession; the frontier which separates them from the middle work is a line, not a gulf: the divine light which irradiates them transfigures but does not re-create. *The Winter's Tale* and *The Tempest* are by the same hand as *Romeo* and *Henry IV*: it does them no honour to throw them into relief by darkening their background.

I am not, of course, denying that the present generation may gain the same permanency of delight from the music of the new idiom; that Schönberg and Bartók and the chamber music of Stravinsky may be to it what Mozart and Beethoven and the Songs of Schubert were to our own. If so, it has double advantage in that it reaps from a wider field. That it knows more than we did is, I think, certain: whether its enjoyment is proportionate to its knowledge it alone can determine. Every age has its own dangers to avoid or encounter; they are among the conditions of progress and may be regarded without misgiving. That of our *nuove musiche* is the prospect of making serious art too esoteric; of striking a breach between the priesthood and the worshippers in the outer court. The essential function of music is to ennoble and purify the soul of man by steeping it in pure and noble pleasure: in that function the whole man is involved—sense and emotion, reason and intuition, and that effluence of the divine spirit which is the central light of our personality. Music can spread its enchantment over mirth and jollity, over intricacy and artifice, over the tragicomedy of action and the mystery of the contemplative life: it best achieves its purpose when it emerges from the laboratory, when it breathes the free air of heaven, when it brings all its gifts of skill and learning and genius as offerings to the service of human happiness.